NEAR TO the heart of GOD

Daily Readings from the Spiritual Classics

Compiled and Prepared for Modern Readers by
Bernard Bangley

Harold Shaw Publishers
Wheaton, Illinois

All Scripture quotations, unless otherwise indicated, are taken from the HOLY BIBLE, NEW INTERNATIONAL VERSION®. NIV®. Copyright © 1973, 1978, 1984 International Bible Society. Used by permission of Zondervan Publishing House. All rights reserved.

Scripture quotations marked CEV are taken from the *Contemporary English Version* of the Bible, ©1991 by the American Bible Society.

Scripture quotations marked JB are taken from THE JERUSALEM BIBLE, copyright © 1966 by Darton, Longman & Todd, Ltd. and Doubleday, a division of Bantam Doubleday Dell Publishing Group, Inc. Reprinted by Permission.

Scripture quotations marked KJV are from *The King James Version* of the Bible.

Scripture quotations marked TLB are taken from *The Living Bible* © 1971. Used by permission of Tyndale House Publishers, Inc., Wheaton, IL 60189. All rights reserved.

Scripture quotations marked THE MESSAGE are from *The Message.* Copyright © 1993, 1994, 1995 by Eugene H. Peterson. Used by permission of NavPress Publishing Group.

Scripture quotations marked NLT are taken from the *Holy Bible,* New Living Translation, copyright © 1996. Used by permission of Tyndale House Publishers, Inc., Wheaton, Illinois 60189. All rights reserved.

Scripture quotations marked PHILLIPS are from the Phillips' Translation. Reprinted with permission of the Macmillan Publishing Company, Inc., from the *New Testament in Modern English,* Revised Edition by J.B. Phillips, © J.B. Phillips, 1958, 1960, 1972.

Scripture quotations marked TEV are from *Today's English Version (The Good News Bible),* © 1966, 1971, 1976, 1992 by American Bible Society. Used by permission.

ISBN 0-87788-824-8

Edited by Lil Copan

Library of Congress Cataloging-in-Publication Data
Near to the heart of God : daily readings from the spiritual classics / compiled and
    prepared for modern readers by Bernard Bangley
        p.   cm.
    Includes bibliographical references.
    ISBN 0-87788-824-8
    1. Devotional calendars.   I. Bangley, Bernard, 1935– .
    BV4810.N38   1998
    242'.2—dc21   98-24970
                                                                   CIP

04   03   02   01   00

10   9   8   7   6   5   4   3   2

For Anna,
whose life is a book of devotion

Contents

# INTRODUCTION

Y ou are holding a unique devotional guide. It makes the most respected spiritual writing of many centuries available for easy reading and meditation. These works have a particular devotional value for our present day. The contemporary importance of these "classics" continually amazes me.

Many of the writers included in these readings are famous. Their books will always be in print and widely available. Others are obscure. Few have ever heard of Evagrius Ponticus, Guerric of Igny, or Gertrude of Helfta. You will understand why a dedicated few have preserved the writings of all these spiritual authors once you have tasted the little samples in this book. An appendix provides a brief biography of each author. A list of books for additional reading will help you to dig deeper. It is my hope that you will be motivated to read some of these writers in their original, complete works.

The sad reality is that some of these great works are difficult to find and exist in English versions that are very difficult to read. Older translations are particularly clumsy. A modern reader, nurtured mostly by television, opens such books and finds them forbidding. This makes the religious thought contained in them seem out of touch with everyday life.

Many of these writers are also held captive by the writing style of their era. They look stuffy and cold on paper. The reader may turn several pages before seeing a paragraph break. Sentences can run on for great length, strung together with semicolons and commas until the eye and the mind grow weary. When such passages are carefully rephrased in our generation's conversational style, we can see the warm, loving spirit behind most of these dark pages. In some cases the release is almost miraculous.

What I have done is to paraphrase their writings into clear, simple, modern English. I wanted to make them accessible to people who might get bogged down struggling with the original versions. I have shortened sentences and expressed their ideas with dignified but commonplace language.

One of the great problems with spiritual literature is the inadequacy of language. It is an enormous challenge to reduce an experience with God to words. In the same way that an eyewitness to a disaster stammers into a reporter's microphone, the mystics fumbled for metaphors and images that might convey a little meaning to others. Human language is orderly. It is a good tool for describing thoughts, asking questions, and reaching conclusions. Even for this purpose it can fall short when it must cross linguistic barriers. Translating Japanese into English, for instance, can be a considerable challenge because of differences in word pattern.

The writers of the material contained in this book have little difficulty analyzing and explaining important rules for Christian living. It is when they begin to pull back the curtain and show us something of their personal experience of an overwhelming reality that they stutter with a kind of colorful language that goes beyond ordinary conversation. I have attempted to preserve as much of this difference in style as possible in these modern paraphrases.

Although I have expressed their thoughts and statements in modern English, I have not put any words into their mouths. Even when I have disagreed with certain aspects of their ideas, I have stayed out of it and let them speak their own minds. The metaphors, examples, and illustrative comments in this book are in the original material. It may be a little startling to read about dieting and family squabbles in works that are hundreds of years old. The reader may well wonder whether or not I have imposed these categories and images in order to make them lively for our day. I have not. Every reference to anything can be found in the original. While freely paraphrasing for quick reading, I have resisted every temptation to introduce new elements. They aren't needed. These pages were lively when they were first written and remain lively today.

There are many ways to use a book like this. Maybe for you it will provide a daily moment of quiet devotion in a busy life. A blessed moment it will be! Prepare yourself for the fact that you may not be able to escape the implications of what you have read for the remainder of that day.

On the other hand, one page might lead to another. You may find it hard to put down. This is beneficial too. Although these pages are not intended for continuous reading, it may be that you can read until you come to the one that speaks to your present circumstance. Then you can slow down and meditate upon what God is saying to you.

Or perhaps you have a particular question, some area of concern, a problem, or an opportunity. Using the topical index, you can quickly find a subject that may speak to your need. The biographical index allows you to find readings by each author. With the Scripture index the reader, pastor, or teacher may investigate ideas that are related to a specific verse of Scripture.

Above all, read prayerfully. God can speak through these writers. The Scripture readings have a close tie to everything that follows. Many were suggested by the original authors. Don't skip the Bible verse. Read it. Think about what it is saying. Then read the meditation with an open mind and spirit. The personal reflections at the end are intended to give you a start in your own time of meditation. Go ahead and give God an opportunity with your soul. Be still and listen. Good things will come of it.

—Bernard Bangley

Getting Started

As the deer pants for streams of water, so my soul pants for you, O God. *Psalm 42:1*

Our soul is like a castle created out of a precious jewel. There are many interesting rooms in this beautiful castle of the soul.

How do we enter? Is that a foolish question? After all, if the castle is your own soul you are already rather intimate with it! What you must realize is that there are many different ways we can exist within this castle. You can remain with the guards in the courtyard outside the gate. You can live your entire life and never discover what it's like inside.

The doorway into the castle is genuine prayer and meditation. Mechanical repetitions of prayers are insufficient. They will leave you like the paralytic who waited beside the pool of Bethesda: He stayed there helplessly for thirty-eight years until the Lord himself came along to help him.

—Teresa of Avila: *Interior Castle*

 A Personal Response

I am spiritually hungry. I have lingered too long in the garden outside. I can only imagine what it is like in the depths of my soul. Maybe I have never really prayed with personal involvement.

Help me now. Help me to turn my face toward this entrance to my soul. Give me the courage to approach it with genuine faith and prayer.

Unjust Accusations

A woman giving birth to a child has pain because her time has come; but when her baby is born she forgets the anguish because of her joy that a child is born into the world. So with you: Now is your time of grief, but I will see you again and you will rejoice, and no one will take away your joy. *John 16:21-22*

If you are caught in a fault you must certainly humble yourself and admit your responsibility. If you are the target of an unjust accusation, politely deny your guilt. You owe it to both truth and your neighbor. If you continue to be accused after you have made a true and legitimate explanation, don't let that bother you. There is no need to try to force anyone to agree with your explanation. After you discharge your duty to truth, then discharge your duty to humility.

Try not to complain. Egotism always thinks the injuries are worse than they are. Most importantly, never complain to someone who is quick-tempered and cranky. If you absolutely must protest to someone in order to correct an offense or to recover your peace of mind, then find a calm person who really loves God. For the hot-tempered person, instead of helping your situation, will stir up even more trouble. Instead of pulling the thorn out of your foot, that person will drive it in even deeper.

The truly patient person neither whines nor seeks pity. If that person must speak of his sufferings he will use a normal tone of voice and not exaggerate. If that person is extended pity for something he does not suffer, he will not accept it. This way he keeps peace between truth and patience.

You have Jesus Christ within your soul. Until this "child" is born you will suffer in labor. Take heart! These sorrows will pass and joy will remain with you.

—Francis De Sales: *The Devout Life*

 A Personal Response

Lord, I offer you all my grief, pain, and weakness. Let them be of service to you.

The Value of Suffering

> Our light and momentary troubles are achieving for us an eternal glory that far outweighs them all. *2 Corinthians 4:17*

It is hard to believe that a loving God could allow us to suffer. Does it please him? Couldn't he make us good without making us miserable? Certainly he could. God can do anything. Our hearts are in his hands.

But he does not choose to spare us sorrow. In the same way that we are not born mature, but have to grow into adulthood, so we must learn to be humble and to trust God. We need our crosses. Suffering can help us loosen some knots that tie us to earth. To resist is merely to delay what God is trying to do for us.

It is not possible for a child to wake from a nap fully grown. God works in the heart the same way he works on the body—slowly, imperceptibly. Physical development is steady and deliberate. And that is how our souls grow: Our heavenly Father sends a series of events that wean us from earth by gradual steps. Learning to deny ourselves is a painful process. But the sick soul must take its medicine. Is the surgeon cruel when he makes an incision? No! It is an act of kindness.

The parental heart of God has no desire to hurt us. But he understands that we must get our priorities straight. We cry. We pout. We sigh and groan. We say unkind things about God. He does not intervene. He lets us continue through the process. And we are saved. A little grief has spared us a much greater sorrow. We can only conclude that God is good, that he is tender and compassionate even when we feel that we have a right to complain that he is unkind.

—François de Fénelon: *Meditations and Devotions*

 A Personal Response

Whatever the source of my difficulties and pains, dear God, work in them for my good. Use them to bring about positive changes in me. Though I would be rid of them, let me find hidden value in them.

January 4   Asking for the Right Things

Take this cup from me. Yet not what I will, but what you will. *Mark 14:36*

It is a mistake to ask God to give you what you want. Your desires are probably not in complete harmony with God's will. Pray instead that God will lead you to want the right things. Ask for what is good and for what is best for your soul. There is no way you could want these things for yourself more than God desires you to have them.

Often when I prayed, I kept asking for things that seemed good to me. I pressured God to give me what I wanted. I did not trust God enough to allow him to provide what would be best for me. When I actually received the thing I had unreasonably sought I would be embarrassed by my own selfish stubbornness. Ultimately, the thing would not turn out to be what I had expected.

Relax your prayers. Do not work so hard to have your request granted. The Lord wants to give you more than you ask. Nothing can be greater than intimate conversation with God, than being absolutely preoccupied with his companionship. Prayer that is not distracted with a wish list is the highest achievement of the intellect.

If you would ask God for something, ask to be cleansed of your passions. Pray to be delivered from ignorance. Plead with God to free you from temptation.

In your prayers, desire justice, virtue, and spiritual knowledge. The other things will be given you as well.

If you will pray for others, you will pray like the angels.

—Evagrius Ponticus: *Chapters on Prayer*

A Personal Response

Lord, show me the way *you* want me to pray. Teach me to desire the things that *you* desire for me.

Walking with God

I stay close to you; your right hand upholds me.
Psalm 63:8

There is nothing in the world as delightful as a continual walk with God. Only those who have experienced it can comprehend it. And yet I do not recommend that you seek it solely because it is so enjoyable. Do it because of love, and because it is what God wants. If I were a preacher, the one thing I would preach about more than anything else is the practice of the presence of God.

Please get started now. I don't care how old you are. It is better late than never.

I can't imagine how any faithful person can be satisfied without the practice of the presence of God. For my part, I spend as much time as possible alone with him at the very center of my soul. As long as I am with him I am afraid of nothing, but the least turning away from him is unbearable.

It is necessary to trust God completely. The various forms of devotion, as good as they are, merely help us on our way to God. But when we are already *with* God, they are of little use.

Don't be discouraged if you find this hard to do. If you just try it a little, you will consider it wasted time. Stick to it! Resolve to persevere in it until the day you die—no matter what!

—Brother Lawrence: *The Practice of the Presence of God*

A Personal Response

Show me, dear God, how to engage in the ultimate spiritual discipline: practicing your presence.

Why Love God?

> How great is the love the Father has lavished on us, that we should be called children of God!
> *1 John 3:1*

Y ou have asked me to tell you why and how God is to be loved.

God himself is the reason why. Without limit is how.

For the wise, that is answer enough.

But now I will speak more elaborately, if less profoundly, for the benefit of less agile minds.

There are two reasons for loving God. First, there is no one more worthy of your love. Second, no one can return more in response to your love.

God deserves our love because he first loved us. His love for us was genuine because he sought nothing for himself. See the object of his love: enemies. "For if, when we were God's enemies, we were reconciled to him through the death of his Son, how much more, having been reconciled, shall we be saved through his life!" (Romans 5:10). God's love was unconditional.

How much did he love? The answer is in John's Gospel: "For God so loved the world that he gave his one and only Son, that whoever believes in him shall not perish but have eternal life" (John 3:16). The Son, speaking of himself, said, "The greatest way to show love for friends is to die for them" (John 15:13, CEV). We, the wicked, then, should love the Righteous One in return.

—Bernard of Clairvaux: *On Loving God*

A Personal Response

Love never asks "What's in it for me?" Reflecting upon what I have read above, I see that genuine love gives. Sacrificially. My love, dear God, is in response to your love. I have received much from you. I respond in kind.

Ways to Eat

One person believes it is all right to eat anything. But another believer who has a sensitive conscience will eat only vegetables. Those who think it is all right to eat anything must not look down on those who won't. And those who won't eat certain foods must not condemn those who do, for God has accepted them. *Romans 14:2-3,* NLT

What shall we say about the belly? It is the supreme passion! If you can kill it, or even half kill it, do so. It can be the cause of downfall.

Our need for physical nourishment varies greatly. One needs only a little food while another needs a lot to sustain natural strength. The same amount does not satisfy everyone. The one who practices silence never allows himself to eat until full, for when the stomach is heavy the mind is clouded. Overeating makes that person drowsy. Prayer becomes difficult.

With the wise use of food—that is through eating all kinds of food—one may accomplish two things. On the one hand you will avoid egotism. On the other, you will not show contempt for any of God's excellent creation.

Eating has three degrees: moderation, sufficiency, and satiety. Moderation means to remain a little hungry after eating. To eat sufficiently means to be neither hungry nor stuffed. Satiety is a condition of being slightly weighed down with food.

Eating beyond satiety opens the door to belly madness. Lust for food will enter. Knowing these things, choose the best for yourself. Understand your own limitations. Say with the apostle, "I have learned the secret of being content in any and every situation, whether well fed or hungry, whether living in plenty or in want. I can do everything through him who gives me strength" (Philippians 4:12-13).

—Gregory of Sinai: *Instructions to Hesychasts*

A Personal Response

If the way I eat is a problem for my soul, help me, dear God. Be in my eating. If eating is not my problem, keep me from feeling superior to those who struggle.

A Pattern for Life

When Jesus spoke again to the people, he said, "I am the light of the world. Whoever follows me will never walk in darkness, but will have the light of life." *John 8:12*

Christ encourages us to pattern our lives after his. In this way we can become spiritually enlightened. The most important thing we can do is to meditate upon the life of Jesus Christ.

Many who have attended church all their lives have not been affected by it. They do not have Christ's Spirit. If you really want to understand and enjoy the words of Christ, you must attempt to live like him.

What is the point of scholarly discussion on a deep subject such as the Trinity, if you lack humility? Deep conversation will not make you holy. God is pleased by a pure life. It is better to *feel* contrition than to *know* its meaning.

If you knew the entire Bible by heart and were familiar with all the philosophers, what good would it be without the love of God and his grace?

Here is the wisest thing you can do: forget the world and seek the things of heaven.

—Thomas à Kempis: *The Imitation of Christ*

 A Personal Response

Help me to balance my life, Lord God. Show me where to put the emphasis. Some things are more important than others. Don't let me miss this.

God's Word Endures

Let these false prophets tell their dreams, but let my true messengers faithfully proclaim my every word. There is a difference between chaff and wheat! Jeremiah 23:28, NLT

Numa Pompilius, Lycurgus, and Minos were kings and were considered to be wise men. With great governments they devised laws to rule people. They indicated their laws were divinely inspired in order to give them more credibility and permanence.

But where are these men now? Where are their books? What has become of their laws? They were unwise and had no knowledge or understanding of God. They and their laws are dead. Their names are forgotten.

God's word will have no end. Over a long span of time it has passed many dangers from tyrants, legalists, heretics, fire, and sword. It continues to exist until this day. This is a wonderful work of God, that having so many and such great enemies, and passing through so many great dangers, it still continues with no alteration of its teachings. No creature was able to do this. It is God's work.

He preserved it. No tyrant could destroy it. No tradition could choke it. No editor could corrupt it. The Word of God has no end. Cities shall fall. Kingdoms will crumble. Empires will fade away as smoke. But the truth of the Lord endures forever. Burn it, it will rise again. Kill it, it will live again. Cut it down by the root, it will sprout again. "There is no wisdom, no insight, no plan that can succeed against the Lord" (Proverbs 21:30).

—John Jewell: *Of the Holy Scriptures*

A Personal Response

In a world that changes with shocking speed and regularity, it is assuring to understand that your word, Lord, is permanent. The Bible is never out-of-date. Help us to interpret it with fresh insight in every generation.

Personal Glory

When pride comes, then comes disgrace, but with humility comes wisdom. *Proverbs 11:2*

People can become proud and arrogant because they ride a handsome horse, or have a feather in their hat, or wear well-tailored clothes. If there is any glory in such things it surely belongs to the horse, the bird, and the tailor!

You can spot genuine goodness the same way you can identify the best balm. If it sinks to the bottom of a container of water and stays there, it is the most valuable balm. Truly wise, educated, generous, noble people will tend to be humble, modest, and eager to help another. If they float on the surface and show off, they are phonies. They are less genuine in direct proportion to their personal display.

Honors, titles, and rank are like saffron. Saffron grows best when it is walked on. Honor is excellent when it is freely given to us by others, but it becomes cheap and degrading when we go looking for it. Beautiful flowers wither when plucked. Generous minds waste no time on such toys as rank or honor. They occupy themselves with other things. The owner of pearls pays no attention to shells.

On the other hand, don't make a pretense of being humble. My advice is that you should never talk about it. Never ask to be given the lowest place if you only intend to start there and work your way to the top.

—Francis De Sales: *The Devout Life*

A Personal Response

I want to please others, Lord. I want them to like me. Spare me from trying to gain their respect by artificial means. Live in me. Work through me. Let others see you when they look at me.

Daily Bread

Give us today our daily bread. *Matthew 6:11*

This is a very good prayer if one should say no more at one time than this. As we see our need, so we shall pray.

When we lack the necessities for the maintenance of life, and everything is important, then we may pray, "Give us today our daily bread."

We should pray for the things we need. It is better to say a short prayer like this, with faith, than to say a whole psalter without faith.

Every word in this little phrase is important. "Bread" signifies everything that is necessary to sustain life. All of these essentials are wrapped up in this little word.

—Hugh Latimer: *Fruitful Sermons*

A Personal Response

Forgive me for thinking that all my prayers must be grand prayers, O God. Show me the power and significance of ordinary, practical, simple prayers.

Tranquility

Oh, that I had the wings of a dove! I would fly away and be at rest—I would flee far away and stay in the desert; I would hurry to my place of shelter, far from the tempest and storm. *Psalm 55:6-8*

There is a serenity of spirit that is extremely valuable in the spiritual life. It is not easy to acquire because we are inexperienced and face powerful foes.

Sometimes we are completely out of control. Our minds are confused. This is the time to get right into prayer. Remember how our Lord prayed three times in the Garden of Gethsemane before his betrayal. It is only in conversation with God that we can find refuge. Pray that God will replace the chaos in us with tranquility.

Don't be bothered by the continuous and meaningless hustle of the business world. When we go to work we can take care of business without getting rattled. We can lighten up a bit. We do not need to be whipped by a crowded calendar. Some work can wait.

The thing we should concentrate on is an awareness of God's holy presence. A desire to please God should be our top priority. If we let other business take precedence, our souls will quickly become fearful and anxious.

Forbid thoughts that depress and distress you from entering your mind. Try to preserve tranquility. Christ said, "Blessed are the peacemakers" (Matthew 5:9). God will surely bless your work and give you a peaceful soul. The only thing he requires of you is a genuine effort to still the storms in your life.

You can't build a house in a day. Neither will you be able to build this castle of inner peace in your soul in an instant. It is a gradual accomplishment.

—Lawrence Scupoli: *The Spiritual Combat*

A Personal Response

Some people I know tend to medicate their way out of stress, Lord. But you have a better way. Help me to discover "this castle of inner peace."

Gradual Growth

. . . Until we all reach unity in the faith and in the knowledge of the Son of God and become mature, attaining to the whole measure of the fullness of Christ. Ephesians 4:13

Spiritual growth does not happen all at once. It is more like a developing fetus. Over time, it becomes like a human shape, but even when it is born it is not perfect. Growth continues for years. Think of the way seeds of grain winter over before they sprout. A fruit tree sapling takes years to bear fruit. Spiritual progress is a continuing process. It is gradual, incremental.

If you want to be a language scholar you have to start with the alphabet. When you rise to the head of the class in reading and writing it is time to begin Latin. At once you are a beginner again. If you master Latin, then you must enter the school for debating and you are reduced to the lowest rank. If you finish with great scholastic success you must still begin a profession as a novice.

The affairs of this world are conducted in a series of steps. In the same way there are many stages in spiritual growth. You will need to pass through many difficulties and tests on your way to perfection. It does not happen in a flash.

—Pseudo-Macarius: *Homilies*

A Personal Response

Discovering you, Lord, can be so exciting. It's like falling in love. I want to sing about it. I want to shout it from the rooftops! But spare me from thinking I have arrived when I am only getting started. And grant me the ability, O Lord, to understand that many others have been on this road longer than I.

January 14 # Reconciliation

For if, when we were God's enemies, we were reconciled to him through the death of his Son, how much more, having been reconciled, shall we be saved through his life! *Romans 5:10*

When two goats meet on a narrow bridge over deep water, what do they do? The bridge is so narrow they can neither turn around nor pass each other. If they fight they may fall into the water and be drowned.

They resolve the problem quite naturally. One lies down and the other passes over. Neither is injured.

People can learn a similar tactic. It is better to yield a little than to fall into raucous discord with others. We turn too quickly to lawyers. When people desire to be reconciled and to reach an agreement, someone must yield, giving way to another.

This is the way we were reconciled to God. God waived his rights and controlled his wrath. Christ mediated an agreement between us. Like all peacemakers, he suffered pain. The one who separates two fighters receives the most blows. For Christ, reconciliation led to the Cross where he died for us.

—Martin Luther: *Table Talk*

A Personal Response

If I don't look out for myself, Lord, who will do it for me? I live in an aggressive and selfish world. If the earth I inherit by being meek is off the bottom of someone's shoes, I have no interest in it. And yet, yielding a little can make a difference. Help me to comprehend the meaning of *humility* and to follow your example.

January 15 · **Remarkable Love**

> Now the betrayer had arranged a signal with
> them: "The one I kiss is the man; arrest him."
> Going at once to Jesus, Judas said, "Greetings,
> Rabbi!" and kissed him. Jesus replied, "Friend,
> do what you came for." *Matthew 26:48-50*

Ponder how Christ loved Judas, who was his deadly enemy. Christ was good to him. He was courteous to one he knew to be damnable. He chose him as an apostle. He sent him to preach with the others. He gave him power to work miracles. He showed him the same good cheer in word and deed that he gave the other apostles.

He washed his feet and sat down at table with him.

He did not speak sharply to him in front of others.

He never said an evil word about him.

When Judas betrayed him with a kiss, Jesus called him his friend.

In all of this, Christ did not pretend or flatter. He showed honest love.

Judas was not worthy of it. He deserved not even a token of love. Our Lord is love and goodness. It is appropriate for him to show love and goodness to all God's creatures, even Judas.

This kind of unconditional love is also required of us. Jesus said, "A new command I give you: Love one another. As I have loved you, so you must love one another" (John 13:34).

You protest. How can you love a bad person the same way you love a good one? Here is my answer. We are to love both, but not for the same reason. If you can love yourself only because you know you belong to God, you can love others the same way. If they are good and virtuous, you can love God who is in them. If they are bad and immoral, you can still love them—not as they are—but for the sake of God who can make them better.

—Walter Hilton: *The Scale of Perfection*

A Personal Response

Lord Christ, you have demonstrated the best way to deal with enemies. I have no doubt of that. It seems so easy for you. Natural. I suppose it will always seem difficult and unnatural for me—until I become more like you.

How To Find Perfect Joy

May I never boast except in the cross of our
Lord Jesus Christ. *Galatians 6:14*

Saint Francis and Brother Leo were walking from Perugia to
Saint Mary of the Angels. It was winter and they were suffering from the cold. Saint Francis said, "Brother Leo, even
if all the Friars Minor lived a life of exemplary holiness and integrity, make a note that perfect joy is not in that."

They walked further and he spoke again. "Brother Leo, even if a
Friar Minor restores sight to the blind, drives out demons, grants
hearing to the deaf, heals the crippled, gives speech to the dumb and
raises the dead, write it down that perfect joy is not in that."

After walking a little further, Francis again spoke out strongly.
"Brother Leo, if a Friar Minor understood all languages and knew
everything about science and the Bible, if he had the gift of prophecy,
write this down and underline it: perfect joy is not in that."

Continuing on their way, he added more. "Brother Leo, even if
a Friar Minor were able to preach well enough to convert every infidel
to Christ, put it on paper that perfect joy is not there."

After about two miles of this, Brother Leo asked him to please
tell him where perfect joy *could* be found.

This is what Saint Francis said: "If, when we get to Saint Mary
of the Angels, cold and wet and hungry, and the attendant comes to
answer our ringing at the gate, and he is angry and asks us who we
are, and we answer that we are two brothers, and he doesn't believe
us and sends us away because he thinks we are thieves and robbers,
and we have to stay out in the snow and rain without any food until
dark; then, if we are able to endure such treatment patiently, without
getting upset and without complaining, and if we will concede that
he is probably correct in his judgment of us, *then,* Brother Leo, write
it down that perfect joy is there!"

—Ugolino: *Actus-Fioretti*

A Personal Response

The greatest gift you can give me, O Christ, is the ability to
conquer myself so that I can accept suffering, insults, and hu-
miliation for your sake.

January 17 ## Truth

I am sending you prophets and wise men and teachers. Some of them you will kill and crucify; others you will flog in your synagogues and pursue from town to town. *Matthew 23:34*

Think about the challenges to truth. If you accuse someone correctly of being drunk or gossiping, they will become angry with you. They will immediately deny it and strike out against you.

On the other hand, we honor lies. If we tell someone he can hold his drink or is in control of any addiction, we will be thanked by a very pleased individual.

See how we adore truth. It is without "form or comeliness" (Isaiah 53:2, KJV) and is nailed to the cross.

Give a warm welcome to truth, as if it were the Lord himself. A lie is to be serenely ignored, or shown to be untrue.

The most profitable thing in the world is truth. It takes a gentle, strong person to welcome the truth. To this person, truth is as appealing as hazelnuts and blackberries.

Truth alone understands the way to avoid evil. Love of truth is the only thing able to do it. You do not escape evil by moving to another place.

Truth is more difficult to endure than any misfortune. Trouble usually comes with only a few pleasures, but truth can hurt all of them simultaneously. "Love truth and peace" (Zechariah 8:19). Peace naturally follows truth.

—Guigo I: *Meditations*

A Personal Response

Lord, truth today is about telling it slant. We shade truth to make it more favorable. We have learned to submit reports that mislead. Political interests, large and small, color the reporting of truth. In such a world, Lord, teach *me* how to tell the truth.

January 18   ## About Prayer

Very early in the morning, while it was still dark, Jesus got up, left the house and went off to a solitary place, where he prayed. *Mark 1:35*

T he proper thing is for us always to think of God and pray without ceasing. If we are not able to achieve this, we can at least set special times for prayer each day. At these designated moments we can focus entirely on God.

Here are some natural opportunities:

- when we wake in the morning
- before we begin our work
- before and after meals
- when we go to bed

This is only a start, of course. We should not think of these times of prayer as a ritual. Neither do they mean we are freed from prayer at other hours of the day. Think of these moments as nothing more than a discipline for your spiritual weakness. It is a stimulation for your groggy soul. There will be times when you are under stress, times when you will be aware of others in difficulty. Immediately turn to God in prayer. Offer prayers of thanks all through the day.

When you pray, do not put any limits on God. It is not your business to tell God how to answer your prayers. This is not a time to bargain or to set conditions. Before you tell God what you want or need, ask that his will may be done. This makes your will subordinate to his.

—John Calvin: *Of Prayer*

 A Personal Response

Lord, sometimes when I read how the great souls engage in prayer, I feel inadequate. Thank you for the reminder that I can begin quite simply.

January 19 ## Our Illogical Ideas about God

How great are your works, O Lord, how profound your thoughts! *Psalm 92:5*

It is not possible for God to want to hurt any creature. No spark of wrath has ever been, or ever will be, in the holy God. If God's wrath was ever anywhere it must be everywhere. If it burned once, it must burn eternally—because everything that is in God is without limit. God cannot be increased or decreased. It makes as much sense to say that God created the universe out of wrath as to say that God ever wrathfully punished any part of it.

God is the unlimited abyss of all that is good. Anything that is not a blessing is contradictory. It is eternally impossible for God to willingly inflict a moment's hurt on any of his creatures. As the sun's nature requires it to give the blessing of light, so God has but one intention toward all creation. His purpose is to pour the goodness of his divine perfection upon everything that is capable of receiving it.

It is the goodness of God, and a desire to communicate this good, that inspired creation. We are designed to receive God's goodness. This is a purpose that cannot change. God must always will what he willed from the beginning. God is a constantly overflowing fountain of good. He is love itself. God is pure love, unmeasurable love. God's only motive is love. He gives nothing but the gifts of love. The only thing God requires of us is that we return love for love.

The attributes we give God are only human ways of coming to grips with a vastness that is beyond our metaphors and terminology. We suit our thinking and speaking about God to our limited selves. This can be a useful thing to do, but to conclude there must be conflicting qualities in God is sacrilege.

—William Law: *Mystical Writings*

 A Personal Response

You exceed my thoughts, O God. My best ideas about you are far from your fullness.

January 20 # Patience

You need to persevere so that when you have done the will of God, you will receive what he has promised. *Hebrews 10:36*

P atience is not to be reserved for only certain kinds of circumstances. Apply it universally to everything that comes your way. Some only want to suffer when it brings them honor. They are wounded in combat or suffer religious persecution. Maybe they are impoverished by a lawsuit they actually win. Such people don't want trouble. They want the sense of honor that goes with it.

A truly patient person will take it all equally. To be picked on and criticized by mean people is of little concern to a courageous person. But to be denounced and treated badly by good people, by our own friends and relatives is a true test of virtue. The sting of a bee is far more painful than the bite of a fly. Attacks of good people are much harder to bear. Sometimes two good people, both with good intentions, have ideas that conflict. They end up attacking each other and slinging mud.

Your patience is required not only for the major parts of the problems that come to you, but also for the little incidental snags that come along with them. Many would be willing to live with an evil if it were not inconvenient. "Poverty wouldn't bother me if it didn't prevent me from educating my children, helping my friends, and living respectfully." "It wouldn't be a problem if other people didn't think it was my own fault." "I don't mind being sick, but I hate to be a bother."

—Francis de Sales: *The Devout Life*

A Personal Response

Give me patience, Lord God. Send me what you will. Let me try to remedy what I can and then wait to see what you can accomplish. If evil is overcome, I will praise you. If evil prevails, still I will bless you, and I will try to be patient.

January 21 **God's Mercy and the Sins of Youth**

> After I strayed, I repented; after I came to understand, I beat my breast. I was ashamed and humiliated because I bore the disgrace of my youth. *Jeremiah 31:19*

May you be blessed forever, Lord God! Although I abandoned you, you did not abandon me. You held out your hand to me. I refused it. I did not attempt to understand why you kept calling me.

As the sins increased I lost my taste for virtue. Goodness left me because I left you. You warned me in many ways with concern and pity. I gave you no attention.

O Lord of my soul! How can I applaud the good will you showed me during those years? When I offended you the most, you prepared me with an extraordinary repentance. You knew exactly what would be the most distressing thing for me. You punished my sins with wonderful gifts!

I had many friends who helped me fall. No one helped me up. It is surprising that I did not remain down. I praise the mercy of God. He alone extended his hand to me.

May God be forever blessed for putting up with me for so long! Amen.

—Teresa of Avila: *Life*

A Personal Response

Lord, what a mess we make of things! In youth we are victims of the life energies that rush through us. We spin out of control. Even at "the age of discretion" we have little discretion. Forgive us, Lord. Forgive us.

Self-Examination

> Live in harmony with one another. Do not be proud, but be willing to associate with people of low position. Do not be conceited. *Romans 12:16*

Knowledge is of little value without respect for God. The most ordinary person who serves God is better than a proud philosopher who neglects himself while studying the stars. If you really know yourself, you will see that there is little to commend.

Great learning can be a distraction. It can make you try to appear wise in order to win praise. There are many things you can know which will be of little value to your soul. It is not wise to waste your time on them.

If you think you know a lot about something, remind yourself that there are many more things you do not know. If you want to learn something worthwhile, attempt to learn how to be a nobody.

The most profound and valuable lesson of all is to truly know yourself and to have a humble opinion of yourself.

Think well of others. If you see someone else engaging in a sinful act or a crime, do not let that make you think you are any better. You will also stumble. All of us are frail. Consider yourself no stronger than anyone else.

—Thomas à Kempis: *The Imitation of Christ*

A Personal Response

There will always be a delightful glow when something is achieved, O Lord. Some accomplishments can be wonderfully satisfying. If I do one or two things well, help me to remember that there are many things I can't do at all. Don't let me become puffed up or consider myself better than others.

Love and Satisfaction

Do not store up for yourselves treasures on earth, where moth and rust destroy, and where thieves break in and steal. But store up for yourselves treasures in heaven. *Matthew 6:19-20*

W e should not have any ulterior motives for loving God even though rewards will come. They are not the results of bargaining or legal transactions. Love is spontaneous. The only reward love seeks is someone to love. If you are looking for something else, it isn't love.

It is the unwilling, not the willing, that we have to ply with favors. Who would ever think of rewarding a person for enjoying himself? You do not have to bribe those who are hungry to eat. Those who love God expect nothing in return. If they did, then they would love that prize instead of God.

God alone can satisfy our desires. A man with a lovely wife may still look lustfully at an attractive woman. A well-dressed person wants more expensive clothes. The rich envy the richer. You can find people who already own much property and have many possessions, still striving, day in and day out, to add another field to their estates. They have a restless ambition for promotion and honors.

It is not very intelligent to desire what can never satisfy. While enjoying wealth, you keep searching for something you still lack. You run back and forth from one pleasure to another, becoming tired, but never satisfied. Who can own everything? Whatever you cling to, you are surely going to lose one day. You are running down a twisting road and you will die before you reach the end of it.

Eventually, we will come to say to God, "Whom have I in heaven but you? And earth has nothing I desire besides you" (Psalm 73:25). Anything else is doomed to failure. Life is too short, strength too limited, competition too fierce. The long road wears us out.

—Bernard of Clairvaux: *On Loving God*

A Personal Response

Help me to organize my priorities, Lord. Let me trust your unconditional love and serve you with my possessions. If I gain more, let me give more.

January 24   ## Tears and Prayers

I decided to study the Bible. But the sacred Scriptures simply
didn't make any sense to me. They seemed to me to be far
beneath the majesty of Cicero.

Then I began to keep company with the Manicheans, a religious
sect that spoke a lot of inflated nonsense. They spoke many of the
right words, but they were only noises without meaning. They kept
talking to me of "truth," but they had none.

O my supreme and good Father, Beauty of beauties, O Truth,
Truth, how my soul longed for you when I heard your name spoken!
But it was all so many words. Those people took me in because I
thought they spoke with authority. But instead of nourishing me, they
starved me. Dreaming of food seems like the real thing, but it will not
fill an empty stomach. I ate, but I was not fed.

You raised my soul up out of that dark pit. My mother wept
faithfully to you more than mothers weep for dead children. You
heard her, Lord. You heard her. Nine years were to pass. All that time
this faithful widow continued her weeping and mourning. She prayed
every hour. But for all her efforts, you allowed me to remain in
darkness.

You gave her at least two grand assurances. In a dream, you told
her that you would be with me. And through a priest, you explained
to her that it was pointless to try to argue me out of my errors. I was
not yet ready for instruction. I was too excited by the novelty of my
heresy. "Leave him alone," he told her. "Only pray to God for him.
He will discover by his reading how great is his error. It is not possible
that the son of these tears should perish."

—Augustine: *Confessions*

A Personal Response

Lord, thank you for those who have been faithful in prayer
for me. Teach me how to be faithful in prayer for others.

Prayer That Makes a Difference

*I am poor and needy; may the Lord think of me.
You are my help and my deliverer; O my God,
do not delay.* Psalm 40:17

First among the beatitudes is the one that says, "Blessed are the poor in spirit, for theirs is the kingdom of heaven" (Matthew 5:3). Being poor in spirit is a holy poverty. If one is sure he is defenseless alone and can survive only with God's help, that person is like the psalmist who confesses he is poor and needy.

Make the Psalms your own. Do not sing them as verses composed by another person. Let them be born in your own prayers. When they come from your lips, understand that they were not merely fulfilled temporarily when they were first written. They are being fulfilled now in your daily life. There are times when you will understand God's Scripture as clearly as a surgeon understands what is seen upon opening a body.

If you have the same attitude that the psalmist had when he wrote or sang this poetry, you will see the meaning before you have thought about it. The force of the words will strike you before you have examined them with your intellect.

The Psalms express every significant religious feeling. These words are like a mirror to our own moral experience. Once we see this we will not hear the words nearly as much as we perceive the meaning. Instead of being recited from memory, they will flow from the depths of our inner being.

—John Cassian: *Conference Ten on Prayer*

A Personal Response

My pride is in the way, Lord, I don't want to accept assistance from anyone. I want to make it on my own. Being poor in spirit would destroy my self-esteem. Teach me to make the Psalms my own. Be with me in my pondering.

January 26 **Prayer at Dawn**

After the Sabbath, at dawn on the first day of the week, Mary Magdalene and the other Mary went to look at the tomb. *Matthew 28:1*

A s soon as you see daylight, begin to pray in this manner:

O Lord, you are the greatest and most authentic Light. The light of this day comes from you.

O Light, you lighten everyone in this world! O Light, you know no night or evening. It is always midday with you. Without you all is darkness.

Enlighten my mind. Let me see only the things that please you. Blind me to all else.

Grant that I may walk in your ways and find light in nothing else.

—John Bradford: *Daily Meditations*

A Personal Response

Lord, teach me to see each day's light as a gift from you and as an expression of your holy character.

Continuing Friendship

> A friend is always a friend, and relatives are
> born to share our troubles. *Proverbs 17:17,* CEV

True friendship is eternal. If it ever ends, it was not true friendship. It only appeared to be friendship. How can friends become enemies? It is not possible.

If your friend blunders or needs correction, it is understood that you must fulfill your responsibility. Some faults may require that the friendship be terminated or at least gradually dissolved. These actions need not result in hatred. There is no need for arguments and name calling. It is not right to fight with someone who has been your friend.

Even if your friend should attack you, you should ignore and endure it up to the point of intolerable abuse. Some people blame their friends for their troubles. They ignore good advice. When they are caught and their flaw becomes public knowledge, they will turn upon their friends. They will whisper slanderous things in dark corners. They will tell lies to excuse themselves and focus the attention on others.

Once a friend, always a friend. Continue to love even the one who hurts you. The conduct of the other person may force the end of active friendship, but never the end of love. Continue to care for your former friend's best interests. Protect the reputation of another even if that person should destroy yours.

—Aelred of Rievaulx: *Spiritual Friendship*

A Personal Response

It's odd, Lord, how things can turn around. People do the unexpected. We are surprised by shocking reversals. Help me in such a situation. Give me the inner strength to continue caring about the person who has intentionally struck out at me.

January 28 **Working and Praising Together**

The Lord works out everything for his own ends. *Proverbs 16:4*

What is made is intended to be useful to the one who made it. Its usefulness is limited, however. A pot is not able to help the potter to think and talk. In the same way, God's creatures can't help God be God. God will be God without any hindrances. In the same way, a barrel does not improve the understanding and language of a barrelmaker. The potter may sell a pot and the cooper a barrel. The profit can be used to buy bread from the baker and meat from the butcher. This social relationship can be very helpful.

God does not need our service. God is complete in himself. He can do without us. His divinity is independent of our existence. The reason God made us and all other creatures is to make his goodness known. He desires that whatever exists because of his goodness should recognize it and sing his praise. This is why we may be of service to him by serving others. Each creature has special gifts that can be used for the good of all creatures. The result is that God is praised everywhere. The psalmist sings to God, "You are good to everyone, and you take care of all your creation" (Psalm 145:9, CEV).

The sun does not shine for itself, but for all God's creatures. The earth produces not for itself, but for everything God made. All plants and animals are directed to use what they are, have, and can do, toward usefulness to all others.

—Martin Bucer: *Instruction in Christian Love*

 A Personal Response

I am not an island. I am a part of a much larger whole. Help me, O Lord, to do my part for others even as I depend upon them to do for me what I cannot do for myself.

Bible Translations

> All scripture is given by inspiration of God,
> and is profitable for doctrine, for reproof, for
> correction, for instruction in righteousness.
> *2 Timothy 3:16,* KJV

Some think that many different translations of the Scriptures make divisions in the faith and in the people of God. This is not true. The best possible thing for the people of God is for every church to have various translations of the Bible. From the earliest centuries there have been many translations in several tongues. The Church Fathers such as Ireneus, Cyprian, Tertullian, Jerome, Augustine, Hilary, and Ambrose did not read the text all alike.

Therefore, it need not be evil that people who have a knowledge of language should express the text of the Bible in their native tongue. They should work hard at it, translating out of one language into another. Instead of taking offense at such labor, we should thank God for their willingness and for the inspiration of his Spirit!

It would have been better if the practice had not been dropped after the time of Augustine. That would have spared us this era of blindness and ignorance so filled with errors and delusions. As soon as the Bible was set aside, people began to write whatever came into their heads. If it seemed good to them, they put it in print without any reference to Scripture. Sometimes they alleged that their ideas were confirmed by the Bible, but few were able to be certain about this because they could not read the original.

—Miles Coverdale: *A Prologue to the Bible*

A Personal Response

Thank you, God, for the people who supply us with Bibles: for the scholars who carefully translate, for the editors who proofread, for the vast army of unseen people who print, bind, and distribute them. May they understand their work is a ministry in your name.

Response or Prepayment?

I tell you, her many sins have been
forgiven—for she loved much. But he who has
been forgiven little loves little. *Luke 7:47*

The Scripture urges us to do good not in order to win God's love, but to do good because God loves us. Faith naturally results in good works. If good works are not the result, then it is only a dream, an opinion, a pretension of faith.

Notice that fruit does not make a tree good. Fruit is testimony that the tree is good already. As Christ says, "Every good tree bears good fruit, but a bad tree bears bad fruit" (Matthew 7:17). A tree is known by its fruit. You can also spot true faith by its fruit.

We may think in reverse, putting what is behind in front. We begin with the effect and then look for a cause. If the moon is dark we want to know why. We discover that the earth is between the sun and the moon. It is the earth's shadow that darkens the moon. Or consider a man who has a son. This makes him a father, and yet the son is not the cause of the father. Quite the contrary! And yet the son is the proof that the man is a father.

The woman who washed and anointed Christ's feet did so to express love and not to earn it. The things we do demonstrate our loving response to love already received.

—William Tyndale: *The Parable*

A Personal Response

We live in a world where we earn and pay for things, Lord Jesus. Your way is still a matter of "this for that," but it works in reverse. We are freely forgiven by your grace. Responding in love, I will do my best to pass your love on to others.

Religious Tolerance

Above all, love each other deeply, because love
covers over a multitude of sins. *1 Peter 4:8*

There are many different points of view regarding religion. This wide variety of opinions has been a problem for Christianity. There have been factions and great divisions among people who are devoted to God. We are like the doctor who prescribes a good medicine in the wrong way. The cure we intend does not result. Our efforts have been ineffectual because we work on the wrong part or focus on the symptoms rather than the illness.

Our attempts to unite people simply add fuel to the fire. If we had a single rule that could find agreement with everyone in the world, the interpretations of that rule would be so diverse as to become a part of the problem we were trying to fix. We want to reconcile differences of opinion. We think there is no room in Christ's kingdom for variety.

As long as we have such a mixture of ideas, differences in level of education, varieties of temperament, and degrees of enlightenment, it is impossible that everyone will agree. If it is not possible, neither is it necessary.

One heaven will hold people of several opinions. What then is the point of all these factions and divisions? These are the tools of hatred, persecution, and war. Such things are not the natural result of different opinions. The problem is that every opinion is made an article of faith. These become the basis of quarrels, and every quarrel results in a faction. Factions are led by aggressive "true believers" who are convinced God agrees with them. When we are working for God nothing is too much for us. We begin to believe that the only way we can love God is to hate a person who disagrees with us. We think we don't have any religion at all unless we persecute all religions but our own.

In this furious effort we preserve the body but destroy the soul of religion. Being enthusiastic for faith, we lose interest in charity. As a result, we lose the reward of both.

—Jeremy Taylor: *The Liberty of Prophesying*

 A Personal Response

Wow! I need to let this one sink into my soul, Lord.

Obstacles to Prayer

Ask and it will be given to you; seek and you will find; knock and the door will be opened to you. *Matthew 7:7*

Resentment casts a cloud over your prayers. This is why Christ told us to leave our offering before the altar and first go be reconciled with an enemy. If you collect injuries and resentments and think you can still pray, you would probably put water in a bucket full of holes!

Learn patience, and your prayers will be joyful. Sometimes, even in prayer, something will occur to you that will seem worthy of anger. But anger helps nothing. Think of ways to avoid displaying it.

Be careful! While attempting to heal another, you may make yourself sick. If you restrain your anger you will discover how to pray well. Anger is like an overcast day for the soul. It will destroy your prayer life.

The one who is in chains cannot run. In the same way a mind that is a slave to emotion will have a difficult time discovering genuine prayer.

You are crazy if you love prayer and give in to anger or resentment. This is as ridiculous as one who wants to see clearly scratching his eyes. If you desire to pray, stay away from everything that harms prayer. This will clear the path and allow God to walk with you.

When we know we are in the Divine Presence, negative thoughts are stilled. Our spirit is wrapped in profound tranquility. Our prayers are pure.

Much of the time, however, we struggle between prayer and disturbing thoughts. Our emotions get in the way of our prayers. Keep trying. If we knock on the door hard enough it will be opened.

—Evagrius Ponticus: *Chapters on Prayer*

A Personal Response

I get in my own way, dear God. My emotions cloud my judgment and scatter my prayers in little pieces. If I am not able to control myself, let your Holy Spirit take charge. Do for me what I cannot do for myself.

With Friends Like These . . .

My enemies are not the ones who sneer and make fun. I could put up with that or even hide from them. But it was my closest friend, the one I trusted most. *Psalm 55:12-13*, CEV

Friends can hurt us more than enemies. Sometimes the very person we are trying to help turns against us. In such a time, hear what the Lord is saying: "Don't be sad. I have permitted this for the benefit of your soul. I enjoy your companionship. A frightened child returns to its mother's arms. You will find the kind of absolute faithfulness in me that you will not be able to find in another person."

Let the Lord lift you to his breast as though you were a little child. Let him hug you and soothe you with divine kisses. He will take whatever has been troubling you and weave it into a necklace of bright flowers.

Then you will think of others who have greater problems than yours. You will be bothered by your own impatience. When the Lord assures you of his tender love for you, placing the lightweight necklace of brilliant flowers around your neck, you will be strengthened. You will praise God with much devotion.

Being able to praise God when you are troubled is a special gift.
—Gertrude of Helfta: *The Herald of Divine Love*

A Personal Response

I don't have to go looking for trouble, Lord. It seems to find me quite easily. I don't fully understand the complexities of human relationships. The behavior of others is not always easy to understand. I want everyone to love me, but not everyone does. Dear God, your friendship is the most profound and the most enduring. Help me to sing your praise even when others misunderstand and mistreat me.

Raging Nature; Loving God

We will not fear, though the earth give way and the mountains fall into the heart of the sea, though its waters roar and foam and the mountains quake with their surging. *Psalm 46:2-3*

God will always help those who are in trouble if they understand that he is the only help available.

This knowledge removes fear during natural catastrophes. The faithful are confident when the earth shakes, the surf pounds the shore, and things are being washed away. In spite of all these frightening disasters, God steadies those who trust in him. There are visible evidences of divine assistance.

We may trust the goodness of God.

—Peter Vermigli: *Sacred Prayers from the Psalms*

A Personal Response

I remember the fury of an approaching thunderstorm when I was a child. My mother was in the backyard, hurrying to remove drying laundry from the line. The greenish darkness, the howling wind, the crackling thunder terrified me as I stood at the door. Though I was very small, I still remember crying in fear. I also remember the warmth and security that came into the house with my mother and her laundry basket.

Jesus teaches me to think of you, Heavenly Father, as a good parent. Come, be with me in frightening and troubling times.

Misguided Devotion

You are full of all kinds of deceit and trickery. Will you never stop perverting the right ways of the Lord? *Acts 13:10*

If you want to unite your spirit with God, you need to understand the true nature of spirituality.

Some consider only appearances. They concentrate on penances, vigils, fasting, and other physical deprivations. Others indulge in long prayers, attend public services frequently, spend many hours in church, and take Communion as often as they can.

They are all misguided. These things are little more than the side effects of true piety. While these tools are useful in the spiritual life, they are not its essence. They help beginners in their struggle against human nature, which is indifferent to good and inclined to evil.

They also are the precious fruits of the spiritual life. Many perform these things with no desire at all for some resulting sensual pleasure. They honestly want to know the grandeur of Divine Goodness and the depth of their own ingratitude. Such people want to increase their love of God while discovering self-denial. They want to follow their Lord, shouldering his cross. They receive the Lord's Supper for no other reason than the honor of God and a closer union with him.

It is quite different when we ignorantly think of our devotion as external acts. There is nothing wrong with these behaviors, but when wrongly applied they become a hazard. We can become so attached to these rituals that we completely neglect to notice any inner movement of our hearts. Then we become filled with empty ideas and think that we have tasted the joys of Paradise and the delights of angels. We think we have seen God when all we have seen is the devil's decoy.

—Lawrence Scupoli: *The Spiritual Combat*

A Personal Response
Lord God, clear my thinking about my own spirituality.

February 5 ## Lost Labor

If you love me, you will obey what I command.
John 14:15

I f you love God, you will do everything possible to serve and
please him. Love is impatient to do good. It is also quick and
active and observant. Faith will encourage you. Hope will set
you spinning like the spring in a watch. Reverence for God will
rouse you out of your sleepiness. Enthusiasm for spiritual things
will set you on fire. The more aware you are of God, the more
involved you will be in working for him.

Those who trifle lose their labor.

If two are running in a race, the one who runs slowest loses both
the prize and the effort. If you are lifting weights and do not put
sufficient strength into it, you might as well not try it at all. How many
duties have Christians lost because they did not do them thoroughly?
"Make every effort to enter through the narrow door, because many,
I tell you, will try to enter and will not be able to" (Luke 13:24). The
difference may be in the dedicated effort. Give a little more diligence
and strength in the application of your faith. That way what you have
already done will not be wasted.

Precious time is already lost. With some of us, childhood and
youth are gone. With some, middle age is also gone. The time before
us is very uncertain. Only a little of our work is done! The time we
have lost cannot be recovered. If a traveler sleeps late or trifles most
of the day, he must travel much faster in the evening, or fall short of
his journey's end. "For God is not unrighteous to forget your work
and labour of love" (Hebrews 6:10, KJV).

—Richard Baxter: *The Saints' Everlasting Rest*

A Personal Response

Thank you, God, for every distant bugle call that reminds us
it is time to get moving. While it brings you no glory for us
to burn ourselves out early in your service, neither is it any
good to offer you only the charred end of a poorly spent life.

February 6 ## A Matter of Degree

I consider everything a loss compared to the surpassing greatness of knowing Christ Jesus my Lord, for whose sake I have lost all things. I consider them rubbish, that I may gain Christ.
Philippians 3:8

Our best efforts are less than perfect. All of our thinking is tinged with a little stupidity. A humble understanding of ourselves is a more certain way to God than the most in-depth study.

But education is not to be condemned! Knowledge is good. It is God's gift to us. However, a clear conscience and a decent life are superior to great learning. The fruitless error comes in desiring to know much, rather than to live well.

If we were as careful in weeding out vices and planting virtues as we are in scholarly research, we would not have so much evil and scandal among us.

You can be sure of this: when the Day of Judgment comes, we shall not be asked what we have read, but what we have done; not how well we have spoken, but how well we have lived.

Tell me, where now are all the great doctors and masters you used to know? Others now sit in their offices. They are forgotten. The world's glory soon fades.

The person who considers himself small, caring nothing about high honors, is genuinely great. The most learned of all is the one who does the will of God with self-denying love.

—Thomas à Kempis: *The Imitation of Christ*

A Personal Response

The world runs on achievement, Lord. I need to fill my résumé with a long list of accomplishments if I expect to be successful. Perhaps it would be wise to pad it a little. What's that? You are looking for something else?

Suffering As an Opportunity

I consider that our present sufferings are not
worth comparing with the glory that will be
revealed in us. *Romans 8:18*

I don't pray that you may be delivered from your troubles. Instead, I pray that God will give you the strength and patience to
bear them. Comfort yourself with him who nails you to the
cross. Happy are those who suffer with him.

The world doesn't understand this. That's not surprising. They
suffer as lovers of the world and not as lovers of Christ. They think
that sickness is a pain of nature and find nothing in it but grief and
distress. But it can be a consolation to those who understand that God
can use illness in mercy.

God is frequently closer to us in sickness than in health. Put all
of your trust in him and you will soon be on the road to recovery.
Medicine will help you only to the degree God permits. When pains
come from God, only he can heal them. Sometimes a disease of the
body will cure a sickness in the soul.

I can't understand how a soul, which is with God and desires only
God, can feel pain. Be courageous. Offer your pains to God. Pray for
the strength to endure. Above all, develop a habit of conversing often
with God. Adore him in your infirmities. At the very height of your
suffering, ask him humbly and affectionately (as a child to a good
parent) to help you to accept his will.

When our minds are filled with God, suffering will become full
of sweetness and quiet joy. I know it is difficult to accomplish this.
But remember, we can do all things with the grace of God. He never
refuses to help those who earnestly ask for his grace. Knock, keep on
knocking, and I promise you that he will open the door to you in due
time and give you what you have wanted for many years.

—Brother Lawrence: *The Practice of the Presence of God*

A Personal Response

If I must suffer, O God, let me suffer in companionship with
Christ.

February 8 — Hooked on God

I stand at the door and knock; if anyone hears my voice and opens the door, I will come into his house and eat with him, and he will eat with me. *Revelation 3:20,* TEV

You cannot become smart enough to really know God. God will reveal himself to us from within. There is no need to go looking for him or call for him. He is as close as the door of your heart. He is waiting there eager for you to open it. He wants this more than you do.

Here is a way to tell when God has been born in you: Everything will point to God. Nothing will be a hindrance anymore. Everywhere you look, you will see God. It is like staring at the sun. The image is burned into your eyes. Regardless of where you look, you see the sun.

The flesh is strong and prominent here in this world. This is its natural environment. The spirit is a stranger here, an alien. Its connections are in heaven. The old acts of penance were an effort to weaken the dominance of the flesh a little. The best way to restrain the flesh is genuine love. God waits for us to learn this love more than anything else.

It is like a fishhook. The fish must take the bait. If the fish swallows it, there will certainly be a catch. It may twist and turn and leap from the water, but it is hooked. The same thing is true for love. The person who is caught by it is strongly bound. None of the acts of penance and mortification of the flesh can approach its effectiveness.

With the love of God, people will be able to accept and endure whatever happens to them. They will gently forgive the harm that is done to them. There is nothing else in human experience that will bring you as close to God or form a more certain bond. If you take this hook, everything about you belongs to God. The more hooked you are on God, the more freedom you will experience.

—Meister Eckhart: *Sermons*

A Personal Response
We want our independence, Lord. Convince us that the only way we can be liberated is to be caught up into you.

February 9   # Evangelism

"Come, follow me," Jesus said, "and I will make you fishers of men." *Matthew 4:19*

It is your duty to excite and help others to respond to Christ. This does not mean that everyone should become a minister and preach in public. There is no reason for you to go beyond the bounds of your particular work. This does not involve promoting a party spirit. It certainly does not urge you to speak of the faults of others behind their backs while being silent before their faces.

This duty is of another nature. It consists of honestly feeling a burden because of the misery of our acquaintances' souls. We are compassionate toward them and yearn that they might have something better. God will bless our efforts when we are motivated in this manner.

This duty also requires us to take every opportunity that we possibly can to lead them to Christ. Teach them. Show them the glory they are neglecting. Help them. Convince them. Aim only at the glory of God. Do not do these things to improve your self-esteem, or to get a name for yourself, or to get a following, or to make anyone depend on you.

To jeer and scoff, to rant and denounce, is not a likely way to reform anyone. Let them see it is the desire of your heart to do them good. Do it simply and plainly. Choose the right moment. When the earth is soft, the plow will enter. Watch for an opportunity. Love, simplicity, and seriousness are effective with everyone.

Fire is not always brought out of the flint at one stroke. People do not respond immediately. If they do, they are not likely to persist very long.

—Richard Baxter: *The Saints' Everlasting Rest*

A Personal Response

Give me the courage, the determination, and the ability to pass on what I have received, O God.

True Glory

I will not boast about myself, except about my weaknesses. *2 Corinthians 12:5*

If you were smart enough to know all sciences, if you could understand every language, and if you were able to see the stars and planets at close range, you still could take no pride in it. If you were better looking and richer than everyone else, and even if you could work miracles and exorcise demons, none of that would do you any good and neither could it be said to be yours. There is no glory for you in such things. The only thing you can glory in is your infirmities, and in daily carrying the cross.

Consider the Good Shepherd who suffered crucifixion to save his sheep. And now his sheep must follow him in tribulation and persecution and shame, in hunger and thirst, in temptation, and in many other ways. In return, the Lord will give them everlasting life.

Often those who sin or experience grief blame their enemy or their neighbor. But this is wrong. You have control over your enemy because your enemy is your body which commits the sins. Blessed is that servant who makes a captive of his enemy and guards himself from it.

We will never know the full depth of our capacity for patience and humility as long as nothing bothers us. It is only when times are troubled and difficult that we can see how much patience and humility are in us.

—Francis of Assisi: *Admonitions*

 A Personal Response

Sometimes I wonder if these great saints are real, O God. Do they really think like this? Are they just saying the things they think saints are supposed to say? Did Francis ever strike his thumb with a hammer? What did he say then?

At the same time, I know Francis would be the first to remind me of his human nature. There can be no denying the depth of his spiritual life and the powerful effect it has on others. In humility I pause and ask you to help me begin to think and pray this way.

A Glimmer of Light

What must I do to be saved? *Acts 16:30*

I dreamed I saw a man clothed with rags, looking away from his home, with a book in his hand and a great burden upon his back. I saw him open the book and read. As he read, he wept and trembled. He cried out, "What shall I do?"

He looked like he wanted to run, but did not know which way to go. I saw a man named Evangelist coming to him. He asked, "Why are you crying?"

"Sir, I see by this book that I am condemned to die, and after that to come to judgment. I am not willing to die and not able to withstand judgment."

"Why not die? This life is very troublesome."

"Because I fear that this burden on my back will sink me lower than the grave."

"Then," asked Evangelist, "why are you standing here?"

"Because I don't know where to go."

Evangelist pointed with his finger over a very wide field. "Do you see yonder Wicket-gate?"

"No."

"Do you see yonder shining light?"

"I *think* I do."

"Keep that light in your eye, and go straight to it. You will find the gate. When you knock, you will be told what to do."

—John Bunyan: *The Pilgrim's Progress*

A Personal Response

You speak of a mustard seed of faith, Lord Jesus. Sometimes it is enough to *think* I see a little light in the distance. That will get me started.

February 12 Heavenly Guidance

Blessed are they whose ways are blameless,
who walk according to the law of the Lord.
Blessed are they who keep his statutes and seek
him with all their heart. They do nothing
wrong; they walk in his ways. You have laid
down precepts that are to be fully obeyed.
Psalm 119:1-4

The captain of a ship uses the North Star to guide his way upon the sea. In the same way we, who are passengers and strangers in this world, must keep our eyes on God. Then no tempest will capsize us. We will be guided past dangers and will arrive safely in our haven of rest.

Jesus said, "I am the light of the world. Whoever follows me will never walk in darkness, but will have the light of life" (John 8:12). This is our rule of faith. Without this our faith is mere fantasy.

Pray for knowledge of God's word. "Show me your ways, O Lord, teach me your paths; guide me in your truth and teach me" (Psalm 25:4).

—John Jewell: *Of the Holy Scriptures*

A Personal Response

Oh, that my ways were steadfast in obeying your decrees!
Then I would not be put to shame when I consider all your
commands. I will praise you with an upright heart as I learn
your righteous laws. I will obey your decrees; do not utterly
forsake me.—Psalm 119:5-8

Sadness

Why are you downcast, O my soul? Why so disturbed within me? Put your hope in God, for I will yet praise him, my Savior and my God.
Psalm 42:11

Godly sorrow brings repentance that leads to salvation and leaves no regret, but worldly sorrow brings death" (2 Corinthians 7:10). Sadness, then, can be either a blessing or a curse. It has many negative effects, but only two positive effects—compassion for others and repentance.

"Is any one of you in trouble? He should pray" (James 5:13). It is also helpful to get busy with some diverting work. Get around spiritual people and talk out your feelings with them. Keep trusting God. After this trial he will deliver you from evil.

Each day is unique. There are cloudy days and sunny; wet days and dry; windy days and calm. The seasons roll by as day turns into night and night into day. This variety makes beauty. It's the same way with your life. There are ups and downs; no two days, no two hours, are ever exactly alike.

A compass needle always points north regardless of the ship's course. If we will aspire toward God, the confusing changes of life will not unsteady us. "If we live, we live to the Lord; and if we die, we die to the Lord. So, whether we live or die, we belong to the Lord" (Romans 14:8).

Nothing can separate us from God's love. When little bees are caught in a storm they take hold of small stones so that they can keep their balance when they fly. Our firm resolution to stay with God is like stability to the soul amid the rolling waves of life.

—Francis de Sales: *The Devout Life*

A Personal Response

Lord, sometimes I am sad and don't know how to turn my sadness into compassion or repentance. I need your guidance through life's confusing changes. I need your steadying hand to give me balance and keep me on course.

The Nature of Prayer

Pray in the Spirit on all occasions with all
kinds of prayers and requests. *Ephesians 6:18*

When you pray, do not aim your heart at earthly things.
Put all of your effort into drawing your thoughts inward.
Let your desires be free of material things. Direct yourself to God. When you can pray like this, you have learned how to
pray well.

Prayer is mainly the desire of the heart rising into God. It is like
fire that blazes away from the lowness of the earth and goes up into
the air. When what you want in your prayer life has been touched and
set on fire by God, it will rise naturally to its source.

We may speak of the fire of love, but it is not easy to describe.
It is not felt in the body. It is felt in prayer and devotion by a soul
who exists in a body. It is a spiritual thing.

There are three kinds of prayer. The first is spoken prayer with a
prepared text, such as the Lord's Prayer and other special prayers. It
is useful to say these vocal prayers as devoutly as possible. Never say
them carelessly or grudgingly. Such prayers can lift you up to God.

The second kind of prayer is spoken, but without prepared text.
This is when a man or a woman feels devout and speaks to God as
though they were standing together. The words match an inward
stirring and reflect the various concerns of the moment. This kind of
prayer pleases God. Because it comes from the heart, it never goes
away without some of God's grace.

The third type of prayer is only in the heart. It is silent and brings
with it great rest of body and soul. Some can pray in the heart
continually, glorifying and praising God.

—Walter Hilton: *The Scale of Perfection*

A Personal Response

Lord, teach me how to pray.

February 15   # The Feminine Side of God

As a mother comforts her child, so will I comfort you; and you will be comforted. *Isaiah 66:13*

God is happy to be our Father. God is pleased to be our Mother. God rejoices that he is our Spouse and our soul is his beloved. Christ is happy to be our Brother, and Jesus rejoices that he is our Savior. These make five great joys.

As truly as God is our Father, so also is God our Mother. God is both the power and goodness of fatherhood and the wisdom and lovingness of motherhood.

There are three ways to consider the motherhood of God. One is in the foundation of the creation of our nature. The second is in the Incarnation, the taking of our human nature. The third is in motherhood at work.

The service rendered by a mother is naturally near, lovingly ready, and truly sure. We know that all our mothers experience pain for us. Jesus is our true Mother. He nourishes us. He alone loves and labors for us to the point of death.

When we realize our sin, we are embarrassed. We hide in shame. But our courteous Mother does not want us to run away. Nothing could be less pleasing to our Mother, who wants us to behave like a child. A hurt and distressed child runs to its mother for help.

Our lives are a wonderful mixture of happiness and grief. We possess both our risen Lord Jesus Christ and the disastrous results of Adam's fall.

We are all feeble children until our gracious Mother brings us up to our Father's joy. Then we will fully understand these words: All will be well. You will see for yourself that everything will be well.

—Julian of Norwich: *Showings*

 A Personal Response

My kind and gracious Mother, I love you. Have mercy on me. I have made a mess of myself. Only you can make it right.
—Julian of Norwich

Good Reading

The word of the Lord is right and true; he is faithful in all he does. *Psalm 33:4*

Reading and meditating upon sacred Scripture will prepare you for both the joy of the love of God and the contempt of worldly people. Read the parts of the Bible that speak of the love of God and that teach you how to live and pray. Leave the more difficult parts to the scholars with long experience in sacred doctrine.

Scripture will help you to become a better person. It will help you to discover both your strengths and your weaknesses. It clarifies the meaning of sin. It will help you determine what to avoid and what to do. With its guidance you can perceive the most subtle activities of temptation.

The Bible will make love burn in your heart. It will sting you to tears. It will prepare you for a banquet with God.

But be careful of your motive! Do not let a desire for the honor and applause of others drive you to gain a knowledge of the Bible. Intend only to please God. Make it your goal to learn how you may love God.

When you teach your neighbor, sharing what you have learned, do so without attempting to appear wise. It would be better to hide your knowledge of the Bible than to show it off for your own praise.

—Richard Rolle: *The Mending of Life*

A Personal Response

My desire is to become more familiar with your Word, Lord God. For my own spiritual welfare I want to be familiar with its contents. Let me be stirred more by the things in it I clearly understand than by its mysteries. May my understanding increase with each passing day.

No Rose Garden Promised

> Blessed are those who are persecuted because of righteousness, for theirs is the kingdom of heaven. *Matthew 5:10*

The Bible assures us that our faith is more precious than gold, and that it is tried by fire. We may suffer for our Lord. If that is our assignment we will do it without complaint. Christ suffered afflictions for us. We can follow his footsteps. He committed no sin. There was no deceit in his mouth. When he was maligned, he did not return anything similar.

Jesus said, "Blessed are you when people insult you, persecute you and falsely say all kinds of evil against you because of me. Rejoice and be glad, because great is your reward in heaven, for in the same way they persecuted the prophets who were before you" (Matthew 5:11-12). We must remember his words no matter what others think of us.

If Christ suffered, why should we expect to be spared? "The disciple is not above his master: but every one that is perfect shall be as his master" (Luke 6:40, KJV). You can be sure that your heavenly Father wishes good for you. Without his knowledge and permission, nothing can harm you. Cast all your care upon him. He will provide what is best. Jesus asked, "Are not two sparrows sold for a penny? Yet not one of them will fall to the ground apart from the will of your Father. And even the very hairs of your head are all numbered. So don't be afraid; you are worth more than many sparrows" (Matthew 10:29-31).

—Nicholas Ridley: *Farewell*

 A Personal Response

When you ask me to follow you, Lord, I have a mental image of a garden path—flowers, fragrances, butterflies, rainbows, smiles, and gentle music. I want to follow you across the sunny hills of Galilee. I want to follow you to the edge of a beautiful lake. If you beckon me to Calvary, give me the strength to follow.

February 18 ## Take Time to Evaluate

It is not good to have zeal without knowledge,
nor to be hasty and miss the way. *Proverbs 19:2*

D on't believe everything you hear or see. Consider things
carefully. Spend some time evaluating things in God's
presence.

We often believe and repeat ugly rumors. It is best not to accept
every report. We have a tendency to evil, and even the most reliable
sources make mistakes.

Be hesitant to believe the things you hear. Don't be quick to pour
it into another's ears.

The more humility you have and the more subject you are to God,
the wiser you will be, and the more at peace.

—Thomas à Kempis: *The Imitation of Christ*

A Personal Response

Avoid hearsay and rumors—that has always been good advice,
Lord, but it seems even more important to hear today. With
digital manipulation I can see people do things they did not
do, hear them speak words that never came from their lips.
The tabloids scream at me with images and headlines that are
comical because of their obvious deception. Help me to understand that the juicy things I pick up over the back fence
or by the office water cooler may be equally tweaked. And
please, Lord God, if I must pass it on, don't let me add my
own new details.

February 19 # Springtime of the Soul

Surely you have granted him eternal blessings and made him glad with the joy of your presence. *Psalm 21:6*

A well-cultivated spiritual life is the best way to find peace and security. Countries in the far north are cold and frozen because they are at a greater distance from the sun. Some Christians are cold and frozen because they live too far from heaven.

Spring sunshine causes all things on earth to revel in its approach. Grass turns green, trees burst out of their buds, dormant plants awake, birds sing, the entire countryside wears a smile. If we tried to live life with God, keeping our hearts on the things above, what a spring of joy would rise within us! We would forget the sorrows of winter. We would get up early singing praises to God.

Won't you try this? Those who have, report that it is warmer there. Probably you have had a little taste of it. When are you happiest? Hasn't it been when you have been close with God and caught a glimpse of heavenly glory? If this is true for you, it is certain that you have a notion of what spiritual joy can be. If David is right when he says that the light of God's countenance cheers the heart more than wine, then surely those who are most aware of God are the happiest.

In the same way that you would thrill a greedy person by showing him some gold, God enjoys his people by leading them to heaven and revealing himself to them. He does not do this when we are busy with other things. He gives the fruits of the earth while we plow and sow and weed and water and fertilize and cultivate patiently. God gives the joys of the soul in the same way. Get busy and learn the art of heavenly-mindedness.

—Richard Baxter: *The Saints' Everlasting Rest*

A Personal Response

Lord, I want to seek your glory. I want to enjoy your presence. Teach me to put other things aside in order to cultivate time with you.

Loving Others

For where your treasure is, there your heart will be also. *Matthew 6:21*

Love is natural. It is not the result of teaching an idea. It is part of our being. To keep our love from becoming self-centered, we are given this commandment: "Love your neighbor as yourself" (Matthew 22:39). Those who share our nature should benefit from shared love. Those who indulge themselves need to remember that their neighbors have identical privileges. Restraint is the safeguard. Instead of serving the enemy of your soul with nature's gifts, serve your neighbor. God will give you the means to do it.

It is not possible to love your neighbor unless you love God. If you love God first, then you can love your neighbor in God.

It is advantageous to love God. Some things we cannot do for ourselves. We need divine help. If we are faced with many difficulties, we will turn to God for help with increasing frequency. As God continues to help, even the coldest heart will be warmed.

Personal familiarity with God's goodness is the best incentive to pure love of him. This is expressed by the Samaritans to the woman at the well: "We no longer believe just because of what you said; now we have heard for ourselves, and we know that this man really is the Savior of the world" (John 4:42). We become like these Samaritans when we can say to our body, "We love God now, not because God can satisfy our needs, but because we have found out for ourselves how good the Lord is!"

If we feel this way we will have little difficulty loving our neighbor. If we really love God, we will love what belongs to God. We will love in the same manner as we have been loved. We care about others even as Christ cared. We love the Lord not because he is good to us, but because the Lord is *good*.

—Bernard of Clairvaux: *On Loving God*

A Personal Response

Help me to see other people as objects of your love, dear God. If I can't love them because they please me, let me love them because you love them.

February 21 Growth

But I don't need to write to you about the
Christian love that should be shown among
God's people. For God himself has taught you
to love one another. Indeed, your love is
already strong toward all the Christians in all
of Macedonia. Even so, dear friends, we beg
you to love them more and more.
1 Thessalonians 4:9-10, NLT

Many of this world seek to increase in their wealth and
riches. They never think they have enough in the bank.
In 1 Thessalonians, Saint Paul is urging us to increase in
everything that is good.

A child that does not grow bigger is pathetic. Soil that does not
produce vegetation is sterile. The tree that is barren is cut down.
Unless we go forward we slip backward.

—John Jewell: *Exposition on the Thessalonians*

 A Personal Response

No matter how much I have achieved, I am not finished. There
are always a multitude of new lessons waiting to be learned,
fresh mountains waiting to be climbed. In doing good for others
and deepening my spiritual life, I have a long way to go. Help
me grow, Lord. Help me grow.

Mother Knows Best

We were as gentle among you as a mother
feeding and caring for her own children.
1 Thessalonians 2:7, NLT

A mother may understand that her little child would like to
take a sparrow in its hand. She is careful to prevent that
from happening, even though she is sure the child would
be glad to have it.

It is certain that we want those we love to be happy. Then why
does the mother not want her child to have it? Why does she work so
hard to prevent its capture? If she wants a happy child, then it makes
little sense to deny it the very thing it wants.

She knows a moment's pleasure with the bird will bring great
sadness later. The child's sadness in the future will be equal to its
delight now. She is guiding the child away from those pleasures which
bring tears. Passing joys can leave us with bitterness.

Wonderful possessions and the opinions of others are in this
category. What we need is a wise mother who will guide us away
from the instant gratifications that ultimately bring regret.

But listen to us complain! All over the world a great fretting and
crying go up in protest and frustration to the One who will not give
us what we demand. Part of the business of the church, and of those
who lead it, is to call us back from damaging desires.

The more the mother loves, the more she grieves. She knows
what is coming to those who want only immediate pleasures.

Without a doubt, many of the tears in this world are in the eyes
of children who are being denied a sparrow.

—Guigo I: *Meditations*

A Personal Response

Why, O God, is it so difficult for me to admit that you may
know more about what is good for me, and for others, than I
do?

Cravings

I have learned the secret of being content in any and every situation, whether well-fed or hungry, whether living in plenty or in want. I can do everything through him who gives me strength. *Philippians 4:12-13*

L et me comfort and strengthen you against the anxious care of the belly. Many in our time are greatly troubled by this.

I am fully aware of the constant cravings of our stomachs. It fears it shall never have enough. That's why it continually knocks at the door of the mind to remind us to provide for it, saying, "Bring here! Bring in!" The idle belly continually consumes and wastes. All it cares about is being fed.

This belly care causes lawyers to corrupt the law. It leads officers to be untrue to their superiors. It motivates hypocrites to corrupt the Holy Scriptures. It makes rich people stingy. Because of it, craftsmen make poor and faulty wares. It prompts landlords to raise rents and innkeepers to gouge their guests. It causes servants to rob their masters and subjects to rise against their overlords. Innumerable evils are the result of this care for the belly.

Belly care, without a doubt, is a great temptation. To resist it, remember that the Holy Scriptures teach us that the Lord is merciful and bounteous. He will not allow us to starve if we place our trust in his fatherly providence.

—Thomas Becon: *The Fortress of the Faithful*

A Personal Response

You made me with a marvelous complexity, Lord God. The needs of my stomach are only the beginning of my primary motivators. It is a simple and very present example, however. Guard me against my cravings.

The Best Way to Fast

Then John's disciples came and asked him, "How is it that we and the Pharisees fast, but your disciples do not fast?" *Matthew 9:14*

I was sitting on a hillside, fasting and thanking God for all his care. The shepherd sat beside me.

He asked, "Why are you here so early?"

"I am fasting."

"You are doing it wrong. This is not the way to fast for God."

"What do you mean?"

He said, "This is not truly a fast you are keeping. It is not enough to limit your eating."

"Sir," I said, "you will do me a great service if you will tell me how to fast in a way that is acceptable to God."

"Listen," he replied. "God does not want a pointless fast like this. This is what you are to do to please God. Avoid evil. Serve the Lord with a pure heart. Keep his commandments and live by his orders. Control your thoughts. If you do these things and behave decently, you will live to God. If you do this, you will keep a great fast that is acceptable to God."

—The Shepherd of Hermas

A Personal Response

The spiritual life is not about skipping meals but about having a pure heart before you, Lord. Teach me to keep that "great fast."

Beginners

> I could not address you as spiritual but as worldly—mere infants in Christ. *1 Corinthians 3:1*

If you have lived far from God, you may think you are very near him when you finally start a life with him. The peasant thinks he has been to court because he saw the king pass by one day.

New Christians give up their worst sins and break fewer laws than they once did, but they are still attached to the world. Instead of judging themselves by the gospel they merely compare themselves with their former lives. If today is better than yesterday, they think this is enough to make them saints. If they can tell you the time and place of their salvation, they probably see nothing remaining to be done.

Such people have a long way to go.

—François de Fénelon, *Meditations and Devotions*

A Personal Response

In my enthusiasm I like to believe I have everything settled. I have good answers for important questions. I can recite a few verses of Scripture. I can even quote chapter and verse! I look at others who have not made the discoveries I have made. I feel sorry for them, maybe even a little superior to them.

I know better, Lord. I know the road is long and I have not traveled far. There are questions I have not yet asked, difficulties I have not experienced, and joys I have not known. Be patient with me, Lord. Keep me growing.

February 26 # The Demands of Inequality

Does not the potter have the right to make out
of the same lump of clay some pottery for
noble purposes and some for common use?
Romans 9:21

Here is a question for the rich. How is it that you happen to be rich? Is it because God has blessed you? By what means did you receive this blessing? Is it through prayer? You prayed for riches and God gave you riches? Very well.

But answer another question. What do others, who are not rich, seek in prayer? Do they not pray the same way you do? If everyone prays for riches then it must be that your riches are not the result of your own prayers only, but also of others who have helped you pray. It is quite possible that some of them are better than you are. It follows that since you did not receive your riches through your own prayers alone, but through the prayers of the poor, then you are obligated to relieve poverty in any way you can.

What is the point of this inequality? Why does God give some a hundred and another thousands and some nothing at all? Here is the meaning. The rich are to distribute riches among the poor. Those who are rich are God's officers, God's treasurers. "It is *God,* not we, who makes things grow" (1 Corinthians 3:6, THE MESSAGE, adapted).

—Hugh Latimer: *Fruitful Sermons*

 A Personal Response

Lord, the problem is that none of us ever think we are rich. Except for maybe a few at the very top, we all wish we had about 10 percent more than we do. But teach me to take a clear look at my situation. Teach me my duty. Do I have anything I can share? Let me be your treasurer and share in your name. Do I have a need? Teach me to receive in your name.

Crossing the Wires

> Woe to those who call evil good and good evil,
> who put darkness for light and light for
> darkness, who put bitter for sweet and sweet for
> bitter. *Isaiah 5:20*

These are the things that produce anger and rivalry:

- hating
- evil suspicion
- false and unreasonable projection
- despising
- misquoting
- unreasonable blaming
- unkindness
- backbiting
- thinking ill of those who speak evil against you—and
  being glad when they are in trouble
- being furious with those who will not do what you
  want—and wanting to hurt them while appearing to
  love them

Many are trapped by this. They choose the bitter instead of the sweet.
They take darkness instead of light. They hate the person instead of
the sin, and think that they hate the sin.

—Walter Hilton: *The Scale of Perfection*

A Personal Response

Whenever I am mean, I like to think it is for a good cause.
Convince me, dear God, that I am mistaken at such times. My
eyes are often clouded by suspicion or blame or bitterness.
Teach me to see with your eyes, away from anger and blame:
Then I will learn to call the good *good* and the light *light.*

Virtuous Patience

Watch and pray so that you will not fall into
temptation. The spirit is willing, but the body is
weak. *Matthew 26:41*

P atience is a cheerful acceptance of frustration. A patient person does not complain about problems. Ordinary people always grumble about difficulties. They are looking for
comfort in the wrong place if they try to find it here in this world.

A faithful person will sometimes have to face the scorn and
slander of others. Patience is the shield against these things. Be ready
to forget and forgive all wrongs done against you. Pray that those who
hate and hurt you may be turned in a better direction.

It is not possible for you to demonstrate whether you are strong
or weak, unless you are troubled when you are at peace. Many may
seem to be patient when they are not being tested. But the slightest
correction will provoke bitter wrath. Any resistance to their ideas and
desires will enrage them.

Run away from the praises of others. Place no value on celebrity
status and good favor. Gladly sustain backbiting and enmity. Look
for your comfort in heavenly places.

When you are tempted or troubled, remember what our Savior
said. "Watch and pray so that you will not fall into temptation." He
did not say, "Pray that you will not be tempted." It is good for us to
be troubled and tempted. God will be with us in such times. He will
sustain and deliver us.

Don't get the idea that you are holy because you have been spared
temptation. The holiest of all are the most tempted of all. The higher
the mountain, the greater the wind. God plays with his child the way
a mother sometimes hides from a little one. Soon enough, there will
be hugs and a wiping away of tears.

—John Wycliffe: *The Poor Caitiff*

A Personal Response

Devout prayer is the sweet incense that drives evil away and
brings me into your presence, O God.—John Wycliffe

February 29 ## Problems with Criticism

Let us stop passing judgment on one another.
Romans 14:13

N o one can be justified in criticizing or condemning another person. No one really knows another. I can see this in myself. I don't know what's going on in the world. My friends don't really know me. I am in a cloud.

Those who know me superficially think less of me than I do of myself. Those who are closer to me think more highly of me. God, who truly knows me, knows that I am nothing. God is not deceived or misled.

Further, no one can judge another, because no one knows himself. We are critical of others when they disagree with what we think is good in ourselves. We commend others only for what seems to reflect our own values.

—Thomas Browne: *Religio Medici*

A Personal Response

There is, of course, another side to this debate. We must stand for something unless we fall for anything. An open mind is an empty mind. But as I play the argument through in my mind, it turns into blah, blah, blah. I am forced to admit the truth spoken by this ancient physician. After all, he got it from you, Lord Christ.

Imperfect Perception

Now we see but a poor reflection as in a mirror; then we shall see face to face. Now I know in part; then I shall know fully. *1 Corinthians 13:12*

Lift your heart up to God with simple love. Let God be your aim rather than the things he can provide. Try to forget the world and everything material. Focus on God alone.

When you begin you will only find darkness. This is like a cloud of unknowing. You will not be able to identify it. As you reach out to God, this dark cloud will always be between you and God. There is nothing you can do about it. It will prevent you from seeing him clearly. Neither the reasoning powers of your rational mind nor the affections of your emotions will permit a complete experience of God.

Accept this as natural. Try to be comfortable and content in this darkness for as long as it takes. Continue to call out for God. If you are going to have any kind of experience with God in this life, it will be in this cloud and in this darkness.

You have a knowing power and a loving power. God, who gave both of them to you, is incomprehensible to the knowing power. But he is entirely comprehensible to the loving power. This is the miracle of love.

Some think they ought to be able to achieve a perception of God by thinking about him. Racking your brain with intellectual effort is useless. You will misguide yourself.

—Anonymous: *The Cloud of Unknowing*

A Personal Response

Lord, my spiritual vision is clouded. I search for you in darkness. Though my ability to perceive you is limited, let my love for you be total.

Why You Are Here

Let the Spirit change your way of thinking and make you into a new person. You were created to be like God, and so you must please him and be truly holy. Ephesians 4:23-24, CEV

God did not put you in the world because he needed you. He made you for the purpose of working his goodness in you. He has given you a mind to know him, a memory to recall his favors, a will to love him, eyes to see what he does, and a tongue to sing his praise.

This is the reason you are here. Anything that hinders that purpose needs to be avoided.

Think of the unhappy people who miss this point and live as though they were here only to construct houses, plant trees, accumulate money, and waste themselves on trifling matters.

Scold your soul with humility. Remind it that until now it has been so miserable that it hasn't thought much about these things. Ask yourself, "What did I think about when I did not think about God? What did I remember when I forgot God? What did I love when I did not love God?"

Hate your previous behavior. "I am through thinking shallow thoughts and making futile plans. I renounce bad friendships, ugly deeds, and self-indulgence."

Turn to God. "My Savior, from now on you will be at the center of my attention. I will stop thinking about evil things. I will remember your mercy toward me every day. The vanities I used to chase after now disgust me."

—Francis de Sales: *The Devout Life.*

A Personal Response

Thank you, God, for my purpose in life. Help me to measure up.—Francis de Sales

Keep On Praying

Be joyful in hope, patient in affliction, faithful in prayer. *Romans 12:12*

With a proper attitude toward God it will be easy to learn to persevere in prayer. We will discover ways to hold our own desires in check and wait patiently for the Lord. We can be sure he is always with us. We can be confident he actually hears our prayers even when the only immediate response is silence.

It is a mistake to be like impatient children who need instant gratification. There are times when God does not respond as quickly as we would like. This is not a time to be despondent. It does not mean that God is angry with you or indifferent toward you. This is certainly not the time to give up praying. Instead of being discouraged, keep on praying.

This perseverance in prayer is highly recommended to us in the Scripture. In Psalms we read how David and others became almost weary of praying. They complained that God was not responding to their prayers. But they understood that persistent faith was a requirement, and they continued to pray.

—John Calvin: *Of Prayer*

A Personal Response

It may seem like a trite religious idea, Lord, but I know it is true. Sometimes your kindest answer to my plea is, "No." Or maybe, "Not yet."

March 4   # A Glimpse of Deep Waters

My soul thirsts for God, for the living God.
When can I go and meet with God? *Psalm 42:2*

Consider prayer this way: two ponds of water have quite different sources. One needs elaborate plumbing with canals and pipes. The other is filled with an unseen, continuously flowing spring. The pipes are like our meditations that bring us the water when we have done our work. But the spring is symbolic of the direct gift of God. I can't explain where or how it arrives. All I can say is that it begins with God and ends within ourselves, producing a great calm and peace.

God enlarges the heart by sending spiritual water from a source deep within us. It is like smelling something good cooking on a distant grill. The spiritual joy is not something we can obtain with our own efforts. We can only receive it as a gift. The best way to experience it, then, is not to strive for it. Simply love God without any ulterior motives. In humility recognize that you are not worthy of such an experience. Desire to suffer the way the Lord suffered, instead of seeking spiritual pleasure. We can be saved without these divine favors. God knows what is best for us. Anyway, how can we make a spring flow water? There is nothing we can do. This experience is given only as God wills, and often the recipient is not even thinking about it.

Let me warn you about a danger. Some persons have such weak physical constitutions they are overcome as soon as they feel any interior pleasure. They misinterpret what is happening to them and call the physical experience "spiritual." They figure it must be a rapture. I call it foolishness. It is a waste of time and bad for their health.

When the experiences are given by God there is no withering weakness in the soul, only deep joy at being close to God.

—Teresa of Avila: *Interior Castle*

A Personal Response

Please, God, don't let me play games with you. I know some prayers reach a profounder depth than others, but I seek no prophet's ecstasy, no angelic visitations. It would be enough if you would simply take away the coldness of my heart.

Three Kinds of Friendship

This is the very best way to love. Put your life on the line for your friends. John 15:13, THE MESSAGE

More people can be loved than can be our friends. We can love our enemies. The only ones we can call friends are those we can trust with our secrets. If we are someone's friend, we are obligated to provide this same good faith and security. If you don't have respect for yourself, it will be impossible to respect another.

There are three types of friendship. *Physical friendship* entertains and captivates many. The one will agree to any crime or impiety imaginable to please the other. It is a sweet friendship bonded by shared likes and dislikes. This kind of friendship is not controlled by reason. It is entirely governed by wild emotion without any consideration of limits or consequences. Primed by furious passions, it either consumes itself or is broken apart as casually as it was formed.

Worldly friendship is prompted by a desire for possessions. It is accompanied by deception and intrigue. It is never settled, changing with circumstances and following the pocketbook. These friends are often called "fair weather friends." If the possibility of getting something is removed, the friendship evaporates.

Spiritual friendship requires neither worldly benefit nor an external motive. Such a friendship is its own reward. This friendship is wisdom. "God is love" (1 John 4:16). While it might be stretching the point to say that God is friendship, we need not hesitate to attribute to true friendship what is attributed to love. We might even go on to paraphrase the remainder of that verse by saying, "Those who abide in friendship, abide in God, and God in them."

—Aelred of Rievaulx: *Spiritual Friendship*

 A Personal Response

Could anything better be said of me than to have someone call me a true friend?

A Prayer for Getting Dressed

He wraps himself in light as with a garment.
Psalm 104:2

When you dress yourself, pray:

O Christ, clothe me with yourself. Be for me a warm garment that will protect me from catching the cold of this world.

If you are away from me, dear Lord, all things will be cold and lifeless. But if you are with me, all things will be warm, lively, and fresh.

As I cover my body with this article of clothing, please become the clothing of my soul. Put upon me mercy, meekness, love, and peace.

—John Bradford: *Daily Meditations*

A Personal Response

Call to mind a little how we are a part of Christ's body. Consider how he clothes us and nourishes us under his wings. Think of God's protection and providence.—John Bradford

Keeping Yourself in Check

The Lord sneers at those who sneer at him, but he is kind to everyone who is humble. *Proverbs 3:34,* CEV

There is no shame in appearing to be poor in the world's eyes and serving others because of your love for Jesus Christ.

Take no glory in money, if you have any, or in influential friends. Glory in God who gives you everything and above all wants to give you himself.

Avoid boasting about the size or beauty of your body, which a little illness can disfigure or destroy.

Have no pride in your native wit and talent. Reject the thought that you are better than anyone else. God knows what is in you. There is no excuse for being haughty.

Pride about our good deeds is pointless. God has his own ideas regarding what is good, and he does not always agree with us. If there is anything good about you, believe better things of others. This will keep you humble.

It will not hurt you at all to consider yourself less righteous than others, but it will be disastrous for you to consider yourself better than even one other person.

The humble are always at peace; the proud are often envious and angry.

—Thomas à Kempis: *The Imitation of Christ*

A Personal Response

Pride is a powerful force, O Lord. Help me to understand that it has a negative effect upon my spiritual life. Most importantly, don't let me fall into the trap of trying to build myself up by putting others down.

Risks of Newness

> You blind guides! You strain out a gnat but
> swallow a camel. *Matthew 23:24*

After a soul is converted to God's service, it is spiritually nurtured and caressed by God. It is as though a loving mother holds a child to the warmth and nourishment of her bosom.

When the child is an infant, the mother carries it in her arms and caresses it. As the child grows bigger, it is weaned and encouraged to walk on its own legs. There is a natural independence that increases each day. Important steps happen: the child ceases being a child and learns to accept more important responsibilities.

A mother's love is similar to God's grace. When souls are warmed with a fervent desire to serve God, they are lead by God to spiritual milk. Without any effort on their own part, they are freely given sweet and delectable spiritual pleasure.

Such souls enjoy long times at prayer and take pleasure in the things of God. But because they are not prepared, not mature, they may be awkward. Their spiritual activity is imperfect. Since they have not had the opportunity to practice spiritual skills, they necessarily stumble like children.

As these beginners are very enthusiastic about the devout life, they often feel a kind of secret pride. In spite of their immaturity and imperfections they may feel a certain satisfaction with themselves. They begin to want to talk with others about spiritual things. They want to teach rather than learn. They look down on others who do not think and feel as they themselves do. Their pride and presumptions grow. Virtues even become vices.

When another religious person questions their activity, they think they are not understood. Eager to be highly esteemed and praised, they imagine their critics are not truly saved.

—John of the Cross: *Dark Night of the Soul*

A Personal Response

A little knowledge is a dangerous thing. Give me, dear God, a passion to know more about you. Grant me the patience to grow in your love.

The Dull Pages

I am not ashamed of the gospel, because it is the power of God for the salvation of everyone who believes. *Romans 1:16*

S ome think that what Paul wrote about gospel power is not true of the whole Bible. They don't believe that *every part* of the Scripture is profitable. There are genealogies and pedigrees, primitive ways of dealing with lepers, and such things as instructions on how to sacrifice goats and oxen. These seem to have little value for today.

They may look pointless to you, but God did not set them down in vain. There is no sentence, no clause, no word, no syllable, no letter that is not written for our instruction. Our understanding is the problem. There is nothing useless in the Word of God.

Scripture is like a drugstore. It is full of all kinds of medicines. There is something for all kinds of diseases, but there are specific uses. Not every drug is for every illness. You need to apply the correct salve and ointment for your malady.

Those oxen and goats that were slaughtered teach you to sacrifice the ugliness of your heart. You may have leprosy of your soul. Those genealogies lead us to the birth of our Savior Christ. Everything in the Bible is there for your sake.

—John Jewell: *Of the Holy Scriptures*

 A Personal Response

The dullness is in me. Awaken my spirit, Lord God, that I may begin to see and hear you in every nook and cranny of the sacred Scripture.

March 10   # To Know Is to Love

If I go to the east, he is not there; if I go to the
west, I do not find him. When he is at work in
the north, I do not see him; when he turns to
the south, I catch no glimpse of him. But he
knows the way that I take; when he has tested
me, I will come forth as gold. *Job 23:8-10*

D on't be in a bigger hurry than God. Holiness is not
achieved all at once.

We can't escape life's dangers without the actual and
continual help of God. We need to pray all of the time. And how can
we pray to him without being with him? How can we be with him
unless we think of him often? And how can we often think of him
unless by a holy habit of thought?

You tell me I am always saying the same thing. You are right. I
say it because this is the best and easiest method I know, and it is the
only one I use. I recommend it to everybody.

We must *know* before we can *love*. In order to *know* God, we
must often *think* of him. When we finally love him, we shall automatically think of him all the time, because our heart will be with our
treasure.

—Brother Lawrence: *The Practice of the Presence of God*

 A Personal Response

Love comes with familiarity. Do not be a stranger to me, O
God. Let me know you well enough to truly love you.

Obedience to God

"I am the Lord's servant," Mary answered. "May it be to me as you have said." *Luke 1:38*

God speaks to us today in the same way that he spoke to our ancestors. In ancient times people found it natural and important to seek God's will. With little spiritual guidance, and in utter simplicity, they heard from God. There was nothing complicated about it. They understood that every moment of every day presented an opportunity for faith to fulfill a responsibility to God. They moved through the day like the hand of a clock. Minute after minute they were consciously and unconsciously guided by God.

Mary's response to the angel who announced the conception of Jesus is an example of this kind of behavior. She was a young and simple person. She completely surrendered herself to God. Her brief answer completely subjugated herself to God's intention.

Her son expressed the identical sentiment when he prayed in the Garden of Gethsemane, "My Father, if it is possible, may this cup be taken from me. Yet not as I will, but as you will" (Matthew 26:39). He teaches us to pray the same thing in the Lord's Prayer: "Thy will be done" (Matthew 6:10, KJV).

—Jean-Pierre de Caussade: *Abandonment to Divine Providence*

 A Personal Response

Why do I look for you in hidden places where I will never find you, Lord? You are right here, throwing yourself at all of us. Let me breathe some fresh air, walk in the park, drink a fresh glass of water, and see your holiness in everything.

March 12   From Brokenness to Wholeness

Who will rescue me from this body of death?
Romans 7:24

We will find happiness when we no longer love anything in ourselves except for God. When will flesh and blood, this clay pot, this earthly house, understand that? When will this new affection be felt? When will this divine intoxication, this forgetting of self, this perception of brokenness that turns us toward God, cause us to cling to him and become united with him in Spirit?

When this happens we can say, "My flesh and my heart may fail, but God is the strength of my heart and my portion forever" (Psalm 73:26). Anyone who tastes something as rare as this, even if only for one brief moment, will be blessed.

To lose yourself, as though you did not exist, to become nothing, is an act of God. When it happens, the sinful world will envy you, evil will disturb you, your body will become a burden, and concern for others will call you back with a jolt.

At this point our personal cares and needs will no longer take first place. We will want God's will to be done in us. We will pray every day, "your will be done on earth as it is in heaven" (Matthew 6:10). O pure and sacred love! It frees us from personal vanity. It is cleansing.

Love of this kind is not won by our efforts. It is a gift from God. We will arrive at this highest love when we are no longer enslaved by any physical desire or upset by any difficulty. It will happen when we are eagerly seeking only the Lord's joy.

—Bernard of Clairvaux: *On Loving God*

A Personal Response

Wholeness is what I want, loving Creator. I need to be together rather than scattered. My life, my health, and my ability to achieve anything worthwhile depend upon this unity within myself.

A Queen's Humble Prayer

Set your minds on things above, not on earthly
things. *Colossians 3:2*

Lord Jesus, help me to want what is most pleasant to you.
You know what is best for me. Give what you will, when
the right time comes, and in the quantity you prefer. Do with
me as you please. Put me where you will. I am in your hands. I am
your servant. I am ready to do whatever you command. You are the
true peace of my heart and the perfect rest of my soul.

If you want me to be in light, I will praise you. If you want me
to be in darkness, I will also praise you.

If you comfort me, I will bless you. If you allow me to be
troubled, I will bless you.

O Lord, make possible by your grace that which is impossible by
my nature.

Sometimes I think I am going to hold together, but when a little
trouble comes it tears me apart. Good Lord, you know my weakness,
my frailness. Have mercy on me.

—Catherine Parr: *Prayers and Meditations*

A Personal Response

Even when we are in positions of power and authority we
remain vulnerable human beings. In control of others, we may
not be in control of ourselves. Lord, take control of us.

March 14   # Cleansing a Life

They said to Moses, "Was it because there were no graves in Egypt that you brought us to the desert to die? . . . It would have been better for us to serve the Egyptians than to die in the desert!" *Exodus 14:11-12*

All of the Israelites left Egypt, but in the desert many of them had second thoughts and wanted to return. In the same way, some resolve to avoid sin, but they look back at Sodom even while fleeing it. They give up their sins, but go right on talking about them, desiring them. If you want to live a devout life, you are required to stop sinning and also to lose your appetite for it.

The first step toward the devout life is the cleansing of your soul. "Your foolish desires will destroy you. . . . You must give up your old way of life with all its bad habits" (Ephesians 4:22, CEV). Remove anything that stands in the way of your union with God. This will be a gradual process. It has been compared with sunrise, which brings light in imperceptible steps. A slow cure is best. Have courage and patience. The work of cleansing your soul will go on for a lifetime. Our perfection consists of struggling against our imperfection.

Think of the time before you were born. Where was your soul then? The world existed, but it saw nothing of you.

God pulled you out of that void and made you who you are out of his own goodness.

Think of the possibilities God has placed in you.

—Francis de Sales: *The Devout Life*

A Personal Response

Oh my soul, you would still be a part of that nothingness if God had not pulled you out of it. You would have neither consciousness nor activity. My good Creator, I owe you a tremendous debt. You made me what I am.—Francis de Sales

Set Your Sights High

But I call to God, and the Lord saves me. *Psalm 55:16*

Perhaps I speak too highly of prayer. I admit that I recommend things I may not do myself. My intention is that you know many of the best ways to pray well. If we fail to fully realize our prayer potential, we can admit our weakness with humility and ask for God's mercy.

When Jesus told us to love God with all our heart, soul, and mind, he gave us a challenging task, impossible for any of us earthlings to accomplish. Nevertheless, our Lord did tell us to love this way. His purpose (as Saint Bernard pointed out) is that we should admit our weakness and seek mercy.

When you pray, intend to make your prayer as complete and honest as you can. If you are dissatisfied with the results of your effort, do not be too angry with yourself. Do not complain that God has not given you the kind of devotion he gives others. Instead, acknowledge your weakness, consider it a valid prayer, and trust that in his mercy God will make it good. Do your part and allow our Lord to give you what he will. You are not praying to teach God anything.

Cry for mercy while trusting in forgiveness. There is no need to struggle. Let it go. Go on to some good work and resolve to pray better next time. Many are never able to be comfortable with the quality of their prayers. They are troubled with their thoughts for a lifetime.

—Walter Hilton: *The Scale of Perfection*

 A Personal Response

Nothing worth doing is mastered quickly. If I want to learn to play a musical instrument, become a surgeon, paint a picture, or put a basketball through the hoop, I must practice. If I want to do anything well I must practice, practice, practice.

Give me the patience to practice prayer, Lord. Keep me at it. Assure me you are listening even when I stammer in my soul.

March 16   Simply Love God

Be very careful to ... love the Lord your God,
to walk in all his ways, to obey his commands,
to hold fast to him and to serve him with all
your heart and all your soul. *Joshua 22:5*

*This is one of several pieces written about Brother
Lawrence. It was included in Lawrence's book* The Practice of the Presence of God:

Brother Lawrence said, "The only motive behind my religious life is the love of God. I have tried to do everything for him. Whatever happens to me, whether I am lost or saved, I will continue to act purely for the love of God. This one good thing I will be able to say: Until I die, I shall have done everything I could to love him."

Brother Lawrence said that whenever he faced any challenge he prayed, "Lord, I can't do this unless you help me." And when he failed, he simply admitted it to God, saying, "I shall never do any better if you leave me to myself. It is you, O Lord, who must prevent my falling. And then he forgot about it.

His life had become simplified since he knew it was his obligation to love God in all things. Since this is what he was trying to do, he no longer needed anyone to direct or advise him. What he needed was someone to hear his confessions. He was very aware of his faults, but he was not discouraged by them. He told everything to God and then peaceably returned to his customary practice of love and adoration.

He also noted that God seemed to have granted the greatest favors to the greatest sinners, and said that the greatest pains or pleasures of this world were in no way comparable with what he had experienced spiritually.

 A Personal Response

Maybe this is possible for me, Lord. Perhaps a regular person can get to know you by being devoted to loving you.

Domination or Cooperation?

Listen to advice and accept instruction, and in
the end you will be wise. *Proverbs 19:20*

It is of great importance to be obedient, to respect authority, and
to let someone else be in control. Moreover, it is far safer to
follow than to lead.

At the same time it is quite natural to want to manage our own
affairs. But if God is among us, it is sometimes necessary to surrender
our personal opinion in order to keep harmony.

Who is intelligent enough to know everything? Don't be too sure
of yourself. Be willing to hear what others think. Sometimes, even if
you have a good idea, it is better to discard it in favor of another, for
God's sake. It is less dangerous to take advice than to give it.

Perhaps your opinion is just as good as anyone's. But if you
stubbornly refuse to yield to others when there is a good reason or a
just cause to do so, all you prove is your obstinate pride.

—Thomas à Kempis: *The Imitation of Christ*

 A Personal Response

It is clear that when we work together, Lord, good things are
accomplished. It is equally clear that if I wish to impose my
will on others, the results may not be the best. Teach me to
cooperate, to be a part of a community, to listen as well as to
speak.

March 18   ## Ecology of Usefulness

God blessed [Adam and Eve] and said to them,
"Be fruitful and increase in number; fill the
earth and subdue it. Rule over the fish of the sea
and the birds of the air and over every living
creature that moves on the ground." *Genesis 1:28*

We are not taking good care of the animals. We make big mistakes in tending and harvesting the plants of the earth. We do a poor job of mining and gathering. Many pay a lot of money for a certain kind of rhubarb and other imported plants that bring them little of medicinal value. They could find as much relief from a pot of cabbage if they comprehended its value.

Because we have lost the knowledge of God, we have lost the knowledge of his creation. We no longer wish to live to serve God. As a consequence, the service of his creatures is being taken away from us. If we ignore the Creator, we will lose the service of the created. We are no longer useful ourselves. We have become universally destructive.

The entire creation, which was intended to be used to the praise and glory of the Creator and for our sustenance and profit, has been disgraced, profaned, and ruined by our thoughtless misuse and self-seeking.

—Martin Bucer: *Instruction in Christian Love*

A Personal Response

If I destroy any part of your world, O God, I destroy a part of myself and bring disgrace to you.

The Soul As Light

The appearance of the living creatures was like burning coals of fire or like torches. Fire moved back and forth among the creatures; it was bright, and lightning flashed out of it. *Ezekiel 1:13*

When God determines a soul is ready, it takes on the light of the Holy Spirit. It becomes God's brilliantly lit place of residence. The soul is clothed with the beautiful glory of the Spirit. It is illumined. In a way similar to those creatures described in Ezekiel, the soul is totally light, face, and eye. There is no place of darkness. It only faces forward. Like the sun, it shines all over.

Our soul is given the privilege of becoming the throne of God. Christ rides it, as it were. Christ drives it, directs it, carries it, nourishes it. He gives it spiritual beauty.

Jesus said, "You are the light of the world. A city on a hill cannot be hidden. Neither do people light a lamp and put it under a bowl. Instead they put it on its stand, and it gives light to everyone in the house. In the same way, let your light shine before men, that they may see your good deeds and praise your Father in heaven" (Matthew 5:14-16). What he means is that we are not to keep our faith a secret. It is to be shared with others who want it.

—Pseudo-Macarius: *Homilies*

A Personal Response

Are you talking about me, Lord? A light for this dark world? Me? The darkness is so overwhelming! But I see you have many who are lights for you. I bring my little candle in and add it to the others. Does it make any difference, Lord? You assure me that it does.

Spiritual Traps

> You have a reputation of being alive, but you are dead. *Revelation 3:1*

In an attempt to open our eyes and show us a way to a deeper spiritual life, God may allow sickness, persecution, and other tests of our fidelity. These things never happen without God's plan or permission.

Our problem is conforming with the will of God. We don't know how to yield to him. We are reluctant to submit to his judgments. We are not able to imitate Christ humbled and crucified. We have not found a way to love our enemies, or to see them as instruments used by God to train us in self-denial.

This is the hazard. Our eyes are blinded by self-love. We do good things and then become proud. We think that we are far advanced as religious people and then look down on our neighbor. Our spiritual pride deepens our blindness. We are beyond help, short of a miracle of grace.

Outright sinners can be reformed with less difficulty than those who hide under a cloak of false virtue.

The spiritual life does not consist in holy practices that are mere outward appearances. It actually consists in knowing the infinite greatness and goodness of God. It includes an admission of our weakness and our proclivity to evil. It is an act of loving God and denying ourselves. It means renouncing our own will and accepting God's will. The only life-giving motive for any spiritual practice is to please God because we love God.

—Lawrence Scupoli: *The Spiritual Combat*

A Personal Response

You will have to change me, Lord. By myself I will never get it right.

Discussion Groups

All the Athenians and the foreigners who lived there spent their time doing nothing but talking about and listening to the latest ideas. *Acts 17:21*

Sometimes it is not advisable to engage in religious discussion. If you are under stress and your thoughts are filled with distractions, you should avoid debate about the Bible. It would be like mixing balm and dirt together. You've got to be able to give your full attention when you talk with someone about biblical concerns.

Also, be careful which audience you choose. If you are among people who are thoughtful and eager to learn, that is good. But if you are with those who take pleasure in debating trifling matters as a pastime, keep silent. All they want to do is to show off their wit.

Another important consideration is how deep you may want to wade. Don't go any farther than your ability allows, and no farther than the weakness or intelligence of the others may bear. In the same way that a loud noise will injure the ear and too much meat will hurt your body, profound thought can injure weak persons. Too much of anything can be a problem. It may be a burden that is heavy to carry.

I don't tell you these things to talk you out of studying the Scripture. That study is as necessary for your soul as breathing is for your body. If it were possible, I would spend all my time with the Bible and do nothing else. Read it! But be careful. It is possible to eat too much honey, as sweet as it is. There is a time for every good thing. If you do it in the wrong way, a good thing can become evil. A flower in winter is out of season. If you must engage in disputes about the Bible, at least do it at the right time, in the right place, and among the right people.

Treat holy things in a holy manner. Let mystical things remain mysterious. Do not utter divine secrets into ears that are unworthy to hear them. Be careful in your talking and in your silence.

—Thomas Cranmer: *Prologue to the Bible*

 A Personal Response

Give me respect, dear God. Respect for your Word. Respect for other minds. Respect for my own ignorance.

March 22   ## Confession of Sin

Father, I have sinned against heaven and against you. *Luke 15:21*

The poison of a scorpion can be turned into its own antidote. Sin is bad, but it can be distilled by confession and repentance. Simon called Mary Magdalene a sinner, but our Lord disagreed. He was pleased with her humble act of anointing him with expensive perfume. When we are sorry for our sin, we honor God, and such sins, distilled by our sorrow, become sweet and pleasant.

It is important to tell the doctor exactly what your symptoms are. In confessing sin, be certain to tell it all, candidly and sincerely. This will greatly relieve your conscience. Then listen for any guidance. Listen inwardly for the Savior's assurance of pardon. Experience the joyous celebration of the angels in heaven.

The low angle of the sun early in the morning reveals the wrinkles in our faces. In a similar manner the Holy Spirit lights our consciences and we see our sins more distinctly. No doubt you can see that you still have some proclivity to sin. We are never entirely free from these tendencies, but we can stop having affection for them.

Spiders are not deadly to bees, but they entangle their honeycombs with webs and make their work difficult. Tiny sins will not kill your soul, but if they wrap a tangle of bad habits around you, devotion will suffer. It is not earthshaking to tell a small lie, or to say or do something slightly risqué, or to dress, joke, play, or dance with a little freedom—as long as you don't allow these spiritual spiders to spin their webs and ruin the hive of your conscience. Although it is not wrong to have a little harmless fun, it can become dangerous. The evil is not in the pastimes; it is in our affection for them. Don't sow weeds in the soil of your heart. Your garden space is limited.

—Francis de Sales: *The Devout Life*

A Personal Response

As you inspire me to be, O God, give me the strength to be.

Honest Peace

> I am the way and the truth and the life. No one comes to the Father except through me. *John 14:6*

Y ou will not find peace in things that do not last. Your satisfaction will be as temporary as they are. This is the kind of
peace the animals have. What *you* want is the peace of angels. It is the truth that produces this kind of peace.

Unceasing peace is the result of truth. Stress and grief are the products of falsehood.

You do not need to defend truth. Truth has no need of your services. But *you* have need of truth.

It makes no difference whether you criticize someone else, or another judges you. You are both at fault. Whether you are giving or receiving is not important.

Have you ever seen an ant nest that has been disturbed? Did you notice how eagerly the ants took hold of the things they valued most? Without fear for their own welfare they grabbed an egg and tried to run with it to safety. You need this kind of love for truth and peace; you need this kind of love for God.

—Guigo I: *Meditations*

A Personal Response

Lord, teach me how to love you and love your truth over everything. Teach me to cling to you irregardless of my safety. Only
in clinging to you and your truth will I meet with the peace
of angels.

Keeping Faith

> Dogs have surrounded me; a band of evil men has encircled me. They have pierced my hands and my feet. I can count all my bones; people stare and gloat over me. *Psalm 22:16-17*

They put me on the rack because I would not reveal the names of others who share my faith. They kept me on it a long time. Because I lay still and did not cry, both my lord chancellor and master troubled themselves to rack me with their own hands until I was nearly dead.

Then the lieutenant released me from the rack. I immediately fainted. They helped me recover consciousness. For two long hours I sat upon the bare floor, talking with the lord chancellor. With many flattering words, he tried to persuade me to leave my opinion. God gave me the grace to persevere.

I was taken to a house and put in bed. My bones were weary and painful. A message came from the lord chancellor that if I would leave my opinion, I would be given every comfort. If I would not, I would be taken to Newgate and burned. I sent him word that I would rather die than break my faith.

—Anne Askew: *Latter Apprehension and Examination*

A Personal Response

O Lord, I have more enemies now than there are hairs on my head. Yet, Lord, let them never overcome me with their arguments. I cast my care on you. Fight for me. They fall upon me with all the spite they can imagine. Let me not respond to those who are against you. In you is my whole delight.

And, Lord, I want you in your merciful goodness to forgive them the violence which they do and have done unto me. Open their blind hearts. So be it, O Lord. So be it.—Anne Askew

Secret Treasure

But when you fast, comb your hair and wash
your face. Then no one will suspect you are
fasting, except your Father, who knows what you
do in secret. And your Father, who knows all
secrets, will reward you. *Matthew 6:17-18,* NLT

Saint Francis had a unique and personal way of contemplation.
The result was that his encounters with God completely
transformed him.

He was careful, upon returning from his private devotions to
human society, to behave quite naturally. He took great pains to hide
every evidence of these intimate meetings with the Lord. Francis told
his brothers that if they should experience anything similar they
should pray this prayer:

Lord, I am unworthy and sinful.

The consolation you have sent me from heaven I now
return into your hands.

If I did not do this, I would feel like a thief, taking your
treasure for myself.

—Bonaventure: *Life of St. Francis*

A Personal Response

Why am I tempted to parade my piety in public, Lord? If it
is between you and me, what does anyone else have to do
with it?

On Meditation

On my bed I remember you; I think of you
through the watches of the night. *Psalm 63:6*

N o specific rule can be given to guide everyone's meditation.
The Lord inspires a variety of meditations in a person's
soul.

When one is first converted there are strong memories of worldly,
fleshly sins. This can make the heart sorrowful. Tears may flow. There
is a fervent seeking for mercy and forgiveness. These sins will put a
heavy weight on the soul. A little pain here is a small price to pay for
the mercy of the Lord, who wills to forgive. David prays this way in
many of his psalms.

Another meditation is on the humanity of Christ. You may be
stirred to devotion in God. Suddenly, your thoughts leave the contemporary world. You can imagine being present when Jesus was ar-
rested, bound like a thief, beaten, and condemned to death. You can
almost see him carrying his cross. Your heart is filled with compassion. You mourn for him. You are amazed by his love, patience, and
humility. You understand he is suffering this pain for you. Then the
Holy Spirit may open your spiritual eye and you will perceive the
divine Christ. A person ordinarily does not contemplate Christ's divinity without first using the imagination to perceive his humanity.

A hound that chases a rabbit only because he sees other dogs
running will stop to rest when he is tired. He will give up the chase.
But if he runs because he actually sees the rabbit, he will never
surrender to fatigue.

There is one thing worth doing, and that is for a person to go into
himself, to get to know his own soul and its abilities, its fairness and
its foulness.

—Walter Hilton: *The Scale of Perfection*

A Personal Response

Help me to discover the reality of the spiritual life, Lord. Show
me how to clearly see my sin and your grace through the
meditations you inspire in my soul.

Living Faith

We see that people are acceptable to God because they have faith, and not because they obey the Law. *Romans 3:28,* CEV

Genuine faith is God at work in us. It changes us. It affects our temper and disposition. It makes us over. This faith is a living, busy, active, and powerful thing! It is always doing good. It never asks if it should do any good works. It has already done them, and continues to do them without thinking about it.

A person without this living faith is forever groping around for faith and good works. Both of them remain hidden. Such a person, searching without any idea of what is being sought, can talk endlessly about the subject.

Faith is a living, firmly held confidence in God's grace. It makes the one who has it joyful, bold, and loving toward both God and God's creation. Eager to do good for everyone, the faithful person has a deep desire to be of service to others and a willingness to suffer if necessary. It is impossible to distinguish between faith and works in such an individual. It would be easier to separate heat and light from fire.

—Martin Luther: *Preface to Romans*

A Personal Response

O God, work your living faith in me. Let it burn in me, giving my life energy and purpose.

Listening for God

It is the spirit in a man, the breath of the Almighty, that gives him understanding. *Job 32:8*

One way God can awaken a soul is with an inner voice. This "voice" comes in many ways and is difficult to define.

The inner voice I speak of can come from God, from the devil, or from one's own imagination. Do not think you are a better person because you sense this inner voice—even if it is genuinely from God. The only good that results is in how you respond to what you hear. If what you hear is not in agreement with the Scriptures, pay no attention to it at all.

There are some clues that will help you to determine if God is the source. The first and best indication is in the *power and authority* of the voice. Things are better because it was heard. Some difference is made—calmness replaces distress, for instance.

The second sign is a *peaceful tranquility* in the soul combined with an eagerness to sing praises to God.

The third sign is that the *words stick in the memory* better than ordinary conversation. There is a strong faith in the truth of what was heard. Even if all the evidence indicates that the soul misunderstood, and much time passes, there is still confidence that God will find his own way to fulfill his promises. Delays may cause doubts. The devil will actually prey upon your doubts. He will work hard to intimidate you if the inner voice spoke of something challenging that will bring honor to God. In spite of all these difficulties, there will remain a glowing ember of faith that God will overcome all obstacles and keep his word.

Now if the inner voice is only the product of the imagination, none of these signs will be present. There will be no certainty, no peace, no joy.

If what you think is an "inner voice" commands an action that will have dire consequences for yourself or for others, don't do anything until you have sought competent counseling.

—Teresa of Avila: *Interior Castle*

A Personal Response

Let your Holy Spirit inspire me. Make me receptive. But please, Lord God, spare me from assigning your name to the complex thoughts, desires, and motives of my own personality.

A Step Farther

"Take care! Don't do your good deeds publicly, to be admired." *Matthew 6:1,* NLT

If you act out of the pure love of God, you will not perform your actions to be seen by others.

You will not even do them that *God* might notice them.

If it were possible that your good works might escape God's attention, you would still perform them with the same joy, and in the same pureness of love.

—John of the Cross: *The Living Flame of Love*

A Personal Response

Lord, I am now seeing the truth of the matter. The reason for good behavior is not to receive gold stars, personal credits, or a good personal evaluation report. The reason is love. Love is unconditional. Love is its own reward. Genuine love can even get along without recognition.

Silent Prayer

All my longings lie open before you, O Lord;
my sighing is not hidden from you. *Psalm 38:9*

P rayer is the most effective means at our disposal for the cleansing of our mind and emotions. This is because it places the mind in God's bright light, and the emotions in his warm love. Prayer is like water that makes plants grow and extinguishes fires.

Best of all is silent, inward prayer, especially if it reflects upon our Lord's loving sacrifice. If you think of him frequently, he will occupy your soul. You will catch on to his manner of living and thinking. You will begin to live and think like him. It is exactly like the way children learn to talk by listening to their mothers and then making sounds with their own voices.

There is no other way in. Prayer is essential. Find an hour each day, in the morning if possible, and pray.

Start every prayer in the presence of God. Be strict about this and you will soon see its value. Don't rush through your prayers. The Lord's Prayer said once with comprehension is better than many prayers said in haste.

If you can do it, inward, silent prayer is best. If you are reciting a standard prayer and find your heart being drawn deeper, by all means leave the spoken prayer behind and move into silence. Don't worry about leaving your formal prayer unfinished. Your silent prayer pleases God the most, and it will be better for your soul.

Be diligent about this. Don't let a morning pass without some time in silent prayer. But if the demands of business or some other responsibility prevents it, then be sure to repair the damage that evening. Make a vow to start your regular practice of morning prayer again tomorrow.

—Francis de Sales: *The Devout Life*

A Personal Response

Dear Lord, thank you for these thoughts on silent prayer. Let my inner prayers take on a vibrant life.

March 31 A Change of Clothes

For you are all children of the light and of the
day; we don't belong to darkness and night.
1 Thessalonians 5:5, NLT

Strong wind blowing in the darkness of night violently disturbs every plant in its path. It is the same way with us when we give way to the power of the night. The devil's wind pounds at us, convinces us, shakes us. We fall victim to the darkness that is in us. We give in to harmful desires.

The Holy Spirit moves in us with a similar strength. But it is a freshening breeze on a beautiful day. It travels through every corner of the soul, bringing light, health, peace.

It is something like a change of clothes. We may be found wearing the heavy, tattered overcoat of bad language, skepticism, boldness, conceit, arrogance, greed, lust, and all the other contaminated adornments of the kingdom of darkness. Jesus takes these burdensome rags off of us. He clothes us with garments that are sparkling clean. We are clothed with confidence, optimism, love, gladness, peace, decency, human warmth, light, and most of all, life. In the same way that God is loving and kind, we may be also.

—Pseudo-Macarius: *Homilies*

 A Personal Response

Glory to you, O God! In your mercy you free me from darkness.
You give light. Your light is my life.

April 1 In the Right Order

Two people were in debt to a moneylender. One of them owed him five hundred silver coins, and the other owed him fifty. Since neither of them could pay him back, the moneylender said that they didn't have to pay him anything. Which one of them will like him more? *Luke 7:41-42, CEV*

Love is not the cause of forgiveness. Forgiveness causes love. The more we are forgiven, the more we love.

If we fill our thoughts with sin and damnation and the wrath of God which condemns us before we are born, we cannot love God. We will hate him as a tyrant, and run away from him. But when the gospel of Christ demonstrates how God loves us first, forgives us, and has mercy on us, then we love again. As the saying goes, "Summer is near, because the trees blossom." The blossoms do not bring summer. Summer brings the blossoms.

We also say, "If you don't love my dog, you don't love me." Maybe the dog does not deserve it. Perhaps he has even brought you displeasure. Yet, if you love me, you will refrain from revenging yourself against my dog. In the first letter of John we read, "We love each other as a result of his loving us first. If someone says, 'I love God,' but hates a Christian brother or sister, that person is a liar" (1 John 4:19-20).

I am commanded to love. If I do not love this commandment, I do not love God.

—William Tyndale: *The Parable*

 A Personal Response

If I love you purely, O God, nothing anyone could do would make me hate or take vengeance. You have ordered me to love and to leave vengeance to you.

Clearly, my love for you needs refining.

Adversity As Friend

It was good for me to be afflicted so that I might learn your decrees. *Psalm 119:71*

Sometimes it is good for us to have trouble and crosses to bear. Adversity can return us to our senses. It can remind us that we are here as refugees, and that we must not place our trust in anything belonging to the world.

It is good that people sometimes misunderstand us. They may have a poor opinion of us even when our intentions are good. Such experiences lead us toward humility and protect us from conceit. We look for God more diligently when we are in difficulty. Our inner life grows stronger when we are under attack.

If you will fully establish yourself in God, you will not need the consolation of others. When we are troubled with temptation and evil thoughts, then we see clearly the great need we have of God, since without him we can do nothing good. Then with weariness and sorrow we may "desire to depart and be with Christ" (Philippians 1:23), for we understand that absolute security and peace do not exist in this world.

—Thomas à Kempis: *The Imitation of Christ*

A Personal Response

Let me learn this lesson well, Lord God. I see it in the hatchling trout that turns to face the current. I see it in the athlete working out. It is true, I know it is. The temptation is to escape the pain. Spare me. Let me truly believe what I have read.

Knowing God

Whoever does not love does not know God, because God is love. *1 John 4:8*

It is odd that we do so little for God, and that such little as we do is done so reluctantly. We do not know him. We are willing to deny his existence. If we say we believe in him, we have done little more than bow to common consent. We have no living conviction of God. We admit that he is, but we avoid finding out for ourselves.

Our thoughts about God are vague. He is mysterious, unknowable, far away. We conceive of him as a powerful being who demands much of us, who does not want us to have a good time, who threatens us with natural disasters, and who has a very low opinion of our worth. If you think like this it may be said that you "fear God." But you only fear him. You do not love him. A student fears the schoolmaster's ruler; a slave dreads the blows of the overlord. Wouldn't you prefer the service of one who loves you as your child?

People think as they do because they do not know God. If they knew him they would love him. If we only think of God as an omnipotent being who created everything and made the laws of the universe, we don't really know God. We only know a part of God, and *that* is not the best part. There is also an aspect of God's being which can transport and mellow the soul. When we discover this we can say that we know God.

—François de Fénelon: *Meditations and Devotions*

A Personal Response

Sometimes I mistakenly hold on to parts of your character as though they represented all of you. Assure me there is more. Much more.

April 4   Speak the Truth in Love

Love does not delight in evil but rejoices with
the truth. *1 Corinthians 13:6*

Love is the only healthy reason for telling the truth. It can be
a healing action. If the one you speak to in truth refuses to
listen to you, pity that person. One who is sick is refusing to
swallow medicine.

Deal with others the way the truth has dealt with you. If it has
been good for you and has helped to make you better, then be good
to others in order to help them become better.

The truth can be a sword. If you use it with the desire to harm
someone, it can actually become an evil. Never use truth this way.
Always be motivated by a desire for good when you wield truth.

If the truth is unpalatable for people, it is not truth's fault. It is
theirs. Truth is like a glaring light to eyes that have grown weak. Be
careful not to make truth even more painful and disagreeable by
neglecting to speak it lovingly.

Love motivates the caring physician who prescribes bitter medicine, the physician who then rubs some honey on the rim of the cup.
The sweetness of the honey allows the patient to eagerly swallow the
unpleasant but helpful medicine. Your job is to do good to everyone.

—Guigo I: *Meditations*

    A Personal Response

Let me answer my own questions honestly, Lord. Have I ever
beat on anyone with the truth? Your truth is a sword. Swords
are made for fighting. Can a sword be lifted in love?

April 5   Yours and Mine

A thief must certainly make restitution. *Exodus 22:3*

The things we buy, or get with our labor, or which are given to us by inheritance are ours by law. They belong to us. Any thing we get by crafty dealings, by guile and fraud, by robbery and stealing, by extortion, oppression, and pilfering are not ours.

What then shall we do with goods we have received by unlawful means? Give them back. That is the only way that pleases God. Unlawful goods ought to be restored again. Augustine wrote: "Robbery, falsehood, or otherwise ill-gotten goods, cannot be forgiven of God, except they be restored again."

Zacchaeus, that good publican who came down from the sycamore tree to have lunch with Jesus, sets the example for us. "Look, Lord! Here and now I give half of my possessions to the poor, and if I have cheated anybody out of anything, I will pay back four times the amount" (Luke 19:8).

I do not encourage owning everything in common. God has set it up so that what is mine is not yours, and what you have I cannot take from you. If all things belonged to everybody there could be no theft and the commandment against stealing would be pointless. But it is not so. The laws of the realm make "mine and thine." If I have things by those laws, then I have them well. Another may not take my belongings from me, but I am compelled to distribute what I have among the poor.

We are supposed to help one another. "If one of you has enough money to live well, and sees a brother or sister in need and refuses to help—how can God's love be in that person?" (1 John 3:17, NLT).

—Hugh Latimer: *Fruitful Sermons*

A Personal Response

I know a little boy who never spoke the word *mine* until his sister was born. Lord, teach me to be exuberant in sharing. Teach me to give of my possessions, of myself.

April 6   A Letter from the Heart

I am always with you; you hold me by my right hand. *Psalm 73:23*

Y ou want to know how I gained a habitual sense of God's presence, which our merciful Lord has granted me, but I must tell you that I am reluctant to do so. I will agree to it only on the terms that you show my letter to no one.

Here is the way it happened. I had read in many books about the various methods of going to God. All of these different ways of practicing the spiritual life confused rather than helped me. What I wanted to know was how to belong entirely to God. I resolved, therefore, to give everything for everything.

After having given myself wholly to God, asking him to forgive my sins, I renounced everything that was not his. I began to live as though God and I were alone in the world.

Sometimes I thought of myself before him as a poor criminal at the feet of a judge. At other times I knew him in my heart as my Father, as my God. I worshiped him as frequently as I could, keeping my mind in his holy presence and calling my attention back to him when it wandered.

This wasn't easy, but I kept at it. I made this my business all day long, not just at special prayer times. At all times, every hour, every minute, even in the height of my business, I drove away from my mind everything that was capable of interrupting my thought of God.

Although I have not been entirely successful at this, I have still found great advantage in it. When we are faithful to keep ourselves in his Holy Presence, and set him always before us, this not only hinders our wandering, it also gives us a holy freedom. By repeating these acts of devotion, they become habitual. The result is that the presence of God becomes a natural thing.

—Brother Lawrence: *The Practice of the Presence of God*

 A Personal Response

My calendar is filled with activities. The telephone rings incessantly. The kids need to be driven to their activities. There is a stack of papers in my IN box. Twenty-four hours are not enough to get it all done. Show me how to keep myself in your presence, Lord. Be continually with me in my busy life.

External and Internal

> We do not lose heart. Though outwardly we are wasting away, yet inwardly we are being renewed day by day. *2 Corinthians 4:16*

It is easy to explain why the saints are not interested in glamorous jewelry and elegant clothes: These things lose their attraction with each passing hour. The focus of attention is on improving and arraying the inner self that is made in the image of God, which can be "renewed day by day."

Nothing is more pleasing to God than to see his own image restored to its original beauty. This glory is not on the surface. It is internal. It will not attract the attention of others, but the Lord observes. The saints agree with the apostle Paul when he writes, "Now this is our boast: Our conscience testifies that we have conducted ourselves in the world . . . in the holiness and sincerity that are from God. We have done so not according to worldly wisdom, but according to God's grace" (2 Corinthians 1:12).

God is the only judge of their conscience. He is the only one they want to please. Pleasing God is their only, true and ultimate glory. Physical ugliness is not a handicap. Nothing about them is without some value. "In all things God works for the good of those who love him" (Romans 8:28). This is how Apostle Paul explains it: "I will boast all the more gladly about my weaknesses, so that Christ's power may rest on me" (2 Corinthians 12:9). Any weakness is desirable if the power of Christ compensates for it. May I be not merely weak, but absolutely helpless, if this will allow me to enjoy the supporting power of the Lord.

—Bernard of Clairvaux: *On the Song of Songs*

 A Personal Response

Why do I protest when I read things like this, Lord? I respond with thoughts that avoid the truth. Do you want me to be sloppy, to ignore my outward appearance? Doesn't it show disrespect for the community when I fail to groom myself? Patiently, you assure me this is not the point. We are thinking together about something going on inside me. It disturbs me that this invisible inner self is so important to you.

April 8   ## Put Out the Light

Your word is a lamp to my feet and a light for
my path. *Psalm 119:105*

The Bible can help you in any condition of life. In adversity
or prosperity. In health or illness. It is a comfort in trouble.
If you must fight, it is your sword. If you are hungry or
thirsty, it is your meat and drink. It is a home for the homeless and
a garment for the naked. If you are in darkness, it is a light upon
your way.

When the Scriptures are not opened, when no one refers to the
Bible, there is great danger. No one knows which way to go, which
person to honor, what to believe, or what to do. They become captives
who understand nothing, see nothing, hear nothing. They are lost
because they have no knowledge of God. Christ told the Sadducees,
"You are in error because you do not know the Scriptures or the power
of God" (Matthew 22:29). Mistakes are the children of ignorance. In
this case there is no plea of ignorance. Ignorance will not excuse us.

When the Philistines cut Samson's hair they took him, bound
him, blinded him, danced around him, and made scorn and games of
him. We are like Samson. The strength of our hair is the knowledge
of the will of God. It is contained in our heads, the highest and
principle part of us. If it is shorn off, if we are kept from hearing,
reading, and understanding the Bible, then we will succumb to super-
stition. Wickedness will get the upper hand and fall upon us. It will
pluck out our eyes, make scorn of us, and utterly destroy us.

—John Jewell: *Of the Holy Scriptures*

A Personal Response

Lord, I live in a modern culture that is falling apart because
few understand and live by your word. Teach me not to discard
the only light I've got in this dark world.

God Can, God Will, God Wants

He alone is my rock and my salvation; he is my fortress, I will never be shaken. *Psalm 62:2*

Psalm 62 assures us God *can* help. God has the ability. When he promised Abraham the land of Canaan, he said to him, "I am God Almighty [El-Shaddai]; walk before me and be blameless" (Genesis 17:1). In the Bible we can learn by his name and by his mighty works that God's strength is not limited. Nothing is impossible with God.

This psalm also declares that God *will* help. In another psalm it is expressed this way: "The salvation of the righteous comes from the Lord; he is their stronghold in time of trouble. The Lord helps them and delivers them" (Psalm 37:39-40). The Gospel of John assures us that "God did not send his Son into the world to condemn the world, but to save the world through him" (John 3:17). The Bible is full of instances when God helped someone in a time of trouble and adversity.

God wants us to *ask* him for help. We are required to call upon him in a time of trouble. It is our job to seek his help. In the same way that we look for water when we are thirsty, we look for God when we need a strength beyond our own. "Come unto me, all you who are weary and burdened, and I will give you rest" (Matthew 11:28). It is God's desire that we ask. He wants us to do it. "Keep on asking, and you will be given what you ask for. Keep on looking, and you will find. Keep on knocking, and the door will be opened. For everyone who asks, receives. Everyone who seeks, finds. And the door is opened to everyone who knocks" (Matthew 7:7-8, NLT).

When you are in a time of great difficulty and understand, by the Word of God, that he commands you to call upon him (and no other), you will take courage. You will be bold enough to turn to God. Even if your sins are many and horrible, they are not as great as God's mercy.

—John Hooper: *Exposition of the Sixty-second Psalm*

A Personal Response

I will not play little nonsense games with you, God. I will not request the ridiculous of you. There are too many important things in my life that need your help. Let me quickly turn to you and join the ranks of those you have helped.

Putting Yourself in God's Presence

> When Jacob awoke from his sleep, he thought, "Surely the Lord is in this place, and I was not aware of it." He was afraid and said, "How awesome is this place! This is none other than the house of God; this is the gate of heaven."
>
> *Genesis 28:16-17*

Perhaps you are not able to pray silently. Many people today are poor at this. Here is an easy way to get started. There are several ways you can place yourself in God's presence.

Consider how God is present in all things and in all places. Wherever the birds fly, they are constantly in the air; wherever we go, God is always there. Instead of merely assenting to this, it is necessary to make the realization of its truth live for us. Since we can't see God physically present, we need to activate our consciousness. Before praying, we need to remind ourselves of God's actual presence. A good way to do this is with Bible verses. "If I go up to the heavens, you are there; if I make my bed in the depths, you are there" (Psalm 139:8).

Remember also that God is not only where you are, he is actually in your heart, in the core of your spirit. "For in him we live and move and have our being" (Acts 17:28).

Think about our Savior watching his children at prayer. "Look! There he stands behind our wall, gazing through the windows, peering through the lattice" (Song of Songs 2:9).

When you know God is present, your soul will bow before his majesty and ask for help. "Do not cast me from your presence or take your Holy Spirit from me" (Psalm 51:11).

—Francis de Sales: *The Devout Life*

A Personal Response

When you seem far from me, dear God, help me to understand how wonderfully near you actually are.

April 11   A Valuable Lesson

Then you will know the truth, and the truth will set you free. *John 8:32*

If we take revenge, we are doing something to another person that we dislike for ourselves. We frequently get even by telling the truth with the intention of poisoning another life. For this reason we do not welcome the truth for ourselves.

Curiously, the cruel comments of enemies can be beneficial if we will accept them with humility. If someone accuses an adulterer of being an adulterer, the words may be spoken viciously, but the adulterer is hearing only what ought to be admitted anyway. It should be accepted without hesitation. The truth is more useful than the motive.

Truth brings life and salvation. Feel compassion for anyone who does not welcome it. That person may be missing out on the best God offers.

Here are the mistakes we make when we speak the truth. Sometimes we want our words to sting. At other times we want to please others, speaking the truth as if we were telling lies or flattering.

Speak the truth, not in order to upset or please someone, but to do another person good. Don't say anything at all if it would hurt.

—Guigo I: *Meditations*

A Personal Response

That's not what I want to hear, dear God! I would rather rationalize, pretend, ignore. Whether the truth is spoken by the Surgeon General, the preacher, my mother, or my child, I am not eager to accept it.

Heavenly Harmony

"Your kingdom come, your will be done on earth as it is in heaven." *Matthew 6:10*

W hy did our Lord teach us to pray that? In the same way the angels in heaven live in harmony, it is desirable for us to live together. Love is shared in heaven. There is agreement. Pride does not interfere. Nothing is pretended. These are things worth praying for here and now.

Whatever we may be doing we can behave in a loving and cheerful manner. The one who is busy working can consider the one who is praying as sharing in the labor. If you are praying and notice another reading a book you can say, "What that person learns from reading is also a gain for me."

"The body is a unit, though it is made up of many parts; and though all its parts are many, they form one body" (1 Corinthians 12:12). You can do your part while others perform their function. The eye sees for the entire body. The hand works and the foot walks for the whole creature. If one member suffers, all suffer.

The ones who pray, therefore, should not criticize the ones who are busy working because they are not praying. The ones who toil are not to judge the ones who are at prayer because they are not working. Let everyone do whatever they are doing for the glory of God.

The highest and most unifying thing for souls is "the bond of peace" (Ephesians 4:3).

—Pseudo-Macarius: *Homilies*

 A Personal Response

Spare me, dear God, from thinking that I am the only one who is doing it right. Don't let me need everyone else to do it my way. Let me do my part the best I can. Let me value the varied contributions of others. Convince me that each way is necessary.

Before You Travel

Let the morning bring me word of your unfailing love, for I have put my trust in you. Show me the way I should go, for to you I lift up my soul. *Psalm 143:8*

When you are going on a journey, pray:

Life is a pilgrimage. I came from the Lord and I will return to the Lord.

I may pass through dangerous places. O Christ, be my guide. Take me in your hand. Open my eyes. Make your highways known to me. Put up some fences to keep me safe.

You are "the way and the truth and the life" (John 14:6). Lead me to the Father. Let me be one with him the way you and God together are one.

—John Bradford: *Daily Meditations*

A Personal Response

Daily I am on journeys. Daily I pass through dangerous places. Millions have lost their lives traveling. Lord, make yourself and your protection known to me continually.

Temptation As a Fact of Life

Be self-controlled and alert. Your enemy the devil prowls around like a roaring lion looking for someone to devour. *1 Peter 5:8*

Temptation is a natural part of life in this world. It is expressed this way in the book of Job: "Is this not the struggle of all humanity? A person's life is long and hard, like that of a hired hand, like a worker who longs for the day to end, like a servant waiting to be paid" (Job 7:1-2, NLT).

Be careful, then, with your own temptations. Pray about them. No one is so good that he is immune to temptation. We will never be entirely free of it.

Still, temptation can be a service to us. It may be a burden, but it can bring us humility and teach us good lessons. All of the saints experienced more than their share of trials and temptations. They grew because of it.

There is no group so holy, no place so far away, that it can shield us from all distractions and difficulties. No one living on earth is entirely free from temptation. The reason is that we are born with the source of temptation within us. We are trapped by our own evil desire.

We are fallen creatures living east of Eden. Therefore tribulation will never leave us, and one temptation will always follow on the heels of another.

Many people try to run away from temptations only to fall even harder. Trying to escape is not the solution. What makes us stronger than any of our enemies is patience and humility. If you only try to avoid temptations outwardly (rather than pluck them out by the roots) you will not get very far. Like weeds in a poorly cultivated garden, they will soon return worse than before.

—Thomas à Kempis: *The Imitation of Christ*

A Personal Response
Help me when I am tempted, Lord God.

Christian Meditation

Mary treasured all these things and pondered them in her heart. *Luke 2:19*

Read a passage from the Gospels. Imagine the scene as though it were actually taking place in front of you. Place yourself, for instance, at the foot of the cross. This will prevent your mind from wandering the same way a cage restricts a bird.

After your imagination has helped you prepare yourself, begin to meditate mentally. If a particular thought catches your interest, stay with it. The bees do not flit from flower to flower. They stay until they have gathered all the honey they can from each. If you find nothing for you after trying a particular thought, move on to the next. But don't rush the process. Take your time.

Meditation will naturally make you feel love of God and neighbor, as well as compassion, joy, sorrow, fear, confidence, and the like. Go ahead and let it happen. But don't stop with such generalized responses. Change them into specific resolutions. For instance, you may be meditating upon our Lord's first word from the cross. This will certainly move you to forgive your personal enemies. But that is a small thing unless you go on to say, "Next time, I won't let _____ bother me so much. I will do everything I can to win that person's love." This will help you correct your faults quickly. Without that specific last step, your progress will be much slower.

Conclude your meditation with humble thanks and an offering of yourself to God. Offer prayers and then gather a devotional nosegay. Let me explain what I mean by that. When people have been strolling through a beautiful garden they usually pick four or five flowers to take with them through the day. They smell them from time to time to cleanse their nostrils of foul odors. When our souls have roamed in meditation through a spiritual garden, we can choose two or three ideas that seemed most helpful and think about them occasionally all day long.

—Francis de Sales: *The Devout Life*

A Personal Response

This is within my ability, heavenly Father. Utter simplicity! I can do this. Practical steps to meditation are exactly what I need.

Watering God's Garden

"The water I give them," [Jesus] said, "becomes a perpetual spring within them, watering them forever with eternal life." *John 4:14,* TLB

Think of yourself as a gardener. You want to cultivate a garden in your soul that will delight the Lord.

How is this garden watered? There are four ways to water the garden of the soul. You can draw the water from a well. This is hard work. You could use a water-wheel with buckets. This is less laborious and yields more water. You could have your garden near a stream or a brook. This will saturate the ground more thoroughly with no effort on your part. You may need to pour on extra water only rarely. But wouldn't it be best of all if rain fell from heaven? You could let the Lord water your garden.

In the same way, there are four degrees of prayer. Beginners draw water out of the well. They must find the well, as it were, in a life full of distractions. If God has put some water in the well, we can water the flowers a little. If the well is dry, there remain moist tears that make virtues grow. If there are not even tears, there can yet be tenderness and an interior feeling of devotion.

The second level of prayer is a condition of the soul that allows itself to be captured by God. It is something like being in love. It brings great joy and requires little effort.

The third "water" that irrigates our soul is incomparably better than the first two. Speaking and silence, laughing and weeping, it is a state of heavenly intoxication. The focus is entirely upon God. There is depth of understanding.

The fourth degree of prayer is almost impossible to describe. It is like rain from heaven. It comes when you least expect it. The soul is in a state of suspension. The soul feels close to God. There is a consciousness of God's presence.

—Teresa of Avila: *The Life of Teresa of Jesus*

 A Personal Response

I must crawl before I walk, and walk before I run and jump. Get me started, dear God. Teach me to pray. I know there is more to it than I have experienced.

Inconveniences and Losses

Naked I came from my mother's womb, and naked I will depart. The Lord gave and the Lord has taken away; may the name of the Lord be praised. *Job 1:21*

Most of us experience inconveniences. Perhaps we are visited by a guest, but we lack the means to entertain that guest. Or maybe we need to appear in public, but our good clothes are somewhere else. What if the wine in our cellar turns sour? Or when we are traveling, we have to spend a night in a cheap hotel? It is easy to lack something, no matter how rich we are. Rejoice in such occasions. Accept them with a good and cheerful heart.

If you lose something to fire, flood, wind, drought, theft, or lawsuits, it is time to practice a little spiritual poverty. Accept your losses meekly and patiently. Be courageous in submitting to such impoverishment.

Esau had natural hair on his arms. Jacob did not. Jacob wore hairy gloves to trick his nearly blind father. If anyone had pulled the hair off of Jacob's arms he would not have felt it. Esau would have screamed with pain, become angry, and defended himself. Because our possessions stick in our hearts we complain loudly when natural catastrophes and crime take them from us. But if we think of our possessions only as something lent from God we won't go crazy when they are taken from us.

—Francis de Sales: *The Devout Life*

 A Personal Response

This goes against the grain, O Lord. Could I actually think and respond in the way he recommends?

Keeping Prayer Focused

Lord, teach us to pray. *Luke 11:1*

Nothing is more essential for the Christian, or more neglected, than prayer. Most people are not excited about praying. They find it a tiring ritual that they like to keep as short as possible. Even when we are led to prayer by responsibilities or anxieties, our prayers are often dull and ineffective.

Many words are unnecessary. To pray is to say, "Not my will, but yours be done" (Luke 22:42). To pray is to lift up your heart to God, to be sorry for your weakness, to regret your constant stumbling. Prayer of this kind requires no special formula. You don't even have to stop doing whatever it is that is keeping you busy. All that is needed is a movement of the heart toward God and a desire that what you are doing may be done for his glory.

You may complain that you have little interest in prayer, that it bores you, that your mind wanders when you attempt to pray. If you are not impressed by grand doctrines, or even by the majesty of God who is always near, at least join me in being sorry for your sins.

It may be more difficult for those who are engaged in business to pray and meditate than for those who live in monasteries, but it is also far more necessary. Take some time out to be with God. Notice how Jesus invited his disciples to a mountain retreat after they had returned from witnessing for him in the cities. If we live and work in a busy place where people talk and behave as though there were no God, it is all the more important that we return to him and restore our faith and love. If he who was without sin prayed without ceasing, how much more should poor sinners like us work at it?

When you pray, ask for what you will with firm faith. If you are not confident when you pray, little will come of it. God loves the heart that trusts in him. He will never ignore those who place their complete trust in him. It is like a father listening to his child.

—François de Fénelon: *Meditations and Devotions*

A Personal Response

Lord, I don't know what to ask of you. You know what I need. You love me better than I love myself. Give your child what he doesn't know how to request.—François de Fénelon

April 19 Taught by a Hickory Stick

You have forgotten that the Scriptures say to God's children, "When the Lord punishes you, don't make light of it, and when he corrects you, don't be discouraged. The Lord corrects the people he loves and disciplines those he calls his own." *Hebrews 12:5-8,* CEV

The best teachers are trouble and affliction. These alone give us understanding.

How can we feel God's goodness when nothing has troubled us and no danger hangs over our heads? These are the things God can help. If we are in good and perfect health do we need a physician? If we are relaxed and in no peril, why would we ever call for help?

As far as I can see, this is the chief reason why God always sharply schools those whom he loves most dearly. The troublesome hazards are effective schoolmasters. An ancient Greek proverb asserts that wisdom can be struck into a student. We are never more holy than when we bear some grievous cross.

—John Fox: *Christ Jesus Triumphant*

 A Personal Response

Lord, I don't like it, but I have to admit it is true. My prayers are most earnest in a time of great need. Teach me that trouble can be a bridge to you, a way for my spirit to grow.

Will and Soul

For our struggle is not against flesh and blood, but against the rulers, against the authorities, against the powers of this dark world and against the spiritual forces of evil in the heavenly realms. *Ephesians 6:12*

Someone will always praise good works. It is more difficult to justify meditation and prayer. You will face a difficult dilemma. You will need to defend yourself against criticism from those who are more active on the social scene. You will also have to fight with your own ideas.

Perhaps you think, *I do not commit adultery or covet my neighbor's property. Therefore I must be OK.* You are forgetting that there are more than two or three categories of sin. The possibilities for sin are vast. Are you arrogant? Angry? Insincere? What is the origin of these things? You are required to be at war with the thoughts of your mind. It's like the frightening discovery of a robber in your home. You resist him, fight with him. In the same way your soul needs to return one blow for another in the combat with your own thoughts.

How can you engage in this kind of contest between will and soul if you think you are already good enough? Maybe you have two or three kinds of sin under control, but dozens more are still chewing on you and you have not even identified them.

If you think the struggle is hopeless, you do God an injustice. An older child can usually win a fight with a younger one. It is an unfair contest. But the soul, if it truly looks for God's help, is equal to the struggle.

You are no match for yourself. Only God can help you. Yes, you can struggle. You can put up a terrific fight against your own nature. You can, as it were, trample down the weeds. Uprooting them is something only God can do. This is why we turn to Jesus.

—Pseudo-Macarius: *Homilies*

A Personal Response

Convince me of the magnitude of my challenge, O Lord. Then help me be victorious.

Spiritual Combat

Follow the Lord's rules for doing his work, just as an athlete either follows the rules or is disqualified and wins no prize. *2 Timothy 2:5,* TLB

If you want the highest degree of spiritual perfection, you will need to wage constant warfare against yourself. It will take all your strength. Prepare for combat. You will need all the determination and courage you can muster.

No war is fought with greater fierceness than spiritual combat. We are both friend and foe. Both sides are equal. A victory gained is therefore very pleasing to God.

Whoever has the courage to control passions, subdue appetites, and repulse even the weakest inclinations of self-will performs meritorious action in the sight of God. Without this victory there is little glory even in the severest discipline, the greatest austerity, or the conversion of a multitude of sinners.

We need to start with ourselves. What does God expect of us?

Begin by equipping yourself with four weapons that are necessary for victory in spiritual combat:

- distrust yourself
- have confidence in God
- use your body and mind properly
- pray

—Lawrence Scupoli: *The Spiritual Combat*

 A Personal Response

At war with myself! Most of the great saints report such a struggle. Lord, that's out of style. I'm supposed to think I'm OK. My need is for self-esteem. This instruction comes from the distant past. It is not in tune with our world today. But wait a minute. Let me think. If it was central to the spiritual life in the past, doesn't it remain valid now?

April 22 ## Shifting Gears

My heart grew hot within me, and as I meditated, the fire burned; then I spoke with my tongue: "Show me, O Lord, my life's end and the number of my days; let me know how fleeting is my life." *Psalm 39:3-4*

After a time of meditation, immediately begin to put into practice the resolutions you have made. Don't wait another day to get started. Without this application, meditation may be useless or even detrimental. Meditate on a virtue without practicing it, and you will mislead yourself into believing that you have actually become someone you are not. If I have resolved to win the heart of my enemy by being gentle toward that person, I will try to find a way this very day to be friendly to him. If I am not able to see that person face to face, I will at least pray for him.

When your silent prayer is over, remain still and quiet for a few moments. Make your transition to other responsibilities gradually. Linger yet a while in the garden. Walk carefully along the path through the gate so that you won't spill the precious balm you are carrying. Don't be unnatural around other people, but keep as much prayer in you as you can.

There is an art to making the transition from prayer to earning a living. A lawyer must go from prayer to the courtroom, the merchant to the store, a homemaker to appointed responsibilities with a gentle motion that will not cause distress. Both prayer and your other duties are gifts from God.

—Francis de Sales: *The Devout Life*

A Personal Response

Someday, perhaps, O Lord, my work and my prayer life will blend. For now, I simply ask that the one will benefit the other.

The Nature of Temptation

My friends, be glad, even if you have a lot of trouble. You know that you learn to endure by having your faith tested. *James 1:2-3*, CEV

Two things increase temptation's hold on you: an indecisive mind and little confidence in God. As a ship without a rudder is driven this way and that by the tossing waves, so the careless and irresolute person is battered by temptations on every side.

Fire tests iron; temptation tests an honest person. Sometimes we don't know what we can do until temptation shows us what we are.

But don't play with fire! It is far easier to deal successfully with temptation in the beginning, when the flames are still controllable. The time to deal with the enemy is while he remains outside the door of your heart. Take him on as soon as you hear the first knock. As Ovid said, "Prevent the illness; medicine comes too late."

First a mere thought comes to the mind; then a strong imagination works on it. Pleasure may come, followed by a tendency to evil, and suddenly we are hooked. Little by little the enemy takes over because we let him get his foot in the door. The longer we put off resisting, the weaker we become.

Some people are tempted most strongly at the beginning of their spiritual life, others near the end. Some are troubled all their lives. Still others receive only light temptation. Such things are decided by God, and we can trust his wisdom.

Therefore, we must not despair when we are tempted. Instead, we need to pray to God all the more sincerely, asking him to help. Saint Paul has assured us, "You are tempted in the same way that everyone else is tempted. But God can be trusted not to let you be tempted too much, and he will show you how to escape from your temptations" (1 Corinthians 10:13, CEV).

—Thomas à Kempis: *The Imitation of Christ*

A Personal Response

It is no great accomplishment for me to be devout when life is running smoothly, Lord. Grant me patient endurance in times of great temptation.

A Capacity for God

One thing I ask of the Lord, this is what I seek: that I may dwell in the house of the Lord all the days of my life, to gaze upon the beauty of the Lord and to seek him in his temple. *Psalm 27:4*

The soul has three vast caverns: memory, understanding, and will. Their capacity is enormous because they are intended for infinite blessings. We know how we suffer when they are empty. We can imagine how great our joy would be if they were filled with their God.

Before these caverns are purged and cleansed from earthly desires, we do not have an awareness of their great emptiness. This is because they have such an enormous capacity. Any little thing in them at all is enough to encumber and distract us. We are not conscious of how much we are missing. We are not able to receive the tremendous blessing God has for us as long as these faculties of the soul are not completely empty.

When they are cleared, we develop an intolerable spiritual hunger and thirst. Because the caverns are deep, the pain is deep. God is the food they lack. The suffering that this emptiness causes is worse than death. This is particularly the case when the soul has caught some glimmer of God. Souls in this condition are agonized by an impatient love. Either they will receive what they desire or they will die.

David expressed it this way: "As the deer pants for streams of water, so my soul pants for you, O God. My soul thirsts for God, for the living God. When can I go and meet with God?" (Psalm 42:1-2).

—John of the Cross: *Living Flame of Love*

A Personal Response

It is awe inspiring to consider that my soul is big enough to receive you, O God. To think that I, a finite being, have infinite spiritual capacity is like gazing at the stars on a clear night. I am hushed with wonder.

April 25   True Friendship

> I no longer call you servants, because a servant does not know his master's business. Instead, I have called you friends. *John 15:15*

Friendship is a union of wills. There is an agreement. This friendship can exist between all kinds of people.

When true friendship is present, long distances between bodies do not separate souls. The strong bond actually relieves the distress of physical distance. As long as their wills are united, they are together. True friendship is when the other person is as valuable as one's self. The friend is loved for his own sake and not for something we hope to receive from that person.

If one of the friends makes a mistake, should the friendship be dissolved by the other? How can true friendship be destroyed even a single time? If the friendship is not perfect it can be whittled down, little by little. But true friendship loves unconditionally, and not for the sake of usefulness or delight. It is not necessary for friends to be changed because of a change in the other. Friendship does not have to dissolve because of an error of one.

On the contrary, true friendship is eager to call back the one who has made a mistake. Friendship becomes love when it wishes good for the friend as it does for itself. No error can destroy it.

Friendships are easily dissolved when they are make-believe. But genuine friendship is not affected by poverty, mistakes, or distortions. This friendship, if it has been shaped by the grace of God and is made whole in God, brings everything back to God. This is holy friendship.

There is no explanation for why a faithful friend is so hard to find today. Everyone seems selfish. Few have a friend of whom it can be said, "That person is to me a part of myself."

—Richard Rolle: *The Fire of Love*

A Personal Response

My greatest friendship, God, should be with you. Use our relationship to shape and influence my relationships with my friends.

April 26　　　## Divine Shadows

The Holy Spirit will come upon you, and the
power of the Most High will overshadow you.
Luke 1:35

Every responsibility, temptation, or difficulty is a shadow upon a particular moment. Hidden in the shadow is the fact that it is an expression of the will of God.

Mary could see this. There is nothing remarkable about this young woman's ordinary life. The Bible records nothing about her that is fantastic or miraculous. She is presented quite simply. The things that happen to her could happen to anyone. The things she had to endure are shared by many.

What bread nourishes the faith of Mary and Joseph? *The sacrament of the moment.* Their perception went beyond commonplace, everyday realities. To all outward appearances their lives were similar to those of others. But their faith recognized God at work in ordinary events. This is heavenly food. This is the bread of angels. They perceive what God is accomplishing right now! "He has filled the hungry with good things" (Luke 1:53). God allows himself to be seen in ordinary things, even when they are darkened by shadows.

　　　　—Jean-Pierre de Caussade: *Abandonment to Divine Providence*

A Personal Response

Divine Love, if we were satisfied with you, we would climb to the highest heavens. If we were smart enough to leave everything to you, we would achieve the summit of holiness. All of us have the opportunity. If we live and behave as you guide us, our ordinariness will be replaced with holiness. It's as simple as that!—Jean-Pierre de Caussade

April 27 Prayer in a Busy Life

Then Jesus told his disciples a parable to show them that they should always pray and not give up. *Luke 18:1*

Perhaps there will be a time when you will not experience the pleasures of meditation. Don't let that bother you. In a time like that, return to familiar spoken prayers. Tell God you are sorry and ask him to help you. The important thing is to stick with it. God grants or withholds his favors as he will. Our responsibility is to continue in a devotional manner before him.

One of the best things you can do is to remember all during the day that God is with you. Birds can return to their nests and deer to their thickets. We can select a place near Christ where we can retreat momentarily during the course of our work. Remember to take a few moments inwardly even as you are busy at your occupation. A crowd of people around will not be able to intrude upon this private act. King David was busy with many responsibilities and yet he often says in his psalms, "I am always with you; you hold me by my right hand" (Psalm 73:23); "I have set the Lord always before me" (Psalm 16:8); "my eyes are ever on the Lord" (Psalm 25:15).

We will not often be too busy to turn aside to God for an instant. In fact, we can present our souls to him a thousand times a day. Sprinkle a seasoning of short prayers on your daily living. If you see something beautiful, thank God for it. If you are aware of someone's need, ask God to help. Saint Francis looked at a stream of water and prayed, "God's grace flows just as gently and sweetly as this brook." You can toss up many such prayers all day long. They will help you in your meditation and in your secular employment as well. Make a habit of it.

—Francis de Sales: *The Devout Life*

A Personal Response

Practice enhances everything I attempt, Lord Jesus. Let me put in the hours it takes to learn to pray.

April 28   To See Ourselves

The eye is the lamp of the body. If your eyes
are good, your whole body will be full of light.
But if your eyes are bad, your whole body will
be full of darkness. If then the light within you
is darkness, how great is that darkness! *Matthew
6:22-23*

Y ou have not noticed that you are chained. You do not struggle as a dog on a leash. Your inner vision has grown dull.
God is in you, but you do not perceive him.

This explains why you abandon your interior self and drift away
from God. It is the darkness in you that makes you uncomfortable
with yourself. You divert your attention with external things and the
opinions of others. These things are not your problem. Your spiritual
blindness is the culprit.

It is when you become dissatisfied with your own false self that
you will begin to return to God.

Pay more attention to your own behavior than to the things other
people do. The person most valuable to others is the one who attends
to his or her own faith and character.

Be careful not to irritate people. Instead of chasing them away,
help them to get rid of their faults. Do this with a loving spirit. The
offensive thing is not human nature, but the vices which blemish it.
The only reason to probe into the wounds of others is to heal them.

If you want to reject an evil person, begin with yourself.

—Guigo I: *Meditations*

A Personal Response

There could not be a more basic lesson than this one, my
Lord. It all begins right here. I see the speck in another's eye
and miss the log in my own.

April 29   # The Sword of the Tongue

All day long they twist my words; they are
always plotting to harm me. They conspire, they
lurk, they watch my steps, eager to take my life.
Psalm 56:5-6

Saint Francis put backbiting in a category with snakebite.
Slandering another person is injurious to the religious life.
He felt strongly that it was an abomination like a devastating
plague. This is because the slanderer feeds on the blood of others
who have been killed with the sword of the slanderer's tongue.

Once Saint Francis heard a friar destroy the reputation of another.
He called for an immediate inquiry. "If you find that the accused friar
is innocent, make an example of his accuser. Correct him severely."

He made it a rule that if a friar stripped another friar of his good
name, the accuser should be stripped and not allowed to pray until he
had done everything possible to repair the damage he had done. It was
Saint Francis's belief that the impiety of detractors is a greater sin
than that of robbers. Christ told us the well-being of the soul is more
important than the well-being of the body.

—Bonaventure: *The Life of St. Francis*

    A Personal Response

Maybe I try to make myself look better by pulling others down.
Forgive me, God, for pointing out the flaws in others while
ignoring my own. Pardon any injury I have caused by the
things I have reported.

April 30 # Can Prayer Be Put in Words?

"Are you still so dull?" Jesus asked them.
Matthew 15:16

My desire is to clearly describe matters related to prayer. This will be very difficult for the uninitiated to understand.

It is best for a soul not to attempt to rise by its own efforts. If the well is dry we are not able to put water into it. Pay attention to this. If the soul tries to go forward it may actually go backward. The foundation for prayer is humility. The nearer we come to God, the more humility we need. There is a kind of pride that makes us want to be more spiritual. God is already doing more for us than we deserve.

When I say that people should not attempt to rise unless they are raised by God, I am using spiritual language. Some will understand me. If you can't understand what I am saying I don't know another way to explain it.

I am sorry for those who begin with only books. There is a big difference between understanding something and knowing it through experience. I have read many religious books that deal with these matters. They explain very little. If one's soul has not already accumulated some practice in prayer, books are not much help.

—Teresa of Avila: *The Life of Teresa of Jesus*

A Personal Response

Everything you do, my Lord, is for the good of the soul you know to be yours already. You know who is willing to follow you anywhere. You know who is determined to bear your cross with you. There is no reason for me to be distressed, nothing to fear.—Teresa of Avila

May 1 # We Are All Imperfect

How can you say, "My friend, let me take the speck out of your eye," when you don't see the log in your own eye? *Matthew 7:3*, CEV

Try to be patient with the defects and blemishes in others. You also have many things about you that they must endure. If you can't make yourself what you want to be, how can you expect to remake somebody else?

While demanding that another person be perfect, we ignore our own faults. We like to see others corrected, but we are reluctant to accept correction. We want the law to apply to everybody but ourselves. It is clear that we don't measure our neighbors and ourselves by the same standard.

If everyone were perfect, there would be nothing in others for us to bear with for God's sake. But God has seen to it that we must "carry each other's burdens" (Galatians 6:2).

For no one is without fault, no one is without burden, no one is self-sufficient, and no one is wise enough to make it alone.

Therefore, we must support one another, comfort one another, help, teach, and caution one another.

—Thomas à Kempis: *The Imitation of Christ*

A Personal Response

O Lord, you know how easy it is to be critical of others. People in responsible positions make inviting targets. And neighbors and people working around me are also within easy judging range. Let me work on myself first. My own faults hide from me. Give me patience and understanding. Above all, make me compassionate.

Quiet Inspiration

After the earthquake came a fire, but the Lord was not in the fire. And after the fire came a gentle whisper. *1 Kings 19:12*

The Scriptures say without hesitation that God's Spirit lives in us, gives us life, speaks to us in silence, inspires us, and that it is so much a part of us that we are *united* with the Lord in Spirit. This is basic Christian teaching.

The Spirit of God is the soul of our soul! We are blind if we think that we are alone in the interior sanctuary. God is actually more present in this place than we are. We are constantly inspired, but we suppress the inspiration. God is always speaking to us, but the external noise of the world and the internal churning of our passions confuse us. We can't hear him speaking. Everything around us needs to be silent, and we must be quiet within. We need to focus our entire being to hear his soft whisper of a voice. The only ones who hear it are those who listen to nothing else.

It is unfortunate that the soul is so infrequently still. Our selfish desires interfere with the voice within us. We are aware that it is speaking to us. We know that it wants something of us, but we can't understand what it is saying. Sometimes we are glad about that!

The inspiration of which I speak is not identical to that of the prophets. They were commanded to speak certain words or to do particular things. On the contrary, this inspiration restricts itself to lessons in obedience, patience, meekness, humility, and the other Christian virtues. It is nothing more than a simple invitation from the depth of our being to be obedient to the will of God.

—François de Fénelon: *Meditations and Devotions*

 A Personal Response

I am quiet right now, Lord. Before I turn away from this page, I pause to listen.

May 3   Precious Friendship

Physical training is of some value, but godliness has value for all things, holding promise for both the present life and the life to come.
1 Timothy 4:8

Friendship has value in this life and the next. Almost no happiness can exist without friendship. To be human we need someone with whom we can laugh and express our thoughts. We need to share our concerns and insights. "If one falls down, his friend can help him up. But pity the man who falls and has no one to help him up!" (Ecclesiastes 4:10).

There is happiness and security in having someone who is able to converse with you on an equal basis. Imagine being able to say *anything* without fear or blushing. Think of the joy of being able to tell the secrets of your spiritual life. Nothing is more pleasant than being able to unite with another spirit so that the two become one. There is then no concern about correction, suspicion, or praise. This is the medicine of life. Medicine can do no more good for a sick body than a friend who meets every misfortune with gladness. "Carry each other's burdens, and in this way you will fulfill the law of Christ" (Galatians 6:2).

Friendship increases the joys of well-being and lessens the sorrows of misfortune by dividing and sharing them. Tullius said that friends are present even when they are absent, rich though poor, strong though weak, and even alive when dead.

Friendship is on the edge of the love and knowledge of God. It is a simple step from true friendship with another person to friendship with God. Jesus said, "I no longer call you servants. . . . I have called you friends" (John 15:15). All the best qualities of friendship begin in Christ, advance through Christ, and are perfected in Christ.

—Aelred of Rievaulx: *Spiritual Friendship*

A Personal Response

Let my friendships be guided by Christ's spirit.

A Spiritual Exercise

Clouds and thick darkness surround [God].
Psalm 97:2

It is worthwhile to think of how much God has blessed you. Love him and praise him for his kindness toward you. And yet, it is far better to think only about his "being there"—to love and praise God for himself alone.

Now you ask, "How can I think of God himself alone? What is God?"

My only answer is, "I don't know." Your question has brought me into your darkness. I call it a cloud of unknowing. It is impossible to think of God himself. What I try to do is to forget everything else and choose, lovingly, the unthinkable. God can be loved, but not imagined. God can be grasped and held by love, but not as a result of rational thought.

Sometimes it is enlightening to remember God's providence in a particular instance. But there is another spiritual exercise worth attempting: Try forgetting. Attempt to penetrate the darkness above you. Toss sharp darts of desiring love at that thick cloud of unknowing.

Don't quit too soon! If a thought strays in between you and that darkness, ask yourself what you really want. Answer that you want God. Nothing but God. And if your thought should ask you who God is, answer that it is the God who made you and ransomed you and has called you to his love. Step on the questions with an impulse of love. Even if the question seems to be a religious one, possibly helpful, force it away.

If God calls you to this exercise, lift up your heart in humble love. A simple reaching out to God is enough. If you want, you can wrap this reaching toward God in a single word of one syllable. Try a word like *God* or *love*. The word can become your shield and spear in peace or in war. With this word you can beat upon this darkness, this cloud of unknowing.

—Anonymous: *The Cloud of Unknowing*

A Personal Response

Dear God, turn my darkness into light, my confusion into understanding, and my lethargy into action so that I may find you alone.

Heaven Is Justice and Joy

Since ancient times no one has heard, no ear has
perceived, no eye has seen any God besides you,
who acts on behalf of those who wait for him.
Isaiah 64:4

When ancient maps were drawn there were often gaps of
knowledge. It would be reported that these unknown
areas were the habitation of giants, witches, and wild
beasts. No explorer could penetrate farther into that country.

We travel as far as we can into the spiritual life with the guides
available to us. Then we can only imagine what is beyond. We say
heaven is inhabited with angels and archangels, with cherubim and sera-
phim. We can look no farther into it with these eyes.

The Holy Spirit accommodates natural human affections. To the
rich he says heaven shall be made of gold and jewels. For those with
aesthetic taste he promises everlasting beauty. To those who delight
in music he promises continual singing, and every minute a new song.
For anyone who is impressed with rank and title he promises a royal
priesthood. To those who need military honor there is the assurance
of a victorious Church. If you enjoy parties there is the image of a
magnificent feast, the sumptuous marriage supper of the Lamb.

But the Holy Spirit goes beyond describing heaven as the improvement of things we have and love here. We have a hunger and
thirst for justice and righteousness. We want both of these now. We
can have them in heaven. Here on earth, justice is not done for the
sake of justice. Justice is done for fear of an appeal or a commission.
Some do justice only to make a good impression at first. In our new
heaven and new earth there will be a love of justice. We shall have
justice in God.

Most of all, there shall be joy. If you look at a map of the world
you will see two hemispheres, two half worlds. If you could crush
heaven into a map, you may find two half heavens. Half will be joy
and half will be glory.

—John Donne: *Sermons*

 A Personal Response

Spare me this mistake of waiting for heaven, dear God. Let
me begin to know its beauty and joy now.

Taking God Seriously

Thou tellest my wanderings: put thou my tears into thy bottle: are they not in thy book? *Psalm 56:8,* KJV

God is in earnest with you. Why are you not so with him? Why trifle with God? Jesus was serious in his work for us. He was so distracted with teaching that he forgot to eat and drink. In prayer, he continued all night. In doing good, his friends thought he was obsessed. In suffering, he fasted forty days, was tempted, betrayed, spit upon, buffeted, and crowned with thorns; he sweat drops of blood, was crucified, pierced, and he died. Shouldn't you be serious in seeking your own salvation?

The Holy Spirit is serious in wanting you to be happy. He is always at work. He is grieved when you resist him. Shouldn't we be serious in obeying and yielding to his motions?

God is serious in hearing our prayers and giving us his mercies. God is afflicted with us. He regards every groan and sigh. The next time you are in trouble, you will beg for God's attention. Do we expect real mercies when we neglect the Giver of mercies?

The servants of the world and the devil are serious and diligent. They work as if they could never do enough. Don't you have a better Master and sweeter employment, greater encouragement and a better reward?

—Richard Baxter: *The Saints' Everlasting Rest*

A Personal Response

Christ assures me of your intimate interest, O God. You are aware of falling sparrows and falling hair. Help me to respond to your interest in me by showing interest in you.

Religious Ecstasy

> I know a man in Christ who fourteen years ago was caught up to the third heaven. Whether it was in the body or out of the body I do not know—God knows. *2 Corinthians 12:2*

Some of the things people consider virtuous are not. I am thinking of fantasies, rapturous insensibility, levitations, and similar magical stunts. These are sometimes presented as the highest spiritual experiences.

If these things happen, they are not virtues; they are nothing more than gifts from God. It is not right for us to seek them. They are irrelevant to loving and serving God. If they come, they come from outside ourselves. All we are to try for is being good, devout men and women. If it pleases God to grant us a moment of angelic perfection, then we shall be good angels.

In the meantime, let's live sincerely, humbly, and devoutly. Let's live patiently, obediently, with tenderness toward our neighbors. Let's learn to put up with their imperfections. Let's desire no chief seats with God, but be glad to serve him in his kitchen or his pantry, to be his janitors or garbage collectors. If later he wants us to serve on his private cabinet, so be it. God does not reward his servants in relation to the dignity of their positions, but in relation to the love and humility they bring to their assigned tasks.

Frankly, ecstatic religious experience is highly subject to make-believe, artificial pretensions. Many who think they are angels are not even good people. They talk higher than they live. If you are awestruck by another's holiness, remain content with your own lower and safer experience.

—Francis de Sales: *The Devout Life*

A Personal Response

Teach me, Lord, to seek humility and faith in all I do. Take away my interest in entertaining spiritual pyrotechnics. Give my devotional life substance rather than glitter.

Meddling

> How can you think of saying, "Friend, let me
> help you get rid of the speck in your eye," when
> you can't see past the log in your own eye?
> *Matthew 7:4*, NLT

At the beginning of the spiritual life it is a common temptation for us to want everyone else to be extremely spiritual. It is not wrong to want this, but it may not be right to try to make it happen. If we do, it is essential that we exercise discretion and give no impression that we are setting ourselves up as a great teacher.

I discovered this for myself. When I attempted to induce others to pray, they would listen to what I had to say. When they then observed that I, the great practitioner of prayer, lacked certain virtues, they would be led astray. My actions were not compatible with my words. A trifling evil can be devastating in a religious community. Across many years only three individuals have gained anything of value from what I have said to them.

We are also tempted to be distressed by the sins and failings of others. We try to fix things. This excites us so much that it keeps us from praying. Worst of all, we trick ourselves into believing we are doing the Lord's work! Good intentions have led to terrible mistakes. Spiritual security comes when we stop being anxious about others and begin to watch after ourselves.

Try to focus on the best in others and the worst in ourselves. This will blind us to their defects. Eventually, we may even think of them as better than ourselves.

—Teresa of Avila: *The Life of Teresa of Jesus*

A Personal Response

Humility does not come easy for me, O God. It is so easy to spot the folly of others and be critical of them. There is a certain grim satisfaction in pulling down people in high positions. When I think of the people around me, I convince myself I would like to help them straighten out their lives. Help me with my own sins, especially the ones I do not notice.

Daily Essentials

We make our own plans, but the Lord decides where we will go. *Proverbs 16:9,* CEV

Christians ought to be as virtuous inside as they appear outside to others. No, they should be *better* in their heart than on the surface. Because God sees every part of us, we should be reverent before him and live as pure as angels in his sight.

Every day pray, "Help me, O Lord God! These are my good intentions in your service. Let me begin this day to settle down to the serious business of living a pure life, for what I have done so far is nothing."

The firmer we stick to our purpose, the more we will advance. If the one who tries the hardest frequently fails, what will become of the less enthusiastic? Remember that our best intentions do not depend upon us for fulfillment, but upon God. We are to rely on him for success in everything.

Even if we do the best we can, we will still fail many times. Yet we must always plan something definite, plot a course, especially as we battle our greatest personal weaknesses.

Determine a plan of action in the morning, and then evaluate yourself at night. How have you behaved today? What were your words, your deeds, your thoughts?

—Thomas à Kempis: *The Imitation of Christ*

A Personal Response

As I try to pay attention to my words and deeds and thoughts, I see the inner me. I would like to be better in my heart than I am on the surface. Change me.

More Than Losing a Pound

I fast twice a week and give a tenth of all I get.
Luke 18:12

A Christian's life is an inward thing. It is between you and God. Your behavior honors God. The good things you do are a way of thanking God.

Take a thing like fasting. Fasting is to abstain from overdoing. The purpose of fasting is to tame the body so your spirit can be closer to God. Too much eating and drinking or, for that matter, too much care about worldly business can press down the spirit. It can choke and tangle the soul.

Now if you fast for some reason other than to subdue your body in order to allow your spirit to quietly converse with God, then you are making a mistake. You are shooting at the wrong target.

If you abstain from eating meat, but drink all day, is that a Christian fast?

Or what if you eat enough at one meal to be sufficient for four?

Some who fast from meat and drink are so busy in the world they cannot once even think of God.

Some avoid butter, some eggs, some all kinds of white meat. Some skip meals on one day, some on another. They all have their reasons. They do it because they have a toothache, or a headache, or fevers, or to be delivered from hell.

Such people have no idea of God and no knowledge of the true purpose of fasting.

—William Tyndale: *The Parable*

A Personal Response

Lord, if I do a good thing for a wrong reason, does it have any spiritual value?

Faith Expands Our Grasp

Jesus said, "Do not hold on to me, for I have not yet returned to the Father." *John 20:17*

Faith is not deceived. It has the ability to understand imperceptible truth. Faith is not limited by the senses. It transcends even the limits of our intelligence. Faith goes beyond nature, beyond experience. We would not ask the eye to hear. There is no point in asking the hand to feel something beyond its reach. Your senses are excellent instructors, but their usefulness is restricted.

Begin to receive with greater trust what faith commends to you. We can touch our Lord with the heart, but not with the hand. We experience him by faith and not by the senses. "Why would you want to touch me now," he asks, "do you want to evaluate the glory of resurrection by a physical touch? Can't you remember that my disciples could not endure even a few seconds of my transfigured glory when I lived on earth? I accommodate myself to your senses by being a familiar servant, but this glory of mine is too extraordinary for you. It is beyond your reach. Don't even attempt to make a rational judgment about it. This is a matter of faith."

—Bernard of Clairvaux: *On the Song of Songs*

A Personal Response

Lord Jesus, I have learned to trust test tubes and computer chips. I want things to add up, make sense. Faith? What is that? Am I to pretend that something is true when I suspect it is not? Do you want me to live on a flight of fancy? Is having faith anything more than hoping or wishing? If these things are so important, why do you leave so much of it to faith? I want to know. I want to be sure.

Conversion of a Saint

Wake up, O sleeper, rise from the dead, and Christ will shine on you. *Ephesians 5:14*

A perverse will produces lust. Lust yielded to becomes a habit. A habit not resisted becomes a necessity. These were like links of a chain hanging one upon the other, and they bound me hand and foot. I had two wills: one old, one new; one carnal, one spiritual. Their conflict wasted my soul. I was like a sleepy man unable to get up.

God convinced me that his words were true, but the only answer I could give was the groggy word: "soon." But the word meant no particular span of time. "What a wretched man I am! Who will rescue me from this body of death?" (Romans 7:24). I refused to follow you, but my soul could find no excuse for not following. I was at war with myself in an agony of indecision. The familiar evil was more powerful than the unfamiliar good.

My introspection dredged up all the misery of my soul and piled it up in full view of my heart. A tremendous emotional storm arose and there was a deluge of tears.

And then I heard the voice of a boy or a girl from the nearby house saying, "Take up and read! Take up and read!" Holding back my tears, I got up, interpreting the child's words as a command from God to open the Bible and read the first passage I should see. I snatched it up, opened it, and silently read the first thing I saw. "Let us behave decently, as in the daytime, not in orgies and drunkenness, not in sexual immorality and debauchery, not in dissension and jealousy. Rather, clothe yourselves with the Lord Jesus Christ, and do not think about how to gratify the desires of the sinful nature" (Romans 13:13-14).

I had no desire, no need to read further. In the instant that sentence ended, it was as if a peaceful light shone in my heart and all the darkness of doubt vanished.

—Augustine: *Confessions*

 A Personal Response

You give us great variety in our religious experience, Lord God, but this saint's account inspires me. If you can work in him, you can work in me. Change me. Make me your own.

Relative Balance

Surely the nations are like a drop in a bucket;
they are regarded as dust on the scales; [God]
weighs the islands as though they were fine
dust. *Isaiah 40:15*

L ove God the same way in everything. Love God as quickly
in poverty as in wealth. Seek God in sickness as well as in
health. Look for God when you are tempted, and look for
him when you are not tempted. Discover God in suffering and in
pleasantness.

It is like carrying two buckets. If one is heavy, the other feels
lighter. The more you abandon yourself, the easier it will be to
abandon. If you love God you will be able to renounce the whole earth
as though it were an egg. The more you give, the easier it is to give.
The followers of Christ discovered that the heavier their suffering,
the easier they could endure it.

—Meister Eckhart: *Sermons*

 A Personal Response

Some of the things I think are mighty important are not. Am
I missing something worthwhile? Could it be, Lord, that the
source of my greatest pains is not worth anything?

A Hike in Dangerous Country

The path of the righteous is like the first gleam of dawn, shining ever brighter till the full light of day. But the path of the wicked is like deep darkness; they do not know what makes them stumble. *Proverbs 4:18-19*

Think of a hiker in the woods. The path is going through a wet and thorny area. With a good eye, the hiker moves carefully through the snags and dangers, able to stay out of mud and keep clothes untorn. The hiker's eyesight is keen, helping avoid stumbling and injury.

Another hiker may be less careful. Passing along the same rough path, this hiker's clothes rip and his skin receives cuts and bruises. He may even fall into deep water and drown.

This is the way it is with the soul. It is dressed in an attractive garment we call the body. It is able to find its way through this world avoiding the thorns of lust and the swamps of vanity. With care it avoids traps that catch others. It does not look for evil. It will not listen to slander. It takes care of itself.

The result is that both body and soul are preserved. This brings praise from God and the angels.

—Pseudo-Macarius: *Homilies*

A Personal Response

It's a precarious road, Lord. "Through many dangers, toils, and snares, I have already come. 'Tis grace has brought me safe thus far, and grace will lead me home."

Distrust of Self

He gives strength to the weary and increases the power of the weak. *Isaiah 40:29*

We easily overestimate our own abilities. It is not easy to spot the error in this.

Distrust of our own strength is a gift from heaven. Sometimes we receive it through the inspiration of God. Sometimes it arrives with afflictions and overwhelming temptations.

There are four things we need to do if we would gain this spiritually healthy distrust of ourselves.

Meditate upon our own weakness. Admit that we cannot accomplish the smallest good without God's help.

Beg God for what God alone can give. Acknowledge that we don't have it and that we can't go somewhere and get it. Let's fall down at the feet of our Lord and plead with him to grant our request.

Gradually discard the illusions of our own mind, our tendency to sin, and begin to see the overwhelming, yet hidden, obstacles that surround us.

As often as we commit a fault, we must take inventory of our weaknesses. God permits us to fall only in order to help us gain deeper insight into ourselves.

God permits us to sin more or less grievously in proportion to our pride. Every time we commit a fault, we should earnestly ask God to enlighten us. Ask him to help you see yourself as you are in his sight.

Presume no more on your own strength. Otherwise, you will stumble again over the same stone.

—Lawrence Scupoli: *The Spiritual Combat*

A Personal Response

Jesus, "I am weak but you are strong."

Success with God

Are not two sparrows sold for a penny? Yet not one of them will fall to the ground apart from the will of your Father. *Matthew 10:29*

Trust God's providence, but cooperate with him. Be like a little child who holds the father's hand while picking strawberries or blackberries in the hedgerows. If you must deal with the world's commerce with one hand, keep the other one with God. Look up to him now and then to see if he approves of what you are doing. Never think that you will be able to gather more if you use both hands. He is your success. Let go of him and you are in peril.

If your business is common enough, focus on God. If it becomes complicated and demands all of your attention, then still look now and then at God, the way sailors look at the sky rather than the water. This way God will work with you, and in you, and for you.

—Francis de Sales: *The Devout Life*

 A Personal Response

Lord, you also show me this truth in the first two verses of Psalm 127: "Unless the Lord builds the house, its builders labor in vain. Unless the Lord watches over the city, the watchmen stand guard in vain. In vain you rise early and stay up late, toiling for food to eat—for he grants sleep to those he loves."

A Prime Thought

So God created people in his own image; God patterned them after himself; male and female he created them. *Genesis 1:27,* NLT

My life is a miracle of thirty years. It is more poetry than history. It sounds to many like a fable. Those who can only see my exterior and think only of my position and experiences are mistaken. The earth is a point not only relative to the heavens above us but also to the celestial part within us.

The flesh that wraps me does not limit my mind. I am a little world, a microcosm. There is surely a piece of Divinity in me. It existed before the elements and owes no homage to the sun. Nature, in addition to Scripture, tells me I am the image of God.

If this idea eludes you, then you have not been introduced to the first lesson. You have not yet started your ABCs.

—Thomas Browne: *Religio Medici*

 A Personal Response

O God. In your light, I can see myself more clearly. Let me perceive your image in myself and others.

A Personal Testimony

He has determined the times of their existence and the limits of their habitation, so that they might search for God, in the hope that they might feel for him and find him—yes, even though he is not far from any of us. *Acts 17:27,* PHILLIPS

For more than forty years my continual concern has been to be always with God, and to do nothing, say nothing, and think nothing which may displease him. I have had no other motive for this than love of God.

I am now so accustomed to that Divine Presence that I am continually nourished by it. My soul has been filled with constant joy. Sometimes I have had to force myself not to let it show too much on the outside.

If I become a little too absent from the Divine Presence, as sometimes happens when I am busy, God soon makes himself felt in my soul and calls me back.

God's treasure is like an infinite ocean, and yet a little wave of emotion, passing with the moment, is enough for many. But when God finds a soul filled with a living faith, he pours into it his grace and good favor. They flow into the soul the way a torrent that has been stopped in its course for a while by some debris spreads its pent-up flood waters.

We often stop this torrent by the little value we give it. Make the most of your opportunity. Redeem the time that is lost. Maybe you don't have much left. Remember, in the spiritual life, failure to advance is going backward.

—Brother Lawrence: *The Practice of the Presence of God*

A Personal Response

If you, O God, are like an ocean, why am I satisfied with a teaspoon? Open me to your greatness.

Prayer beyond Prayer

When you pray, don't be like those show-offs who love to stand up and pray in the meeting places and on the street corners. They do this just to look good. I can assure you that they already have their reward. *Matthew 6:5,* CEV

When you pray, try to determine whether you are really aware of being in God's presence or are simply trying to be noticed by others. It is natural to seek attention and approval, but if this is the goal of your extended prayers, you are not actually praying.

Whether you are praying with others or alone, try to make your prayer more than routine. Desire it to be an authentic spiritual experience. If your spirit is distracted during a time of prayer, then you are not really getting into it. You are like a business executive doing a little puttering in the garden.

Keep a tight leash on your memory when you pray. Do not allow it to suggest fanciful things to you. Let it carry an awareness of reaching out to God. Be constantly aware that your memory has a strong tendency to trouble your spirit during a time of prayer. You will recall all kinds of distressing events that will stir your passions. These passions are irrational. When they burn you are not free to pray.

Suppose you do not have any disturbing emotions. You still may not actually engage in prayer. It is possible to have only the purest thoughts and remain far from God.

If you want to pray, you need God. God will turn ordinary prayer into exceptional prayer. He will take you beyond praising him for *what he does* to praising him for *who he is.*

—Evagrius Ponticus: *Chapters on Prayer*

 A Personal Response

It is amazing, Lord, that even prayer comes in varying degrees of quality. It is not a matter of language or style, but of spirit. Help me to be honest with myself about this.

Religious Conversion

[Jesus said,] "All of us must quickly carry out the tasks assigned us by the one who sent me, because there is little time left before the night falls and all work comes to an end." *John 9:4,* NLT

Turn to God quickly and completely. Be converted to him. Do not keep procrastinating. It is a huge sin to expect God to be merciful while we continue a sinful life. It is a common mistake to think that the mercy of God is so great that there will be no punishment.

We live inside a tiny moment of time. All of our time, compared with eternity, is nothing. It is a serious waste to let a day go by without allowing God to change us.

Conversion is a total turning to God. This means we turn away from the world with its sin. If we choose to turn away from God we ignore the good that never changes. Our affections and our behavior need to be changed.

You will be converted when you have made a complete turn toward God. Your mind will meditate upon him. You will understand that you live your life under God. The psalmist writes, "I have set the Lord always before me" (Psalm 16:8). Notice that he says, "Always." This is different from an occasional glance in God's direction while preoccupied with the things of this world.

Again the psalmist declares, "My eyes are ever on the Lord, for only he will release my feet from the snare" (Psalm 25:15). These words make it clear that if we do not habitually focus our interior eyes on Christ we will be caught in the snare of temptation. In fact, if our soul's attention is not riveted on God, being completely converted to him, there are going to be some traps along the way for us.

Many claim to be willing to turn toward God but believe that responsibilities in this world prevent it. If they were touched in the slightest way by the love of Christ they would immediately try to find a way to serve God. They would keep looking until they find it.

—Richard Rolle: *The Fire of Love*

 A Personal Response

Convert us, O Lord. We are neglecting our souls. Turn us completely toward you. Our lives will be mended if you save us.
—Richard Rolle

Putting the Community First

> The entire law is summed up in a single command: "Love your neighbor as yourself." If you keep on biting and devouring each other, watch out or you will be destroyed by each other. *Galatians 5:14*

I f you want to follow Christ, changing your perspective and behavior, take all of the love and concern you have for yourself and put it all on others. Genuine love, which fulfills every law, does not seek its own profit at the expense of the welfare of others. "Love is not rude, it is not self-seeking, it is not easily angered, it keeps no record of wrongs" (1 Corinthians 13:5).

This is emphasized in all Scripture. It may be applied to those who share our faith and to those who do not. Jesus said, "You have heard that it was said, 'Love your neighbor and hate your enemy.' But I tell you: Love your enemies and pray for those who persecute you" (Matthew 5:43-44).

The best, the most perfect and blessed condition is that in which we can most usefully and profitably serve others. Keep in mind that spiritual service is superior to material service and that the community is more important than individuals.

This responsibility of service to others rests upon both spiritual and secular leaders. There can be no greater plague than people seeking their own advantage. The more a profession is useful to the needs of a community, the more it is honorable.

We are living in those last days that Christ spoke about. "Because of the increase of wickedness, the love of most will grow cold" (Matthew 24:12). People want to live on the work of others. Christianity demands exactly the opposite. The Christian gives up even what is rightly due, is always ready to help others, holding on to the words of Jesus: "It is more blessed to give than to receive" (Acts 20:35).

—Martin Bucer: *Instruction in Christian Love*

 A Personal Response

It would be wonderful, O Lord, if the things I do blessed others. Help me to give all I can and to carry what I am able.

The World Is a Biased Judge

If the world hates you, keep in mind that it hated me first. *John 15:18*

Once it becomes evident that you intend to live a devout life, secular people will laugh at you and criticize you. The worst of them will say that because of some hard experiences you have run to God as an escape. Your friends will warn you of the unhappy consequences of your choice, saying that you will lose your reputation, become difficult to work with, or age prematurely. They will tell you that if you are going to live in the world, you must be a part of the world. They will call you an extremist and urge moderation upon you.

These foolish babblers are not concerned about you. "If you belonged to the world, it would love you as its own. As it is, you do not belong to the world, but I have chosen you out of the world. That is why the world hates you" (John 15:19).

Let some throw away many nights playing chess or cards and no one says anything about it. But if we give an hour to meditation they are ready to go for the doctor to cure us of our illness. The world is a biased judge, approving its own and dealing harshly with the children of God.

While light is a good thing, it can blind us after we have been in the dark. The change in your style of life may create some problems. Be patient. The strangeness will eventually wear off.

—Francis de Sales: *The Devout Life*

A Personal Response

The great saints usually admit they feel a little like strangers in this world. Help me, my Lord, to live here without being an *alien.* Let me fulfill some useful purpose in this time and place. But never let me forget the larger context of spiritual things.

May 23 # The Value of the Church

You will know how people ought to conduct themselves in God's household, which is the church of the living God, the pillar and foundation of the truth. *1 Timothy 3:15*

God will not come down from heaven. He will not send his angels to bring us revelations from above. He will make himself known to us by his Word. God could do it another way if he desired. This is not the only way open to him. But this is the way he has chosen to do it.

God has imprinted his image in his Word. He presents himself to us there and we can behold him, as it were, face to face. We have no need to soar above the clouds. We need not travel up and down the earth or go beyond the seas. We are not required to go down the bottomless pit or open the door of paradise. We can go to church and hear the promises that are made to us in his name.

It is as though God reaches out his hand visibly and receives us as his children. The church is the house of God. The church maintains his truth.

When we participate in the Lord's Supper we should examine ourselves that we may become a part of his Body and truly be made one with him. We must understand that he is our life, that we live in him, and he dwells in us. Call upon him. Trust in his goodness. His Holy Spirit will guide us.

May we listen to what God tells us. He wants to show his grace to more than just one city or a little handful of people. This is for the world. Everyone may serve and worship him in spirit and in truth.

—John Calvin: *Behavior in the Church*

 A Personal Response

Help me to understand that my faith is not an isolated thing. I need to be a part of a community of the faithful. Even though I may experience intimate companionship with you, O God, I need a healthy relationship with others in your church.

Trust God

Offer right sacrifices and trust in the Lord. *Psalm 4:5*

The best way to gain divine assistance is to place complete confidence in God.

With great humility and faith, contemplate the enormous power and wisdom of God. Nothing is too difficult for him. His goodness is unlimited. He is always ready to give those who love him the necessities for their spiritual life, and for gaining a complete victory over themselves. The only thing required of us is that we turn to him with complete confidence. What could be more reasonable?

For about thirty-three years Jesus, the Good Shepherd, looked for lost sheep in difficult terrain. Ultimately, it cost him his life. Is it possible for such a devoted shepherd to ignore a returning stray? Would it matter if the sheep had only a weak intention of following him? No. He would look on it with pity, listen to its cries, and take it up upon his own shoulders to return it to the flock.

Remember what the Holy Scriptures tell us in a thousand different places. No one who puts trust in God will be defeated.

Before attempting to do anything good, think about your own weakness and the infinite power, wisdom, and goodness of God. Balance what you fear about yourself with your faith in God.

—Lawrence Scupoli: *The Spiritual Combat*

A Personal Response

It is surely possible, heavenly Father, to merely presume that I have confidence in you. I can imagine I have a faith that is not in me. It is only as I am absolutely sure that a challenge is greater than I am that I will absolutely trust you.

May 25 Devotional Diversity

> There is a time for everything, and a season for
> every activity under heaven. *Ecclesiastes 3:1*

S ome people believe that devotion will slip away from them if
they relax a little. Recreation is good for the soul. We will be
stronger when we return to prayer.

Do not spend all of your time in one method of prayer. You may
have found an excellent method of prayer that you really enjoy.
Maybe you need a kind of Sunday. I mean a time of rest from your
spiritual labor.

You think you would lose something if you stop working at
prayer. My view is that your loss would be gain. Try to imagine
yourself in the presence of Christ. Talk with him. Delight in him.
There is no need to weary yourself by composing speeches to him.

There is a time for one thing and a time for another. The soul can
become weary of eating the same food over and over again. There is
a great variety of food that is wholesome and nutritious. If your
spiritual palate becomes familiar with their various tastes, they will
sustain the life of your soul, bringing many benefits.

—Teresa of Avila: *The Life of Teresa of Jesus*

A Personal Response

Make my prayer as natural as breathing, dear God. Give me
an openness that will welcome the fresh, the new. While I do
not seek novelty, I would at least like to be sure that I have
opened every possible door to my soul.

Professional Courtesy

[Apollos] began to speak boldly in the synagogue. When Priscilla and Aquila heard him, they invited him to their home and explained to him the way of God more adequately. *Acts 18:26*

I have taken the responsibility of preparing a special translation of the Bible. I have not done this because I find fault with the work of others. Among many efforts to render the Scriptures in English I have found none that is not worthy of great thanksgiving unto God.

I have faithfully followed my interpreters and accepted correction. There must still be mistakes because all humans are fallible and miss something. Christian love will assume the best without any harsh judgment.

There is no one living who can see everything. God has given complete knowledge to none. One sees more clearly than another, one has more understanding than another, and one can express a thing better than another. But no one ought to envy or despise another. The one who can do better than others should, instead of denigrating another's work, remember that the gift is not his but God's. God has given the ability to teach and to inform the ignorant.

If you have the knowledge therefore to judge where any fault is made, help to amend it. Let love be joined with your knowledge.

—Miles Coverdale: *A Prologue to the Bible*

A Personal Response

I recall something I read in the Psalms: "When you discipline people for their sins, their lives can be crushed like the life of a moth" (Psalm 39:11, NLT). Teach me, dear Lord, the art of constructive criticism.

Malicious Gossip

> I am the Lord, the one who encourages you.
> Why are you afraid of mere humans? They dry
> up and die like grass. *Isaiah 51:12,* CEV

It is impossible to satisfy everyone. Paul said, "I try to find common ground with everyone" (1 Corinthians 9:22, NLT). And yet he said, "I care very little if I am judged by you or by any human court; indeed, I do not even judge myself" (1 Corinthians 4:3).

He did everything he could to lead others to Christ, but he still had plenty of detractors. Here is how Paul preserved his sanity: he turned it all over to God who knows everything.

When necessary, Paul faced those who tried to raise their own status by climbing over him. He answered their charges with humility and patience in order to protect others who might be hurt by his silence.

What power does anyone have to injure you with words? He hurts himself, not you. And he will not be able to escape God's judgment, regardless of who he is. Keep God in sight, and if anyone condemns you, ignore it.

Stay near God and don't worry about what others think of you. It is a good thing to suffer such judgment.

—Thomas à Kempis: *The Imitation of Christ*

A Personal Response

It hurts. I feel the knot in my stomach. I have difficulty sleeping. My appetite is diminished. I become irritable. There is a long list of physical and emotional disturbances that chew on my being when I know I am the subject of such verbal sabotage. I can't smile and say it doesn't matter, Lord. Help me, then, to turn to you for strength.

May 28 A Variety of Crosses

So even though Jesus was God's Son, he learned obedience from the things he suffered. *Hebrews 5:8,* NLT

God is a clever designer of crosses. Some are as heavy as iron or lead. Others are as light as straw. He constructs impressive crosses of gold and jewels. He uses all the things we like best. In spite of their great variety, crosses have two things in common. They are hard to carry and they crucify.

A poor, hungry person bears a leaden cross. But God can bring suffering just as unpleasant to the wealthy. The poor can at least beg for a handout! The well-to-do have nowhere to turn. If poor health can be added to the glittering cross, the crucifixion is complete. Then we see both our frailty and the worthlessness of our wealth. The things that impress those looking on from the outside are invisible to the ones who possess them. One may be crucified while the world envies his good fortune! Prestige can be more painful than arthritis.

—François de Fénelon: *Meditations and Devotions*

 A Personal Response

Whatever form my cross takes, O Lord, let me, like Christ, carry it willingly.

May 29 A Demanding Job

[They] made me take care of the vineyards; my own vineyard I have neglected. *Song of Songs 1:6*

When I read these words in the Song of Songs, I usually criticize myself for accepting a responsible position. How can I care for the souls of others when I am not fit to care for my own? The people who made me a keeper of the vineyards should have noticed how I kept my own.

When I became a Christian I made a little improvement, but not much. I am only human. "Unless the Lord watches over the city, the watchmen stand guard in vain" (Psalm 127:1). O my vineyard! How many grapes were stolen from you by subtle fraud just as I was beginning to take better care of you! So many valuable clusters of good works were blighted by anger, stolen by boasting, and contaminated by egotism! I was tempted by craving for food, mental idleness, timidity of spirit, and the storm of passion!

In spite of this they made me a keeper of vineyards. They never considered what I was doing with my own. They ignored the teacher who asked, "If anyone does not know how to manage his own family, how can he take care of God's church?" (1 Timothy 3:5).

Since I am involved in so many concerns for the vineyard I have been assigned, I am in all the more danger of neglecting my own. There is no time for me to build a fence around it or to construct a winepress. I am too busy! Its wall is broken down. Anyone who comes along may pluck some grapes. There is nothing to shelter it from sorrow. Anger and impatience have pounded a path through it. Important tasks, like little foxes, chew on it constantly. Anxiety, suspicion, and worry rush in from every direction. There is hardly an hour when bickering groups are not clawing at me with their fatiguing quarrels. I have no way to escape them. There is not even time for prayer. Will tears be enough to irrigate the desert of my soul?

—Bernard of Clairvaux: *On the Song of Songs*

A Personal Response

O good Jesus, let my broken spirit be a sacrifice to you. Do not disdain this crushed and broken heart, O God.
—Bernard of Clairvaux

White Lies

You use your mouth for evil and harness your
tongue to deceit. *Psalm 50:19*

I s it ever necessary to lie? Some think so. Even in religious matters it seems good to them to speak falsely. I believe every lie is
a sin, though it may be a matter of degree. The intention and
the topic need to be considered. Telling a lie in an attempt to be
helpful is not the same as deliberate wickedness. Speaking falsely
when you really think you are telling truth is not lying. In this case
you are yourself deceived. It is rashness, not prevarication, when
we accept as true what is false.

We lie when we speak the truth, if we actually thought it was a
falsehood. Our intention was to lie. Consider the intentions rather than
the content. We lie when we have one thought secured in our heart
and another prepared for our tongue.

Some lies do no harm. It is a small thing. Good may result. But
it is a mistake to deny that evil is bad, or to approve something false
as though it were true, or to disapprove the truth as though it were
false, or to hold what is certain as if it were uncertain, or the opposite.
It is one thing to suppose that a particular road is the right one when
it is not. It is something else entirely when that wrong road leads to
something good.

—Augustine: *Enchiridion*

A Personal Response

Lord, give me your heart for what is right and your anger
against what is evil. Proverbs 6:16-19 teaches, "There are six
things the Lord hates, seven that are detestable to him: haughty
eyes, a lying tongue, hands that shed innocent blood, a heart
that devises wicked schemes, feet that are quick to rush into
evil, a false witness who pours out lies and a man who stirs
up dissension among brothers."

Misuse of Scripture

Why do you boast of evil, you mighty man? Why do you boast all day long, you who are a disgrace in the eyes of God? *Psalm 52:1*

Debate about the Scriptures hurts those who argue their point. It is like setting your own house on fire, beating your parents, or killing your children. What is the origin of this itching tongue? Why do we enjoy such clattering talk?

What are we trying to communicate? Hospitality? Love? Chastity? Alms? Are we singing God's praise or lamenting our sins? Are we praying? We talk of Scripture, but we do not meditate upon life and death, we do not attempt to control our appetites and affections, we do not try to pull down the proud and high-minded, we have no desire to control our lusts and lechery. All our holiness consists of talking. We forgive each other for not living well in order to stay together in order to argue, as though this chatter were the way to heaven. Religious speculation leads not to heaven, but to unnecessary contention and sophistication.

Gregory of Nazareth wrote that a Christian's learning ought to begin in fear of God and end in matters of high speculation. Some think it works the other way, beginning with speculation and ending in fear.

Anyone who attempts to read the Bible should begin with a genuine respect for God. Then there needs to be a firm desire to reform one's life according to its teaching. If you will be a sober and fruitful hearer and learner, then you will one day be able to teach. Your teaching will not be done with your mouth, but with holy living and good example.

—Thomas Cranmer: *Prologue to the Bible*

A Personal Response

Lord, if I have anything to teach others, let my instruction flow from a quality of life that will underscore and give credibility to the things I say.

Happiness

God blesses those people whose hearts are pure.
They will see him! God blesses those people
who make peace. They will be called his
children! *Matthew 5:8-9,* CEV

The pure of heart are those who care nothing for earthly things and always look for heavenly things. They never stop adoring and contemplating the living God with a pure heart and mind.

The genuine peacemakers are those who remain at peace in their souls and bodies when they suffer in this world for the love of our Lord Jesus Christ.

Happy is the person who bears with neighbors, understanding their frail natures, as much as he would want to be borne with by them.

Happy is that devout person who experiences no pleasure or joy except in holy conversation and the works of the Lord, and who uses these means to lead others to the love of God.

Happy is the servant who never speaks merely to get a reward, who always carefully considers what to say. Unhappy is the religious person who, instead of keeping the good things that the Lord has spoken to his heart and demonstrating them by a life of quality, tries to make it known by talking about it. That person may receive nothing more than an earthly reward and those who regarded that person's words will take away little fruit.

Happy is that brother who loves his brother as much when he is sick and not able to help him as he loves him when he is well and able to carry part of the burden. Happy is the brother who loves his brother as much when he is far away from him as he does when he is close by.

—Francis of Assisi: *Admonitions*

A Personal Response

Lord, are we looking for happiness in the wrong places? The saint's finger does not point in an often traveled direction.

June 2 # Temptation

You are tempted in the same way that everyone else is tempted. But God can be trusted not to let you be tempted too much, and he will show you how to escape from your temptations.
1 Corinthians 10:13, CEV

There is a vast difference between being tempted and yielding to it. And yet, if I know in advance that certain places will tempt me and I go there anyway, I am guilty of each temptation that comes my way.

The way to deal with temptations is to look away from them and at the Lord. If you are still subject to them, continue to resist. There is no sin as long as you say "No."

For every great temptation there will be many small ones. Wolves and bears are more dangerous than flies, but we are bothered most by the latter. You may never murder anyone, but you will certainly become angry. You may avoid adultery, but it is not easy to control your eyes. You may never steal anything from your neighbor, but you may covet it.

Let these flies and gnats buzz around you. Instead of fighting with them, do the very opposite of what the temptation is suggesting. For instance, if you are tempted to be vain, think about the troubles of others. If you are greedy, remember how death will take it all away from you, and then go give something away or pass up a profit. Make the effort and you will be hardened against future temptations.

—Francis de Sales: *The Devout Life*

A Personal Response

When I begin to take a little pride in the fact that some of the grossest temptations have never come my way, along comes a reminder that I still have plenty to work on. Lord, do not abandon me in a time of temptation.

June 3   ## God Waits

The Lord said: "People of Jerusalem, when you stumble and fall, you get back up, and if you take a wrong road, you turn around and go back. So why do you refuse to come back to me? Why do you hold so tightly to your false gods?"
Jeremiah 8:4-5, CEV

Because we are immature and ignorant, we ignore the best and choose the poorest. God is patient with us. He understands that being virtuous is not easy for us. When we fall, God picks us up and gives us another chance.

When we demonstrate that we really desire a good life, God begins to truly convert us. God is being good and kind to us at this very moment. Even though we hurt him with our sin he waits calmly for our conversion. When we return to God there is an outpouring of love and joy. This is what Jesus meant when he said, "I tell you, there is rejoicing in the presence of the angels of God over one sinner who repents" (Luke 15:10).

—Pseudo-Macarius: *Homilies*

A Personal Response

It's almost laughable, Lord, the way I stumble along. For some inexplicable reason, I fail to make the obvious choice. Thank you, God, for your mercy. Thank you for your long-suffering patience. Make me equally patient with others.

Misery and Weakness

How frail is humanity! How short is life, and how full of trouble! *Job 14:1,* NLT

Why are you upset when things don't go the way you wish? Who gets everything his way? I don't. You don't. No one does. Not one person on earth—not even a king or a pope—has a problem-free life.

Do you know who can deal with troubles best? It is the person who is willing to suffer something for God.

Thoughtless people say, "Look at the happy life that person leads! Money! Prestige! Power!" But if you consider the riches of heaven, you will see that these earthly things are inconsequential, undependable, and more a burden than a privilege. They are always accompanied by anxiety and fear. Our happiness does not depend upon owning a lot of things. Having enough to get along will do.

Life on earth involves misery. The spiritually perceptive person is even more aware of this because that person sees clearly the effects of human corruption. For that matter, to eat and drink, to sleep and wake, to work and rest, and to be forced to obey the other requirements of nature can become a great annoyance to a devout person who would almost prefer to live without a body!

Friend, don't give up your spiritual journey. You still have time. Why do you keep putting off your decision day after day? You can start immediately. You can say, "This is the moment to start moving. Now is the time to begin the fight and to change my ways."

How great is our weakness of character! Today you will confess your sins; tomorrow you will commit the same ones again. Right now, you intend to do better. In an hour, you will behave as though this moment never happened.

We have every reason, therefore, to be humble. We are weak and unstable.

—Thomas à Kempis: *The Imitation of Christ*

A Personal Response

My best resolutions are often no more than straw in a fire. Do for me, Lord God, what I cannot do for myself.

Something for Everyone

They will neither hunger nor thirst, nor will the
desert heat or the sun beat upon them. He who
has compassion on them will guide them and
lead them beside springs of water. *Isaiah 49:10*

The Bible is a shop that contains the wisdom, knowledge,
power, judgments, and mercies of God. Wherever we look
we will see displayed the works of his hands. We will see
his work of creation and his preservation of everything. We will see
his severe justice upon the wicked and his gracious redemption of
the believer.

If we want pleasant music and beautiful harmony, it is there. If
we would learn, it is a school giving understanding to the simple. It
contains words that will satisfy the heart, the ear, the eye, the taste,
and the smelling. It has the savor of life. "Taste and see that the Lord
is good" (Psalm 34:8).

Some think that the Scriptures are not for the people, saying,
"They may not read them who are not able to wield them." They
remind us that Christ taught us not to cast pearls before swine (Matthew 7:6). Indeed, the Bible is a string of pearls. But people are not
swine.

They say the Scriptures are hard, above the reach of ordinary
people. They are fit only for a few highly educated people. But God
says otherwise. "Now what I am commanding you today is not too
difficult for you or beyond your reach. It is not up in heaven so that
you have to ask, 'Who will ascend into heaven to get it and proclaim
it to us so we may obey it?' Nor is it beyond the sea, so that you have
to ask, 'Who will cross the sea to get it and proclaim it to us so we
may obey it?' No, the word is very near you; it is in your mouth and
in your heart so you may obey it" (Deuteronomy 30:11-14).

There is no need to beat your brains out in searching. The word
and commandment of God will sufficiently teach you.

—John Jewell: *Of the Holy Scriptures*

A Personal Response
Speak to my need, Lord God. Speak to me through the pages
of the Bible.

Tied Down by Threads

When we put bits into the mouths of horses to make them obey us, we can turn the whole animal. Or take ships as an example. Although they are so large and are driven by strong winds, they are steered by a very small rudder wherever the pilot wants to go. Likewise, the tongue is a small part of the body, but it makes great boasts. Consider what a great forest is set on fire by a small spark. *James 3:3-5*

The soul can become entangled with bad little habits. We never completely conquer them. We become attached to certain clothes, a book, a specific food, gossip, or a desire for any number of things. Any of these little imperfections can stand in the way of spiritual progress.

Unfortunately, when we receive strength from God to break the stronger cords that bind the soul, the childish little things remain hard to shake off. It may be nothing more than a thread or a hair, but it binds us.

If a log is placed in the fire it may not catch if only one degree of necessary heat is missing. In the same way a soul with one of these minor imperfections will be hindered. The soul has only one will. If that will is trapped by the slightest thing, it will be embarrassed because it is not free and pure.

—John of the Cross: *Ascent of Mount Carmel*

 A Personal Response

Lord, I'd rather focus on the major issues—the things I'm not really hindered by. But when you start picking lint off of my soul, I become aware that I am not perfect. I want to ignore the trifling things! But I know they are not trifles if they tie me down. I see my soul as some Gulliver in custody at Lilliput. Lord, make me willing to be freed. And free me.

Awareness of God

The peace of God, which transcends all understanding, will guard your hearts and your minds in Christ Jesus. *Philippians 4:7*

This is one of several pieces written about Brother Lawrence. It was included in Lawrence's book The Practice of the Presence of God:

Brother Lawrence said that when he began his religious life, he spent the hours set aside for private prayer in thinking of God. He wanted to convince his mind and heart of the Divine existence. He resolved to live every moment aware of God's presence. He attempted to pray without ceasing.

When he had some job to do he would pray, "O my God, since you are with me, and I must now obey your command and apply my mind to these outward things, I pray that you will continue to be with me, assist me, receive all my works, and possess all my affections."

Brother Lawrence said, "We can do *little* things for God. I turn the cake that is frying in the pan for the love of him. And when I have turned it, if there is nothing else to call for my attention, I worship God. I have arrived at a state where it is as difficult for me not to think of God as it was at first to get used to it."

As Brother Lawrence had found such comfort and blessing in walking in the Presence of God, it was natural for him to highly recommend it to others. But his example was a stronger inducement than his words. His very appearance was a benediction! Even when he was in his greatest hurry in the kitchen, he still preserved his serenity. He neither rushed nor loafed, but did everything in its turn, with an even composure and a tranquility of spirit.

"The time of business," he said, "is not different from the time of prayer. In the noise and clatter of my kitchen, while several persons are at the same time calling for different things, I possess God in as great tranquility as if I were upon my knees at the Blessed Sacrament."

A Personal Response

Make all of my life a prayer, O Lord. Help. me to direct my thoughts toward you. Let me listen for your still, small voice.

Prayer Is Life

Pray continually. *1 Thessalonians 5:17*

Silently descend into the depths of your heart. Call on the name of Jesus Christ frequently. This is the way to experience interior illumination. Many things will become clear to you, even the mysteries of the kingdom of God. You will discover a depth of mystery, a brightness, when you learn to descend into yourself!

The truth is: we are aliens to ourselves. We have little desire to know ourselves. We run after many things in this world, and by doing so run away from ourselves. We exchange truth for trinkets. We kid ourselves. *I would like to have time for prayer and the spiritual life, but the cares and demands of life take all my time and energy,* we think.

Which is more important? Which is temporary? Which is eternal? Making this decision will lead you to wisdom or keep you in ignorance.

Prayer is the heart of Christian life. It is essential. Prayer is both the first step and the fulfillment of the devout life. We are directed to pray always. Particular times may be set for other acts of devotion, but for prayer there is no special time. We are to pray constantly.

Sit alone in a quiet place. Take your mind away from every earthly and vain thing. Bow your head to your chest and be attentive, not to your head, but to your heart. Observe your breathing. Let your mind find the place of the heart. At first you will be uncomfortable. If you continue without interruption it will become a joy.

The most wonderful result of this kind of mental silence is that sinful thoughts which come knocking at the door of the mind are turned away. Pray and think what you will. Pray and do what you want. Your thoughts and activity will be purified by prayer.

—Anonymous Russian: *The Way of a Pilgrim*

A Personal Response

Let prayer be as natural for me as breathing. Fully conscious, O God, let me be aware of you as regularly as I inhale and exhale.

Prayer for Healing

Be merciful to me, Lord, for I am faint; O Lord,
heal me, for my bones are in agony. *Psalm 6:2*

The sixth Psalm is a prayer of David. It is a natural thing for us to run to God when we are in trouble. Even if God appears to be our enemy we seek his help. Although your pains are horrible and you can find no release or comfort, either in spirit or in body, you can still sob to God. He will not ignore you. There is a secret seed of God hidden in you. A sincere sobbing to God is an acceptable sacrifice. "Have mercy upon me, O Lord, and heal me!"

Some people think it is wrong to ask God for bodily health. They do not understand that sickness is a trouble to the body, and that God wants us to call for his help in all our troubles. Our prayers in such a difficulty are the greatest glory that we can give to God.

—John Knox: *Exposition of the Sixth Psalm*

 A Personal Response

Lord, give me a confidence and trust that will seek and accept your healing hand.

More Than Skin Deep

The men who had gone up with [Caleb] said, "We can't attack those people; they are stronger than we are." And they spread among the Israelites a bad report about the land they had explored. They said, "The land we explored devours those living in it. All the people we saw there are of great size." *Numbers 13:31-32*

The naysayers who discouraged the Israelites from entering the Promised Land said it was an unhealthy place. They reported bad air and monstrous inhabitants who would eat them like locusts. This is the way the world puts down a devotional life. It characterizes religious persons as having gloomy, sullen expressions on their faces. It reports that a devotional life is depressing.

Joshua and Caleb disagreed with the report of the spies. They believed the Promised Land was good and beautiful. In the same way the Holy Spirit reports to us through the saints that the devout life is healthy, happy, and enjoyable. Our Lord said, "Come to me, all you who are weary and burdened, and I will give you rest" (Matthew 11:28).

The world notices that devout people pray, fast, withstand harm, care for the sick, support the poor, keep vigils, control anger, subdue passions, avoid extreme sensuality, and perform rigorous and sometimes painful actions. What the world doesn't see is the heartfelt inward devotion that makes all of these things pleasant, sweet, and easy.

Look at the bees in a garden of thyme. The nectar there is very bitter, but they have the ability to change it into honey. Yes, it is true that devout souls meet with great sadness, but it is transformed into something better. Devotion can sweeten the sourest torments.

Sugar sweetens green fruit. Devotion is a spiritual sugar. It takes discontent away from the poor, and worry from the rich. It removes sorrow from the oppressed, and pride from the exalted. It destroys melancholy in the person alone, and fatigue from those living in society. It acts as fire in winter and dew in summer. Devotion makes both honor and contempt useful to us.

—Francis de Sales: *The Devout Life*

 A Personal Response

Let my devotion be genuine, dear God. Don't let me be misguided by what the world thinks about the life of devotion.

Self-Knowledge

> If you reject criticism, you only harm yourself;
> but if you listen to correction, you grow in
> understanding. *Proverbs 15:32,* NLT

Nothing can be closer to you than yourself. Yet it is amazing that you can know other things *better* than you know yourself. If you are holding an object in your hand and start to look for it, you will make others laugh. What is more at hand than your own soul? How can it know anything better than it knows itself?

In fact, you can't know anything at all if you do not know yourself.

We need to look at our own souls as a physician would look at a patient. A physician's first responsibility in treating a patient is to correctly diagnose the illness. The next job is to prescribe the correct treatment.

If nothing can be improved without the physician's review and criticism, then the one who opposes review and criticism doesn't want to improve. It is written, "To learn, you must love discipline; it is stupid to hate correction" (Proverbs 12:1, NLT).

—Guigo I: *Meditations*

 A Personal Response

Lord, if I really took an honest look at myself, I would have to change. Change can be painful. I'm not sure I really want it. Help me.

Confident, Humble Prayer

Therefore I tell you, whatever you ask for in prayer, believe that you have received it, and it will be yours. *Mark 11:24*

Even the humblest prayer is to be prayed with confidence that God will answer. Be sure you will succeed. There is no contradiction between humility and confidence. They are in perfect harmony with each other, like repentance and faith.

This confidence is not a soothing freedom from anxiety. The saints did their best praying when they were stimulated by difficulties and driven to despair. It is precisely when they are in turbulent times that faith comes to help them. It is while they groan in the agony of some calamity that the goodness of God shines upon them. In fearful times they trust God. This has the dual effect of both increasing their endurance and comforting them with the hope of an ultimate deliverance.

It is important, then, for a believer's prayer to be the product of both feelings. Although we may struggle with some present distress and dread evils yet to come, we can trust that God will not hesitate to help us. God is irritated by our distrust.

James compares the power of faith with the weakness of doubt: "If you need wisdom—if you want to know what God wants you to do—ask him, and he will gladly tell you. He will not resent your asking. But when you ask him, be sure that you really expect him to answer, for a doubtful mind is as unsettled as a wave of the sea that is driven and tossed by the wind. People like that should not expect to receive anything from the Lord. They can't make up their minds. They waver back and forth in everything they do" (James 1:5-8, NLT).

God often declares that he will give to us in proportion to our faith. The logical conclusion is that we receive nothing without faith. Everything that results from prayer is obtained by faith.

—John Calvin: *Institutes*

 A Personal Response

I am sure, O God, that the faith referred to here must be genuine faith. It is not a mere clutching at straws.

June 13 Our Own Way

Dear friends, pattern your life after mine, and learn from those who follow our example. For I have told you often before, and I say it again with tears in my eyes, that there are many whose conduct shows they are really enemies of the cross of Christ. *Philippians 3:17-18,* NLT

Get this straight. We are not to follow the saints in *their* vocation. We are to follow God in *our* vocation. If we try to do what the saints did we may miss our own calling. This will be wrong.

Saint Paul was a good man. He was an enthusiastic supporter of God's cause. He was a weeper. It grieved him to see the dishonor of God among those he had instructed in the Word of God. Such a thing doesn't bother us. If we lose something we valued or sustain damages, then we weep from the bottom of our hearts. We can be very sorrowful at the loss of possessions. But when we hear that God is dishonored, that sexual sins are committed, or other horrible sins done, we don't shed a tear. It is clear we do not have the heart of Paul.

—Hugh Latimer: *Fruitful Sermons*

A Personal Response

Christ wept over Jerusalem when it would not listen and respond to him. There is no way I will ever experience the depth of sorrow of Christ or Paul. At the very least, O Lord, let me feel enough to do my part in your grand scheme of things.

Being at Peace

I have learned to be content whatever the circumstances. *Philippians 4:11*

If you are at peace yourself, you will be able to help others become peaceable. An excitable person distorts things, and easily believes the worst. A calm person can turn even bad circumstances into good ones.

If you are at peace, you will not be suspicious of others. If you are agitated and discontented, you will not trust anyone. You will not be able to remain quiet yourself, and you will not let anyone else rest either.

Accuse yourself and excuse another. Love and humility do not know how to be angry or indignant. It is easy to live with good and gentle people. It takes a special gift to get along with obstinate, disorderly, and contrary people.

The person who knows how to suffer will enjoy the most peace. Such a person has conquered himself and has become a friend of Christ.

—Thomas à Kempis: *The Imitation of Christ*

A Personal Response

Does Christianity come down to my disposition, Lord? We are all so different! Some are energetic, others are calm. You made us in this rich diversity. It must be a desirable thing. Help me to understand that the peace you have for me does not mean excitability or lethargy. It is something else, something you offer me in the stormiest of times.

June 15 # The Divine Orchardist

I am the true vine and my Father is the gardener. He cuts off every branch in me that bears no fruit, while every branch that does bear fruit he prunes so that it will be even more fruitful. *John 15:1*

Consider an orchard in spring. See how the trees are taking on new life. Soon they will blossom and bear fruit. It is good to think of your soul as such a place. Imagine the Lord walking in it. Ask him to increase the fragrance of the little virtuous buds that are beginning to appear. Beg him to keep them alive until they can bloom to his glory. Invite him to prune away whatever he thinks needs to go. The trees will be better if he does.

A time will come to the soul when it is like an overgrown orchard. Everything seems dry and lifeless. It is hard to believe it was ever thriving and flourishing. The soul suffers many trials. The poor orchardist thinks that it is out of control and lost.

This is the proper time for cultivation. Remove the weeds. Root out sickly plants. Make room for the healthy trees. If we do this we can gain much humility, and then the blossoms will come again.

—Teresa of Avila: *The Life of Teresa of Jesus*

A Personal Response

My soul is a living thing. It needs nourishment, cultivation, and pruning. There are forces in this world that would turn it into a desert. Come to me, Jesus, with all your life-giving power. Cleanse me. Shape me. Direct me. Live in me that I may live for you.

Independent Wisdom

I thought to myself, "Look, I have grown and increased in wisdom more than anyone who has ruled over Jerusalem before me; I have experienced much of wisdom and knowledge."
Ecclesiastes 1:16

Our most important ambition is to see the crucified Christ always before us. Don't look for anything beyond this. Real friends of the Master only ask for what will help them to be able to fulfill his commissions. Any other desire or task is little other than self-love, spiritual pride, and encirclement by the enemy.

Disciplined conduct will fortify us against all assaults. When a skilled opponent sees the fervor of someone beginning spiritual exercises, he tries to warp their understanding.

As a distraction, he inflates their imagination in moments of prayer, hinting at elevated sentiments. Those who are subject to self-conceit and are fond of their own ideas are easy targets. Drugged with a false sense of appreciation of God, they forget to cleanse their hearts and to examine themselves. They think they know something others do not. They no longer rely on the advice or assistance of others.

This is a deadly—an almost incurable—spiritual disease. It is much more difficult to remedy mental pride than pride of the heart. Intelligence can sometimes overrule the emotions. But those who think they are wiser than their superiors are in trouble. How will they discover their error? To whom will they listen when they think they are wiser than everyone else in the world? If the understanding is the searchlight of the soul, and it becomes blinded and swollen with pride, who is able to cure it? Light has become darkness.

Be on guard, then, against this fatal attack. Train yourself to respect the judgment of others. Don't let your ideas of spirituality go too far. Learn to love the simplicity recommended so highly by the New Testament. Do this and you will become wiser than Solomon.

—Lawrence Scupoli: *The Spiritual Combat*

 A Personal Response

Message received, Lord. Message received.

June 17   ## It Starts Here

> While Jesus was in one of the towns, a man
> came along who was covered with leprosy.
> When he saw Jesus, he fell with his face to the
> ground and begged him, "Lord, if you are
> willing, you can make me clean." *Luke 5:12*

How is it that the lame and blind, the lunatic and leper, the publican and sinner, are helped by Christ? It is because they have a real desire for the thing they seek. They come to Christ in true faith.

Christ's typical response is, "According to your faith will it be done to you" (Matthew 9:29). This is still Christ's answer today. As our faith is, so it shall be done. In this we can find the entire reason for falling short of salvation in Christ. It is because we have no desire for it.

"But," you ask, "don't all Christians desire to have Christ to be their Savior?" Yes. But here is the catch: many want this only for the *next* world. They want Christ to help them into heaven when they die. This is not wanting Christ to be your Savior. It must be had in *this* world. If Christ saves you it must be done in this life, by changing and altering everything about you. It means a new pattern of thinking and acting. The change will be as radical as when the blind see, the lame walk, and the mute speak.

Being saved is nothing other than being made like Jesus. It is to gain his humility, meekness, and self-denial. It means to take on his renunciation of the spirit and honors of this world. It involves his love of God, his desire of doing God's will, and seeking only God's honor. To have these attitudes and perspectives born in your heart is to have salvation from Christ.

If you don't want these things and are not able to plead for them with the same intensity of the sick who came to Christ, then you are clearly unwilling to have Christ to be your Savior.

—William Law: *Mystical Writings*

A Personal Response

Convince me of this, Lord Jesus. Help me to comprehend that this business of being Christian, of being saved, is as important here on earth as it is in heaven.

Personal Tastes

> If our minds are ruled by our desires, we will die. But if our minds are ruled by the Spirit, we will have life and peace. *Romans 8:6,* CEV

Sometimes we are more careful about the things we eat than we are about our behavior. The Greek philosophers teach us to save our lives in this world. Christ teaches us to lose them. One or the other will be our master.

You will know exactly which one you are following if you complain, "This is bad for my eyes. That gives me a headache. This affects my heart. That upsets my stomach." You were not taught to pick and choose like that by the Gospels, or the prophets, or from the letters of the apostles. "Our desires fight against God" (Romans 8:7, CEV).

I am not teaching the lessons of Hypocrites, Galenus, or Epicurus. I am a follower of Christ. Jesus says, "If you love your life, you will lose it" (John 12:25, CEV). These words of my Master condemn the wisest of this world who urge sensual gratification and hypochondria. True wisdom is not found in the place where people live for pleasure.

Why should anyone bother to abstain from sensual pleasures only to spend a lot of time wondering what to eat? "Beans cause gas," they say. "Cheese causes constipation. Cabbages produce melancholy. Onions upset my stomach. Fish from the pond or from muddy water do not agree with me."

Remember that you are a monk and not a physician. Be concerned first with your own peace, then for the grief you cause those who serve you. Beware of being a burden. Keep your neighbor's conscience in mind. How can your neighbor enjoy offering a meal to you if you do some strange kind of fasting? The neighbor is embarrassed by your weird behavior, your insistence on a special diet.

—Bernard of Clairvaux: *On the Song of Songs*

 A Personal Response

Dear God, make me flexible without being a pushover. Let the things I consider vital be truly *important.*

Sun of My Soul

For the Lord God is a sun and shield; the Lord bestows favor and honor; no good thing does he withhold from those whose walk is blameless.
Psalm 84:11

One of the brilliant minds of our century teaches that the sun, not the earth, is the center of our world. He says that the sun is essentially motionless and that the earth revolves around the sun. This is hard for us to understand. It seems contrary to everything our senses tell us, for we see the sun in continual movement around the earth all day long. This is a new opinion. It is not well-known among astronomers.

When it is understood, it can be applied very usefully in the science of salvation. Jesus is the sun. In his greatness he remains motionless, but moves all things. Seated at the right hand of God he is immovable, but he puts all else in motion. Because he is the true center of the world, the world needs to be in continual motion toward him.

Jesus is the sun of our souls. We receive light from him. We are influenced by him. The earth of our hearts should always be moving toward him. Then we may receive the grace and gifts of this great luminary.

—Pierre de Berulle: *Grandeurs de Jesus*

 A Personal Response

I am sure this is the secret, Lord. Christ needs to be at the center of my being. I need to be able to say with Paul, "I have been crucified with Christ and I no longer live, but Christ lives in me" (Galatians 2:20). It won't be easy. My world still revolves around me.

June 20　Religion As a Noise

There are many rebellious people, mere talkers and deceivers. *Titus 1:10*

In a dream I saw a man named Talkative. He was a tall man who looked a little better at a distance than he did close up. Another man, Faithful, began to talk with him.

"Come, let's walk together to the heavenly country. As we go along we can talk about useful things."

"I like to talk about good things," said Talkative. "What can be better than to talk of God? In the holy Scripture we can gain an understanding of the necessity of a second birth, the insufficiency of our works, the need of Christ's righteousness, etc. By this we may learn what it is to repent, to believe, to pray, to suffer, or the like. We can discover the great promises and consolations of the gospel. We can learn to refute false opinions, to vindicate the truth, and to instruct the ignorant."

"All this is true," replied Faithful. "I am glad to hear your words."

"It's too bad so few understand the need of faith and ignorantly live in the works of the law. We can receive nothing unless it is given us from heaven. All is of grace, not works. I could give you a hundred Scriptures to prove this."

Impressed, Faithful stepped over to Christian, who had been walking by himself. "We have an excellent companion with us!"

Christian smiled modestly. "This man is best when he is away from home. He is like a painting that does not show well up close. He is a saint abroad and a devil at home. Religion has no place in his heart, or home, or business. All he has rests on his tongue. His religion is something to make a noise with."

"Then I am deceived."

"Yes. Remember that 'the Kingdom of God is not a matter of talk, but of power'" (1 Corinthians 4:20).

"I see that saying and doing are two different things."

—John Bunyan: *The Pilgrim's Progress*

A Personal Response

Lord, never let me speak of you in order to prove that I am a wise, prudent, or holy person.

June 21 # Love Directs Our Thoughts

Take captive every thought to make it obedient to Christ. *2 Corinthians 10:5*

Gather, O Lord, my senses and the powers of my soul together in yourself. Pardon me and forgive me as often as I pray without concentrating on you. Many times I am not really at the place where I am standing or sitting. My thoughts carry me to some other place. I am where my thought is. I love what I think about.

If I love heaven, I speak gladly of the things of God.

If I love the world, I love to talk of worldly things.

If I love the flesh, I imagine things that please the flesh.

If I love my soul, I delight in talk about things that are for my soul's health.

Whatever I love, I gladly hear and speak of it. I fantasize about it. Jesus was right when he said, "For where your treasure is, there your heart will be also" (Matthew 6:21).

—Catherine Parr: *Prayers and Meditations*

 A Personal Response

Is it too much, O God, to think that you could become for me a "consuming thought"? The object, I am sure, is to be occupied with the divine. Don't permit me to be merely pre-occupied with you.

Tailor-Made Devotion

Then God said, "Let the land produce vegetation: seed-bearing plants and trees on the land that bear fruit with seed in it, according to their various kinds." And it was so. *Genesis 1:11*

In the same way that God commanded plants to produce distinctive fruits, he commands Christians (the living plants of his church) to have different kinds of devotion. A gentleman will have a different religious expression from a laborer. The servant, the prince, the widow, the young woman, and the married woman will each have their own style of devotion.

Religious practice must be adapted to the strength, activities, and responsibilities of each individual. A bishop can't be a hermit. A married man can't be a monk. A skilled worker can't spend all day in church. It would be laughable! Impossible!

Aristotle pointed out that bees extract honey from flowers without harming the flower. The flowers are left as healthy and fresh as when the bee found them. True devotion does even better than that. Not only does it do no harm to one's occupation, it also improves it. Stones take on a luster when they are dipped in honey, each according to its own color. Every vocation improves when it is united with devotion. Family life gets better. Love grows. Service is more faithful. Every kind of job becomes more pleasant and agreeable.

It is a great error to forbid soldiers to be faithful. The mechanic's shop, the royal court, the home of a married couple are not off limits for devotion. There are many creative styles of devotion suitable for any occupation. Wherever we work we can and should aspire to a devout life.

—Francis de Sales: *The Devout Life*

 A Personal Response

Because the world is very much with me, Lord, I am glad to be reassured that I do not have to turn my back on it in order to be with you. Diminish its force and dominance in my soul, but let me do a good job of my work *and my prayers.*

Simple Openness

The law of the Lord is perfect, reviving the soul.
The statutes of the Lord are trustworthy, making
wise the simple. *Psalm 19:7*

Since God is always speaking within all of us, no one is exempt. He speaks within the most incorrigible sinner. And he speaks in the hearts of the scholars who are too full of their own wisdom to listen to God. They depend entirely upon reason. They have a self-inflated notion of their ability.

I have often said that any common sinner who is beginning to be converted through honest love of God will understand more about this interior word of the Spirit than those who are set in their own wisdom. God wants to communicate with those who see themselves as wise, but they are too full of themselves to listen.

His presence is with the simple. Who are they? I have not met many. But God knows who they are, and he is pleased to live with them.

—François de Fénelon: *Meditations and Devotions*

 A Personal Response

It is far easier to listen to myself than to listen to you, my God. Grant me the kind of childlike trust that will simply make me open to your prompting.

June 24 # Human Nature and God's Grace

> He lifted me out of the slimy pit, out of the
> mud and mire; he set my feet on a rock and
> gave me a firm place to stand. *Psalm 40:2*

Human nature and grace move in opposite directions. Here is how to tell the difference between them:

- Human nature is tricky and often misleads and traps. It only cares about itself. Grace avoids guile and cares about God.

- Human nature puts up a fight and dies reluctantly. It is not easily changed or held under control. Grace brings orderliness and does not abuse freedoms.

- Human nature works for its own profit and advantage. It takes everything it can from others. Grace does not think about itself, but about what is good for others.

- Human nature gladly accepts flattery, honor, and adulation. Grace passes on the honor to God.

- Human nature hates to be shamed or rejected. Grace is pleased to endure such things in the name of God and accepts them as special favors when they come.

- Human nature desires exotic and exclusive things. Grace enjoys the ordinary.

- Human nature is greedy and finds receiving more blessed than giving. Grace is generous to the poor and content with little.

- Human nature wants recognition and admiration for good deeds. Grace hides its good works and gives all praise to God.

Grace is a gift from God. It is the mark of a truly spiritual person. As nature is restrained, grace increases.

—Thomas à Kempis: *The Imitation of Christ*

A Personal Response

Am I at war with myself? Which will dominate? My flesh or my soul? This writer has drawn the line so distinctly there can be little doubt about the truth of it.

Objects of Affection

[Jesus said,] "How do you benefit if you gain the whole world but lose your own soul in the process? Is anything worth more than your soul?" *Matthew 16:26,* NLT

G reed for the things of this world and the love of God are opposites. They cannot exist in the same individual simultaneously. The more you can rid yourself of greed, the more you can love God. Greater greed results in weaker love.

We are deceived by five things we relish: riches, dignity, pleasure, power, and honors. These things chain us to sin and tie us up in faults. The bondage is not broken until death. Then it is too late.

The world itself leads us to disrespect it. It is filled with so many miseries. Here we will find hostility, oppression, jealousy, and backbiting. There is crime and scandal. Justice is ignored. Truth is not affirmed. Fidelity is rare and friendship is painfully fickle.

There are other things in this world that inspire contempt for it. Time is changeable and our life here is brief. Death is inescapable. Eternity, on the other hand, is stable.

The choice is yours! Love the world and you will perish with the world. Love Christ and you will reign with him.

—Richard Rolle: *The Fire of Love*

A Personal Response

Miserable soul, what do you want with the world? Everything here is short-lived and deceptive. Why do you passionately desire things that will perish? You will never be satisfied with them.—Richard Rolle

Assembling a Choir

Praise the Lord with the harp; make music to him on the ten-stringed lyre. Sing to him a new song; play skillfully, and shout for joy. *Psalm 33:2-3*

I place before my inward eyes everything there is about me—my body, soul, and abilities. I gather around me all the creatures which God ever created in heaven and on earth. I touch each element, calling it by name. I include the birds of the air, the beasts of the forests, the fish of the sea, the leaves and grass of the earth, the innumerable grains of sand, and all the little specks of dust that dance in the sunbeams. I embrace every little drop of water which falls as dew, snow, or rain.

I wish that each of these had a sweetly sounding musical instrument made of my heart's inmost blood, the sounding of which might send up to our dear and gentle God a new and lofty strain of praise.

And then the loving arms of my soul stretch out and extend themselves toward the innumerable multitude of all creation. In the same way that a choral director can stir up singers, I would incite them to sing joyously, offering up their hearts to God.

—Heinrich Suso: *The Life of Blessed Henry*

 A Personal Response

Such music, Lord God! Let me, too, offer up my whole world to you. Let it resonate in harmony with heaven.

The Words of My Mouth

Set a guard over my mouth, O Lord; keep watch over the door of my lips. *Psalm 141:3*

Saint Francis was with Brother Leo in an isolated place where they could find no breviary for their morning prayers. Francis instructed Brother Leo to respond to his extemporaneous prayers by repeating and affirming what he heard. Leo agreed to do so and told Francis to begin.

The saint then said to himself, "Brother Francis, you are guilty of much sin and ought to go to hell."

Leo answered, "God will do so many good things through you that you will go to heaven."

"Don't say that, Brother Leo! I told you to repeat what I said."

Leo agreed that he would do so the next time.

Beating his breast and crying and sighing, Saint Francis prayed, "Oh, Lord God, I have sinned against you and deserved to be damned!"

Brother Leo answered, "Oh, Brother Francis, God will distinguish you among the blessed!"

Francis became impatient with Leo. He commanded him under the rule of holy obedience to respond as directed. "Then you, Brother Leo, Little Lamb, say, 'surely you are not worthy of God's mercy!'"

Assured that Leo would speak as he was instructed, Saint Francis knelt and raised his hands toward heaven. He said, "Francis, you are a wicked sinner. How can God have mercy on anyone as bad as you?"

When Brother Leo responded, he said, "God's mercy is infinitely greater than your sins. He will be merciful to you and bless you."

This created a gentle wonder in Saint Francis. He asked Leo, "Brother, why do you break the rule of obedience?"

With much humility and reverence Leo replied, "God knows I have tried to answer as you want, but God makes me say what he likes and not what I like."

They kept up this beautiful contest all night.

—Ugolino: *Actus-Fioretti*

 A Personal Response

Help me to understand, O Lord, that sometimes I represent you, speak for you, act for you.

One Day at a Time

> For I know my transgressions, and my sin is always before me. *Psalm 51:3*

The rising of devotion in an ordinary soul is like the dawning of a new day. Darkness is not driven away immediately. Light comes in small increments, moment by moment. The saying is that a slow cure is best. Sicknesses of the soul are like those of the body. They come galloping in on horseback, but depart slowly on foot.

Have courage and be patient. Many see themselves as still imperfect after trying to be devout for a long time. They become discouraged and are tempted to give up. The opposite temptation is far more hazardous. Some figure everything is fixed on the first day! They have scarcely begun. They want to fly without wings. They are taking a great risk of relapse if they stop seeing the doctor too soon.

Purging the soul is a lifetime effort. There is no reason to be upset by our imperfections. Perfection is nothing more than fighting against them. How can we resist them unless we see them? How can we overcome them unless we face them?

—Francis de Sales: *The Devout Life*

A Personal Response

Teach me the patience of unanswered prayer, my Lord. I often want everything set right in a flash of lightning. Often I am annoyed by everything about me that is missing the mark. Let me understand the value of knowing I am not perfect. Let your sun ever rise in me.

June 29 A Clean Conscience

Paul looked straight at the Sanhedrin and said,
"My brothers, I have fulfilled my duty to God
in all good conscience to this day." *Acts 23:1*

A clear conscience is a good person's glory. Keep a clean conscience and you will be happy. A good conscience is able to bear a heavy load and it will encourage you when you are under attack. A bad conscience is always afraid and uneasy. Your sleep will be sweet if your heart does not accuse you.

Scoundrels are never really happy. They have no peace. "'There is no peace,' says the Lord, 'for the wicked'" (Isaiah 48:22).

The praise of the world is short-lived and always accompanied by sorrow. The glory of the good is in their consciences, not in the praises of others.

Anyone who goes looking for stardom and does not count fame unimportant reveals little fondness for heavenly things. The most tranquil person of all is the one who cares about neither the praise nor the fault-finding of others. You are not a better person because you are praised. You are not any worse if someone denigrates you. You are what you are. Words can't change that. God knows what you are. If you really get to know your inner self, you won't care what anyone says about you. People consider actions, but God evaluates intentions.

—Thomas à Kempis: *The Imitation of Christ*

 A Personal Response

I get it, my Lord. It is not what others think of me. It is not even how I regard myself. It is when you think well of me that I am really approved.

Ghost Town

Other seed fell among thorns, which grew up and choked the plants. *Matthew 13:7*

God once became angry with his chosen people. Jerusalem was invaded by their enemies who "lorded it over them" (Psalm 106:41, KJV). Public worship was no longer a part of life. There were no feasts, no offerings at the temple.

It can be the same way with the soul. If we disobey God the enemies of the soul will take it over. Passions can seduce it. The day will come when we cease to pray or even think of God. The soul can become a desolate place, a ghost town. The grand monuments along its avenues crumble from neglect. Snarling animals prowl the deserted parks. A house with no one living in it deteriorates rapidly. The soul that does not celebrate God becomes a dark, ruined, deserted place.

It's sad to think of a road no one travels.

It's sad to see an abandoned house.

It's sad to come upon a farm grown up in weeds.

It's sad to see a derelict ship.

It's sad to find a soul in the stormy sea of life who is not navigated by Christ.

It's sad to discover a soul that is not carefully cultivated by Christ, bringing forth good fruits.

Christ is a Master Gardener. The Cross is his tool. He can take a soul that is overgrown with thorns and briars and turn it into a beautiful paradise of the Spirit.

—Pseudo-Macarius: *Homilies*

A Personal Response

Come, Lord Jesus. Cultivate my soul. Fill me with the best fruits of your divine Spirit.

July 1 # Flatterers

Honest correction is appreciated more than
flattery. *Proverbs 28:23,* CEV

There are three kinds of flatterers.

The first kind praises and encourages someone's good behavior. But they overdo it. They make a person feel better
than they really are. Lavish praise is the first type of flattery. It is
evil enough.

The second kind takes an openly soiled reputation that is beyond
denial and makes light of it. "You are not the first person to do this.
Many others do things that are worse."

The third kind of flatterer is the worst of all. They praise an evil
person's conduct. To a knight who has robbed the poor they will say,
"That's not a bad thing to do. Prune a willow and it will sprout even
better." Such misguided flatterers actually blind the ones who listen
to them. They cloak a foul odor with perfume. This is too bad. If they
smelled it, it would make them sick. They would hurry to confession
and avoid it in the future.

—Anonymous: *A Guide for Anchoresses*

 A Personal Response

All of us have done some of this, O Lord. We try to be nice.
We do not want to condemn. We know that you say the truth
about people and freely forgive sinners.

Now help me to learn the healthy way you do this, Jesus,
Master. You never praise or rationalize sin. You know that people are not perfect. You gently correct, clearly lead, and inwardly strengthen.

July 2 · **Introspection? Maybe Not!**

So when those came who were hired first, they expected to receive more. But each one of them also received a denarius. When they received it, they began to grumble against the landowner.
Matthew 20:10

I was given permission from Rome to establish a convent. Unfortunately, they did not provide any money for it. This whole business gave me a lot of trouble. When I finished it, there was a sense of accomplishment. I praised the Lord for having used me in such a positive way.

Then I began to think of what I had been through. I could find fault with everything I did. The imperfections of the task were clear. I recalled times of doubt and a lack of faith. The Lord had assured me that all would be well, but I would not let myself absolutely believe it. I wanted to think the job would get done, but sometimes it seemed impossible. Eventually I saw that God had done all the good things and I had made all the mistakes.

So I stopped thinking about it. I have no further need to remember these things. Bless God who can bring something good out of my poor work! Amen.

It is dangerous to review the years during which we have prayed. We may come to think that we have won some prize by serving God. It's not that our service doesn't have any merit or that it may not be rewarded. The problem is that if a spiritual person dwells on these things it may not be possible to reach the summit of spirituality.

The more we serve God, the more we are in debt to him. We pay him back a few pennies and he gives us thousands of dollars! For the love of God, let's leave all this to him. Sometimes he will give the same pay to the last workers as to the first.

—Teresa of Avila: *The Life of Teresa of Jesus*

A Personal Response

You have blessed me with a memory, God. Help me to determine the best material to file away for future reference. Show me what belongs in a mental trash can. Let me use more of my memory to remember your faithfulness, not my failures.

July 3   ## Prayer

In all my prayers for all of you, I always pray with joy. *Philippians 1:4*

Prayer is a longing, a desire of the spirit toward God. It is like someone who is sick longing for health.

Faith prays constantly. The spirit is always attentive to the will of God and knows its own fragility. It also remembers the infirmities of others, understanding that there is no strength and no help anywhere other than in God. A neighbor's grief is no less than your own.

Suppose someone who is weak in the faith asks for your prayers. Lead such a person to the truth and promises of God. Teach that person how to trust God.

If you give me a thousand dollars and ask me to pray for you, I am no more bound than I was before. I could not pray more for you if you gave me all the world. If I see a need, I pray. I can't help praying when God's Spirit is in me.

—William Tyndale: *The Parable*

A Personal Response

Let prayer become a natural thing for me, dear God. Let it flow like a river between us. Let it hum with the energy of a soul that is awake. Let it glow with the light of your divine presence. Let it securely anchor my life. Let it radiate to others.

Sickness and Health

> Then your light will break forth like the dawn,
> and your healing will quickly appear. *Isaiah 58:8*

There is one word for all that you seek, desire, and find. In that word is all you have lost. The word is *Jesus*. This does not mean the word *Jesus* painted on a wall, written with letters in a book, or formed by the lips with sound from the mouth. I mean *Jesus:* all goodness, wisdom, love, and sweetness—your joy, your worship, your Lord, and your salvation.

This name *Jesus* in English is nothing other than *healer* and *health*. Everyone who lives this life is spiritually sick. There is no one alive without sin, which is sickness of the soul. John says of himself and others, "If we claim to be without sin, we deceive ourselves and the truth is not in us" (1 John 1:8). We can never approach the joys of heaven without first being made well from this spiritual illness.

This healing is available only to those who desire it, love it, take delight in it. No one can be made whole in the spirit unless that person loves and desires spiritual health. It is the same way with physical illness. If you offered a sick person riches and honors without making that person well (if you could), your offer would mean nothing. So it is for one who is sick in spirit. Nothing is more desirable than spiritual health—and that is *Jesus*.

If you feel a strong desire in your heart for Jesus, either by remembering his name or by a prayer or anything else you may do, then you are doing well in your search. You have found something of Jesus, not yet himself as he is, but a shadow of him. The closer you come to him the more you will desire him.

If the question comes into your mind asking what you have lost and what you seek, lift up the desire of your heart to Jesus—even though you are blind and can see nothing of him—and say that you have lost him and he is what you want. Nothing else.

—Walter Hilton: *The Scale of Perfection*

A Personal Response

Lord, let me seek all that is good and healing in Jesus Christ. Let my spiritual health be in him. Build in me a strong desire for Jesus—not the word, but the person.

July 5   # A Kiss Is Not a Kiss

Let him kiss me with the kisses of his mouth—for your love is more delightful than wine. *Song of Songs 1:2*

We can't live without food and air. We might survive for a while without food, but without air we will not live an hour. In order to live we inhale and exhale our breath. In a kiss the breath of two meet, mingle, and unite. This is a pleasant experience to share. It rouses and joins together the affection of those who embrace.

There is a physical kiss, a spiritual kiss, and an intellectual kiss. The physical kiss is an actual touching of lips. The spiritual kiss is a union of spirits. The intellectual kiss is an infusion of God's grace.

A physical kiss is inappropriate unless it is given and received as a sign of reconciliation when enemies become friends again, or as a mark of peace, or as a greeting between friends after a long separation, or as when guests are received, or as a symbol of love between bride and groom. The misuse of this kiss is commonplace.

A spiritual kiss is the kiss of friends who do not need to make physical contact. It is an affection of the heart. Rather than a meeting of lips, it is a meeting of spirits. There can be one spirit in many bodies. "It is truly wonderful when relatives live together in peace" (Psalm 133:1, CEV).

—Aelred of Rievaulx: *Spiritual Friendship*

A Personal Response

As long as I delight in any evil, as long as sensuality is more gratifying than purity, indiscretion than moderation, flattery than correction, how can I even aspire to friendship which springs from an esteem for virtue?—Aelred of Rievaulx

God Is Far and Near

The high and lofty one who inhabits eternity, the
Holy One, says this: "I live in that high and
holy place with those whose spirits are contrite
and humble. I refresh the humble and give new
courage to those with repentant hearts." *Isaiah
57:15,* NLT

We seek evidence of God in the natural world. The wonders of nature are remarkable and instructive. But we must not forget to look for him in the depths of our soul. There is no need to go down into the earth, or to travel beyond the seas, or ascend into heaven to find God. God is nearer to us than we are to ourselves.

For worldly people there is no place more remote, more unknown, than the depths of their own heart. They do not know what it means to enter into themselves. They have never tried it. They can't even imagine that they possess such an inner sanctuary in the impenetrable regions of their soul where God can be worshiped in spirit and in truth.

Even though God is glorious, he is still intimate. God is high and yet low, enormous and yet within us, awesome and yet lovable. Will we ever cease being ignorant of God? When we advise people to look for God in their own hearts, they are as mystified as if we had told them to look in some unexplored territory in a distant land.

—François de Fénelon: *Meditations and Devotions*

 A Personal Response

Command me. Forbid me. What do you want me to do? What do you want me to refrain from doing? Whether I am lifted up or cast down, comforted or suffering, working for you or doing nothing worthwhile, I continue to love you. I yield my will to you. With Mary I say, "May it be to me as you have said" (Luke 1:38).—François de Fénelon

Morning Prayer

In the morning, O Lord, you hear my voice; in the morning I lay my requests before you and wait in expectation. *Psalm 5:3*

There are some useful short kinds of prayer. One of them is morning prayer. It is a way to prepare for the day's activities. Here is how it is done.

Begin by really adoring God. Thank him for preserving you through the night. Acknowledge that this day is given to you as another opportunity to prepare for eternity.

Look for chances to serve God today. Are there possible temptations lying in wait? Do you think something might make you angry or vain? Resolve to make the best of every opportunity to serve God and increase devotion that comes your way. Prepare carefully to avoid, resist, and overcome harmful things. It is not enough simply to resolve to do this. Make a plan of action. For instance, if I know I will have a conference with an emotional, angry person today, I will resolve to avoid offending him. But then I will try to think of gentle words to speak to him, or try to find someone who can help me by keeping him in good humor. If I know I will be visiting someone who is sick, I will choose the best time and consider what little gift I might take with me.

Then, be humble before God. Admit that you can't do any of this on your own. Offer all of your good intentions to God, as though you were holding out your heart in your hands. Ask him to be involved in your plans for the day.

These prayerful thoughts should be taken care of quickly in the morning, before you leave your bedroom. God will bless your day.

—Francis de Sales: *The Devout Life*

 A Personal Response

Lord, here is my wretched heart. With your inspiration it has made some good plans. It is too weak to accomplish what it wants. Give your blessing through Christ, in whose honor I dedicate today and all the remaining days of my life.

—Francis de Sales

The Real Questions

> For you know that God paid a ransom to save you from the empty life you inherited from your ancestors. And the ransom he paid was not mere gold or silver. *1 Peter 1:18,* NLT

Do not ask whether something is enjoyable. Ask if it is worthy of love. Ask if you should depend upon it.

How will you find an answer? Is there an infallible argument or a verse of Scripture that will enlighten you? Can you think of any example or axiom or sacrament that will prepare you to discover these things?

You can tell if something is made of gold. But how can you know if it is worth your love, or if you can depend upon it? Being gold is one thing, but being worthy of love is something else.

Desiring exquisite food and clothing is like painting firewood. These things are consumables. Clothes keep you warm regardless of their color. Common foods will satisfy your hunger. Desire what is right for you.

—Guigo I: *Meditations*

A Personal Response

O God, please fix my "wanter." I see dazzling sights, hear tempting sounds. They are all around me. I make poor choices. Help me to want what is best for my soul. Lead me to good tools for self-expression. Speak louder than my storms of passion. Give me the grace to follow Jesus.

Christ As Friend

You are my friends if you do what I command.
John 15:14

L ife without Jesus is like a dry garden baking in the sun. It is foolish to want anything that conflicts with Jesus. What can the world give you without Jesus? His absence is hell; his presence, paradise. If Jesus is with you, no enemy can injure you. Whoever finds Jesus has discovered a great treasure. He is the best of all possible good. The loss of him is a tremendous misfortune. Living without Jesus is poverty.

If we want to live intimately with Jesus, we will need to develop our skills. Be humble and peaceable, and Jesus will be with you. Be devout and quiet, and Jesus will reside with you.

Make many friends. Love them dearly. But love Jesus in a special way. Love others because of Jesus. Love Jesus for himself. For him, and in him, love both your friends and your enemies. Pray for them all, asking God to lead them to know and love Jesus also. Never seek this kind of devoted love for yourself. Such devotion belongs to God alone.

If discouraging and unpleasant days come your way, don't be despondent or defeated. Stand strong in God and bear whatever you must to the glory of Jesus Christ. For after winter, summer comes. After night, day returns. After a storm, calm is restored.

—Thomas à Kempis: *The Imitation of Christ*

 A Personal Response

I tend to want to hide from you, Jesus. I don't feel like a worthy companion of yours. But you come to me without any hesitation. Instead of putting me down you lift me up. Near you I discover acceptance, forgiveness, unconditional love. What a friend!

July 10   Peaks and Valleys

Have you considered my servant Job? *Job 1:8*

Our body is like a beautiful purse that encloses our soul. When it becomes necessary, the purse is opened and closed again. It is God who does this. He comes to us at the lowest part of our need. He has no contempt for what he has made. It does not bother him to take care of our simplest physical requirements.

As the body is clad in clothes, the flesh in skin, the bones in flesh, and the heart inside all that, so are we enclosed in the goodness of God. It is an intimate relationship. God is our heavenly lover. He desires that our soul attach itself to him.

It is a valuable thing for us to experience the valleys as well as the peaks. God wants us to know that he is with us in both good times and bad. For our spiritual benefit we are sometimes left to ourselves. We may be allowed to suffer misery. Both happiness and sadness are expressions of the same divine love. Of all the pains that lead to salvation, the greatest is to see your love suffer.

All of us experience a wonderful mixture of both well-being and woe. It is necessary for us to fall. If we did not fall, we would have the wrong idea about ourselves. Eventually we will understand that we are never lost to God's love. At no time are we ever less valuable in God's sight. Through failure we will clearly understand that God's love is endless. Nothing we can do will destroy it.

A mother may allow her child to stumble and fall for its own good. Her love will not, however, allow her child to perish. God wills that even when we act the way a child does we can run to him and cry for mercy. If we don't feel any relief, we can be sure he is acting like a wise mother. It is good for us to shed some tears. It is allowed with compassion and pity.

—Julian of Norwich: *Revelations of Divine Love*

A Personal Response

I would like to be spared pain, dear God. It comes after me anyway. Sometimes it's physical pain. Often it's emotional. Occasionally it may be intellectual or spiritual. Let me know that I am never away from your love, no matter how miserable my circumstances.

Not What They Seem

There are also heavenly bodies and there are earthly bodies; but the splendor of the heavenly bodies is one kind, and the splendor of the earthly bodies is another. The sun has one kind of splendor, the moon another and the stars another; and star differs from star in splendor.

1 Corinthians 15:40-41

When making choices among the virtues, prefer the ones that are more excellent rather than those that are more obvious. Comets may seem to be larger than stars. They catch our attention. But comets are nowhere near the size of a star. They seem bigger because they are closer to us. They are composed of inferior material.

A few religious practices are highly esteemed by ordinary people because they are close at hand and easy. These are the physical rather than spiritual disciplines. They wear hair shirts, fast, go barefoot, etc.

Choose the best virtues rather than the most popular practices. The best are not the most spectacular.

—Francis de Sales: *The Devout Life*

A Personal Response

If a book is not to be judged by its cover, neither should I judge the spiritual realm by mere appearance. Sometimes when I think I am doing something great for you, my Lord, I'm really not doing much at all. At other times when I feel that an assignment is pointless and a waste of time, you make something worthwhile of it.

Before You Eat

Taste and see that the Lord is good. Psalm 34:8

When you sit down to eat, pray:

This is a wonderful mystery of your work, O Maker and Governor of the world. You sustain life with food! How great a thing it is that you are able to sustain so many creatures. "The eyes of all look to you, and you give them their food at the proper time. You open your hand and satisfy the desires of every living thing" (Psalm 145:15-16).

I ask you to continue life in my body through this food.

You are a liberal distributor of your gifts. You give us all kinds of good things to use. Because you are pure, the things you give are pure. Grant that I may not misuse them. Don't let what you have given for the preservation of my body become the poison of my soul.

The meat and drink before me is for my use and not for me to abuse. You have given them to help me and not to hurt me.

—John Bradford: *Daily Meditations*

A Personal Response

Think a little how great is God's power that made us. Think also how great is his wisdom to preserve us. Most of all, think how many things are given for our use.—John Bradford

Tides of Emotion

Why are you downcast, O my soul? Why so
disturbed within me? *Psalm 43:5*

If you should temporarily lose your sense of well-being, don't
be too quick to despair. With humility and patience, wait for
God, who is able to give you back even more profound
comfort.

There is nothing novel about this to those who are familiar with
God's ways. The great saints and ancient prophets frequently experienced the alternation of up and down, joy and sorrow. One of them,
while he was enjoying a mountain-top experience said: "When I felt
secure, I said, 'I will never be shaken.' O Lord, when you favored
me, you made my mountain stand firm; but when you hid your face,
I was dismayed" (Psalm 30:6-7).

And yet, even while he was going through this, he did not feel
crushed. With renewed passion he prayed: "Hear, O Lord, and be
merciful to me; O Lord, be my help" (Psalm 30:10).

In time, his prayer was answered. This is his report: "You turned
my wailing into dancing; you removed my sackcloth and clothed me
with joy" (Psalm 30:11).

If the great saints are exposed to such variations, we who are poor
and weak should not be discouraged if our spiritual life fails to be
uniformly ecstatic. The Holy Spirit gives and takes according to his
own divine purpose. I have never met anyone so religious and devout
that he has not felt occasionally some withdrawing of grace.

—Thomas à Kempis: *The Imitation of Christ*

 A Personal Response

Where shall I place my hope except in your great mercy, dear
God? The best of friends and possessions are of little help
when you seem far from me and I am alone in the poverty of
my being.

The Limits of Prayer

This is the confidence we have in approaching
God: that if we ask anything according to his
will, he hears us. *1 John 5:14*

Our prayers are to be confined to what God permits. Although he invites us to "pour out [our] hearts to him" (Psalm 62:8), God does not extend it *carte blanche*. He does not give us a limitless range of foolish and depraved ideas. When he promises to give us what we wish, this does not include nonsense and caprice.

It happens all the time. Many pray to God about frivolous things. They have neither modesty nor reverence. They present all kinds of dreams before God's throne. They are so crass that they stupidly bring their follies to God when they would blush to tell someone else what they were thinking about.

In the pagan world the ambitious prayed to Jupiter, the greedy to Mercury, would-be writers to Apollo and Minerva, warriors to Mars, and the licentious to Venus. In our time people feel complete freedom to pray about their unlawful desires. Prayer for many is the equivalent of telling jokes among friends. God is not mocked.

The solution to all this is for our heart to gain the same affection for God as our mind has. To help us with this, God's Spirit guides our prayers. He can tell us what is right. He can regulate our desires. "The Spirit helps us in our weakness. We do not know what we ought to pray, but the Spirit himself intercedes for us with groans that words cannot express" (Romans 8:26). God stimulates good prayer. Correct prayer is a gift from God.

This is not to imply that we can be careless in our prayers and let the Spirit do our praying for us. What I am trying to communicate is that when we become tired of our own heartlessness and sloth, we can long for the assistance of the Spirit. The Spirit does not do our work for us.

—John Calvin: *Institutes*

A Personal Response

I will pray with my spirit, but I will also pray with my mind;
I will sing with my spirit, but I will also sing with my mind.
—1 Corinthians 14:15

July 15   # Very Human Church Leaders

The priests did not ask, "Where is the Lord?"
Those who deal with the law did not know me,
[the Lord]; . . . The prophets prophesied by
Baal, following worthless idols. *Jeremiah 2:8*

Our prayer for those who give us light should be unceasing. With the storms that rage in the Church today, what would we do without them?

If some have gone bad, the good ones shine more brilliantly.

May it please the Lord to keep them under his care. God help them that they might help us.

—Teresa of Avila: *Life*

A Personal Response

I praise you, Lord, because you awaken so many to awaken us.—Teresa of Avila

Doom, Defeat, and Despair

I loathe my very life; therefore I will give free rein to my complaint and speak out in the bitterness of my soul. Job 10:1

There was a castle, called Doubting Castle, inhabited by the Giant Despair. Christian and Hopeful were sleeping on the castle grounds. The giant caught them and took them inside. He put them into a very dark and nasty dungeon. He flogged them, beating them senseless.

On Friday the Giant Despair asked them, "Why do you want to live when life is so bitter?" He explained that since they would never escape his dungeon it would be best if they killed themselves with knife, rope, or poison. His prisoners asked to be free. Enraged, the giant rushed toward them, intending them harm. He suddenly fell into one of his fits and withdrew. (Sometimes in sunshiny weather he falls into fits.)

Left alone, the prisoners began to decide what to do. They agreed that the grave would be easier to take than this dungeon. And yet, they considered that the God who made the world might also cause the Giant Despair to die, or at least to be careless about locking them up. They decided to be patient and to endure.

On Saturday the Giant Despair took them outside and showed them the bones and skulls of those he had already dispatched. "These," he explained, "were pilgrims like you. I tore them to pieces. In about ten days I will do the same to you." Then he beat them all the way back to the dungeon.

About midnight that Saturday they began to pray. They continued in prayer until almost sunrise.

"What a fool I am!" shouted Christian. I am in this stinking dungeon when I could be free! I've got the key right here with me. It's called Promise, and it will open any lock in Doubting Castle."

—John Bunyan: *The Pilgrim's Progress*

A Personal Response

Cheer me when I am blue, dear God. Lift up my spirit within me.

Never Lost

My yoke is easy and my burden is light.
Matthew 11:30

Every soul, regardless of its condition—
even if it is encumbered with sin,
trapped by debauchery,
snared by pleasure,
exiled as a captive,
jailed by the body,
slavishly worrying,
preoccupied by business,
sick with sorrow,
restless and deviating,
full of fear and suspicion,
"an alien in a foreign land" (Exodus 2:22)
—every soul that stands under condemnation with nothing to say
for itself, has the power to turn and discover it can yet breathe the
fresh air of God's pardon and mercy.

Why would it hesitate to confidently enter the presence of God?
Why should it fear the majesty who gives it reason to be confident?
Beauty is the soul's birthright.

—Bernard of Clairvaux: *On the Song of Songs*

A Personal Response

Often I don't want to change. Often I avoid the light because
I prefer the darkness. Dear God, bring me to my senses. Let
me see the desirability of a beautiful soul.

Being Fully Human

Whatever is true, whatever is noble, whatever is right, whatever is pure, whatever is lovely, whatever is admirable—if anything is excellent or praiseworthy—think about such things.
Philippians 4:8

Live up to the dignity of your nature. Let there be no doubt at the end of your life that you have been human. You are entitled to a Divine particle and to union with the invisible. Don't throw that away. Let this knowledge tell the lower world you are a part of the higher.

Think about things that do not enter beastly hearts. Think about things of long ago. Think about the future. Acquaint yourself with the movement of the stars and the vast expanses beyond them. Let your brain perceive what cannot be seen through a telescope. Catch a glimpse of the incomprehensible. Think about the unthinkable. Fill your mind with abstractions. Ascend to the invisible. Fill your soul with the spiritual. Dig into the mysteries of faith, the huge concepts of religion.

Then your life will honor God. Without this, though you have gigantic wealth and dignity, you are but a dwarf and pygmy of humanity. Though human souls are said to be equal, there is yet no small inequality in their operations. Some are far below others. Others have been so divine as to approach the peak of their natures.

—Thomas Browne: *Religio Medici*

 A Personal Response

There is so much pressure on me that pulls me down. From popular culture to the daily conduct of business, I am encouraged to ignore every possibility mentioned above. It makes me dizzy to consider the possibilities waiting for my attention. Let me take a moment right now and swim in that vast ocean. Let its warmth become familiar and inviting.

The Basis of Love

Stop being angry and don't try to take revenge. I am the Lord, and I command you to love others as much as you love yourself. *Leviticus 19:18,* CEV

Love yourself, not out of personal conceit but because God is the object of your love. Another person should not be angry with you if you love that individual as God's child.

Jesus said, "Love the Lord your God with all your heart and with all your soul and with all your mind" (Matthew 22:37). This means that every thought you have, your entire life and understanding, should be focused on God. When he says "with all your heart, soul, and mind," he does not leave any part of you free to love anything else.

If something other than God seems lovable to you, channel it into that river of divine love.

If you truly love your neighbor, let your behavior toward that person be based on a total love of God. Then, when you love your neighbor as yourself, you put both loves into that stream of the love of God, the way creeks feed rivers. All of them lead into the larger body of water and none diminish it.

Love others for the sake of God. Love God for his own sake.

—Augustine: *On Christian Doctrine*

 A Personal Response

Help me to love even the unlovable, dear God. Give me the grace to care for the uncaring. Teach me how to love the way you love. Make it possible for me to see your divine image even in the most untrustworthy and frightening people I meet along the way.

Tiny Prayers

"Well done, my good servant!" his master
replied. "Because you have been trustworthy in a
very small matter, take charge of ten cities."
Luke 19:17

Make frequent, short little prayers to God. Express your
appreciation for his beauty. Ask him to help you. Fall at
the foot of the cross. Love his goodness. Give your soul
to him a thousand times a day. Stretch out your hand to him like a
child. If such prayerful, intimate thoughts become habitual, you will
gain a beautiful familiarity with God. When you really love God,
you won't be able to stop thinking about him.

Saint Gregory walked along the beach and noticed the shells and
weeds which the waves had deposited on the sand. Another wave
would come along and take some of them back into the sea. The big
rocks of the coastline stood firm and immovable even though the
waves beat upon them violently. He thought how some people were
tossed about by afflictions and other courageous souls stood firm and
unmoved. It brought to his mind the psalm: "Save me, O God, for the
waters have come up to my neck. I sink in the miry depths, where
there is no foothold" (Psalm 69:1).

On one very clear night a devout person stood by a brook watching the sky. The stars were reflected in the water. That person said,
"O my God, in the same way the stars of heaven are reflected here on
earth, so are we on earth reflected in heaven." Saint Francis knelt in
prayer beside such a beautiful brook and became enraptured. "God's
grace flows as gently and sweetly as this little stream." Another saint
watched a mother hen gather little chickens under her. He said, "Lord,
keep us all under the shadow of your wings."

Many little prayers like this can make up for the lack of all other
prayers. They are essential. Without them rest is mere idleness and
labor is pure drudgery.

—Francis de Sales: *The Devout Life*

 A Personal Response

If I set my mind to it and if I had your help, Lord, I could
pray as easily as I breathe.

The Only Way to Get It Done

> The wolf will live with the lamb, the leopard will lie down with the goat, the calf and the lion and the yearling together; and a little child will lead them. *Isaiah 11:6*

How do we do it? How do we return to the life for which we were created? How can we live not for our own benefit but for that of others and for the glory of God?

Only by faith. A return to the life God intended for us must begin here and now. It will happen when we believe in Christ. The restoration will reach you in proportion to your receptivity and responsiveness. Christ will do for us what our faith allows. He said to the blind men, "Do you believe that I am able to do this?" (Matthew 9:28). They replied that they did. When he touched their eyes he said, "According to your faith will it be done to you" (Matthew 9:29).

We have fallen away from God's intention that we live to serve others and to praise him. Sadly, we now love only ourselves and seek only our own profit. The result is that we ruin ourselves, hurt our neighbor, and insult God.

But God has brought "all things in heaven and on earth together under one head, even Christ" (Ephesians 1:10). God has restored the original character of his creation. If we truly believe this, it will affect our thinking and behavior. The spirit of true love will return to us. Our faith will lead us to consider the welfare of others. It is through faith that we become children of God. The result is that we will regard all others as kin to us and we will place ourselves at their service. Only faith can detach us from ourselves.

—Martin Bucer: *Instruction in Christian Love*

A Personal Response

You love me, O God, as though I were your only child. Yet your love is so big for everyone. Help me to understand that I am a joint heir in Christ—and that your love for all others is as complete as your love for me.

Plain and Simple

[The grace of God] teaches us to say "No" to ungodliness and worldly passions, and to live self-controlled, upright and godly lives in this present age. *Titus 2:12*

Human knowledge is dark and uncertain. Philosophy is dark, astrology is dark, geometry is dark. Those who teach these disciplines often get into difficulties. They lose themselves and wander far afield. They seek the depth and bottom of natural causes, the change of the elements, the impressions in the air, the causes of the rainbow, of blazing stars, of thunder and lightning, of the motions of the planets. They measure the size of heaven and count the number of stars. They go down into mines and search the bowels of the earth. They rip up the secrets of the sea. Such knowledge is difficult and uncertain. Few are able to reach it. Most of us are not able to understand it.

But the Holy Spirit of God, like a good teacher, applies himself to the dullness of our understanding. He leads us not to the unknown places of the earth, air, and clouds. He writes his law on our hearts. He teaches us that we should not participate in ungodliness and worldly lusts and that we should live soberly and righteously in this present world. This good lesson comes in plain words.

There is no denying some things in Scripture are hard. This is good for us. It makes us work at it. We will gain by effort what we could not get by negligence. We need to be more diligent in our reading, more eager to understand, more fervent in prayer, more willing to ask someone else for an opinion, and to presume less upon our own judgment.

It is a pretense to say that the Bible is difficult to read. It is a cover for ignorance. For how many hundred places are there in the Bible that are as clear as noonday?

—John Jewell: *Of the Holy Scriptures*

A Personal Response

Lord, gently lead us to ask the significant question: "What profit is it to gain the whole world and lose your soul?" Teach us that, and all the other good, clear, simple, devastatingly important questions.

Secret Prayer

*When you pray, go into your room, close the
door and pray to your Father, who is unseen.*

Matthew 6:6

Avoid all worldly praise and profit when you pray. Really pray!
Christ does not forbid open prayers. Sometimes we need a
place to come together for group prayer. We can share thanks
or requests to God. We can pray for peace and safety as a community.
We have common interests in weather and fruits. In a congregation
we can pray that we may be spared pestilence and plague.

But we need a secret place of prayer. This will keep us from
showing off. It leaves us free to use any words we please. If we want
to make gestures that increase our devotion no one else will know.

Go boldly to God. He desires your prayers and has commanded
you to pray. He promises to hear you, not because you are good but
because he is good.

It is false prayer that Christ condemns. The tongue and the lips
are busy, the body itself may be in pain, but the heart is not talking
with God. It feels no sweetness at all. It has no confidence in God's
promises. Its only respect is for many words, and the discomfort and
tediousness of the length of the prayer.

There is no greater labor in the world than false prayer. When
the body is compelled, and the heart unwilling, when everything is
against it, then it will hurt. True prayer comforts and encourages. The
body, though it were half dead, revives and is strong again. Even if
many minutes pass, it seems short and easy.

—William Tyndale: *Exposition upon the Sermon on the Mount*

A Personal Response

Alone with you, O God, I close my mouth and listen. Enlighten
me. Inform and edify me. Assure me you know what I need
even before I ask.

True Poverty

You still lack one thing. Sell everything you have and give it to the poor, and you will have treasure in heaven. Then come, follow me. *Luke 18:22*

Not everyone who leaves the things of this world behind comes to Christ. Some become actually worse after they abandon their possessions! They are plagued with jealousy and bitterness. They think they are better than others. They praise themselves and look down on everyone else. They do not hesitate to destroy a neighbor's reputation. What is worse than a proud pauper or a covetous panhandler? They have neither the world nor Christ.

There is a better approach to poverty. When Christ says "sell everything," he means change your point of view. If you are proud, now you must become humble. If you are angry, learn how to forgive. If you are greedy, be transformed into a generous person. If you are a glutton or a drunkard, then reverse that with fasting. If you are in love with this world, give yourself entirely to loving Christ.

This kind of poverty, chosen freely, will accomplish much. "Blessed are the poor in spirit, for theirs is the kingdom of heaven" (Matthew 5:3). Being poor in spirit is having a humble attitude that allows you to see your own folly. In the same way that many branches spring from one root, poverty of spirit will produce many good habits and virtues.

Poverty is not a virtue in itself. It can be a misery. Poverty becomes worthy of praise only when it becomes a way to gain virtue.

Those who are willingly poor but lack the humility and mercy Jesus teaches are worse off than others who are quite rich. On the other hand, those who are strong in humility and mercy in spite of their great wealth will be judged favorably by God.

—Richard Rolle: *The Fire of Love*

A Personal Response

I would be untruthful if I said I held the good things of this world in contempt. There are things I need, and things that will hurt me. There are things I want and things I can do without. Help me to understand the difference.

What God Requires

Respect and obey God! This is what life is all about. *Ecclesiastes 12:13,* CEV

You may be wrong when you say that being religious is difficult. The truth is there is only one thing required of you. Total faithfulness to God.

This devotion can become a part of your life in active and passive ways. You are actively loyal to God when you keep his commandments. Passive loyalty is a loving acceptance of whatever God sends you every moment of every day.

God does not require of us more than we can deliver. Could anything be fairer or more sensible? He will not push you beyond your strength and capacity.

Your life is made up of innumerable trivial activities. If they are done in the right spirit, this is enough to satisfy God. We do our part and God does the rest. He will bless us with his grace and allow us to accomplish wonderful things we can't even imagine! "No eye has seen, no ear has heard, no mind has conceived what God has prepared for those who love him" (1 Corinthians 2:9).

We need to accept what we can't avoid.

We are to endure tiresome and distressing circumstances with a sense of humor.

This is what it means to be holy. It may be difficult to see, but there is nothing hidden or secret about it. God offers it to us everywhere, all the time. We will receive it in great quantity from both friends and enemies. There is no better way to be "religious" than by finding God in everything that comes our way each moment.

—Jean-Pierre de Caussade: *Abandonment to Divine Providence*

A Personal Response

Help me, Lord, to fulfill the simple duties of faith, to accept cheerfully the troubles that come my way, and to suffer without troubling others.

July 26   A Thorny Path

Then Jesus said to the disciples, "If any of you
wants to be my follower, you must put aside
your selfish ambition, shoulder your cross, and
follow me. If you try to keep your life for
yourself, you will lose it. But if you give up
your life for me, you will find true life."
Matthew 16:24-25, NLT

The road to heaven is narrow and full of obstacles. But even
if you could find another road, a burning love will prevent
you from considering it. Remember, the Son of God, and all
the saints after him, took no other road than the thorny path to the
cross.

Keep these things in mind. God loves you so much that he is
pleased with every heroic act of virtue you perform. He welcomes the
return of your fidelity and courage. The more unjustly you suffer, the
more grievous your troubles, the greater your merit in the sight of
God.

Could it be that you deserve the unpleasantness you are now
experiencing? Did you bring it upon yourself? If you are in any way
to blame then you should patiently endure the pain.

—Lawrence Scupoli: *The Spiritual Combat*

A Personal Response

Joining Christ on the road to Calvary is not very attractive at
first sight. And yet, it is road that has been eagerly sought by
many of the greatest of souls. They must know something of
its value. Help me, Lord Jesus, to esteem your sacrifice.

Your Reputation

> We serve God whether people honor us or despise us, whether they slander us or praise us. We are honest, but they call us impostors. . . . We live close to death, but here we are, still alive. . . . Our hearts ache, but we always have joy. We are poor, but we give spiritual riches to others. We own nothing, and yet we have everything. *2 Corinthians 6:8-10,* NLT

C hristians who are too sensitive about their good names and reputation are like those who take medicine for a slight indisposition. They think they are taking care of their health, but they are ruining it. When we are overly protective of our reputation, we may lose it completely. This is because our tenderness makes us argumentative and unbearable. This provokes our detractors even more.

Ignoring a negative comment about yourself is a better remedy than becoming resentful and planning revenge. Contempt for injuries makes them vanish. If we become angry we tacitly admit the truth of the accusation. Fear of losing our good name is the result of not trusting its foundation—a good life. Souls firmly anchored on Christian virtue can pay little attention to the torrent of a critical tongue.

Reputation is like a sign. It points to virtue. If your reputation is taken away by wagging tongues, don't be disturbed. Like a beard, it will grow out again. If God permits it to be taken from us, he will either give us a better one or help us with holy humility.

I would make only a few exceptions. If the unjust accusation refers to horrible crimes, no one should be expected to put up with it. Let the accused justly acquit himself of it. Additionally, if an individual needs a spotless reputation in order to help others, that person should quietly seek a correction.

—Francis de Sales: *The Devout Life*

A Personal Response

Lord, let my accusers bay at the moon. I won't listen. It's *your* voice that matters. It's how I listen when you speak that matters.

July 28 Necessities for the Trip

Because he himself suffered when he was tempted, he is able to help those who are being tempted. *Hebrews 2:18*

If you want to cross a large body of water, you will need a boat. Without it you will drown. It's the same way with life: you need the uplifting Spirit of Christ to carry you through your journey. With his help you will arrive safely at the harbor on the other side.

People taking a voyage at sea carry their own provisions. They have a supply of fresh water, food, and clothing. Likewise, Christians are supplied with divine nourishment in this life. This gives them secure passage through some very rough waters.

A boat requires a good wind and a good pilot. For a faithful person, the Lord himself provides these things. He knows how to calm the storm and steer the ship. The psalm describes it vividly:

Others went out on the sea in ships; . . .
    They saw the works of the Lord,
his wonderful deeds in the deep.
    For he spoke and stirred up a tempest
that lifted high the waves.
    They mounted up to the heavens and went down to
    the depths;
in their peril their courage melted away. . . .
    Then they cried out to the Lord in their trouble,
and he brought them out of their distress.
    He stilled the storm to a whisper;
the waves of the sea were hushed.
    They were glad when it grew calm,
and he guided them to their desired haven.
(Psalm 107:23-30)

—Pseudo-Macarius: *Homilies*

 A Personal Response
Jesus, Savior, pilot me over life's tempestuous sea.

The Tie That Binds

If you love those who love you, what reward will you get? Are not even the tax collectors doing that? Matthew 5:46

We are to love everyone equally, but there is no way we can help everyone. There are many people and the world is large. The ones we can do something for are the ones closest to us. It is almost as though they are chosen by lot.

The desirable thing is that we should want everyone to enjoy God with us. Whether we give or receive assistance, the goal is recognition of God. Entertainment fans enjoy being with other fans of a favorite star. They love each other, not for who they are but because they love someone together. The more captivated the fans, the more they wish many others would also share this affection. When people are unenthusiastic about their favorite star, those fans will try to excite a more positive response by pointing out the celebrity's special qualities. If someone actually dislikes the object of their affections, they will be troubled to the point of distraction.

That is the way it is among those who love God. It is love for God that makes it possible to love our enemies. We are not afraid of them because they are not able to take our love away from us. We feel sorry for them. The more they hate us, the more distant they are from the object of our love. If they turned to God and loved him, they would have to love us too.

—Augustine: *On Christian Doctrine*

A Personal Response

Now I begin to see it clearly, Lord God. You, and you alone, bond us to others. Anything or anyone less than you will result in a relationship that is shallow, dependent, and temporary.

God's Timetable

None of us know when we might fall victim to a sudden disaster and find ourselves like fish in a net or birds in a trap. *Ecclesiastes 9:12,* CEV

Waiting for the Lord can make us impatient. The delay cools our hope. We begin to join those who have brief faith and then fall away. God gives us faith and God tests our faith. He crowns what he has tested. By hoping for something unseen we learn patience.

"I am still confident of this: I will see the goodness of the Lord in the land of the living" (Psalm 27:13). Do you also believe this? Then wait for the Lord. Have courage and give God time.

There is no need to be troubled. Though it may seem long to you, the time will be short. He will surely come. He says, "Behold, I am coming soon! My reward is with me, and I will give to everyone according to what he has done" (Revelation 22:12). With words like these Christ encourages perseverance, strengthens the tiring, prods the careless, and stimulates the idle.

Think of him as already at your door, ready to knock. This will give you some respect for your Judge who is about to enter his court, and some forbearance if he should delay. But he who is both dreadful and desirable will surely come.

—Guerric of Igny: *Liturgical Sermons*

A Personal Response

Let me discover the pleasure of anticipation. Give me what it takes to wait without complaining. Show me that there is more faith in waiting for what is unseen than in believing what is in front of my eyes.

July 31 ## "Danger, Toils, and Snares"

It will be as though a man fled from a lion only to meet a bear, as though he entered his house and rested his hand on the wall only to have a snake bite him. *Amos 5:19*

If we run from one danger, another one will catch us. If we recover from a fever, we have merely been spared to suffer paralysis or something.

After you have struggled to preserve your life and limbs, you are helpless to hold on to it. Death is inevitable. During the time when Christians were martyred, some denied their Lord to save their lives. Are any of them still alive? They lost everything.

Consider events in the future as already done. They will result in little or nothing, just like events in the past. Think about what remains for you. Either you have God or you have nothing.

—Guigo I: *Meditations*

A Personal Response

Lord, these seem like the thoughts of a pessimist, like the thoughts of the weary author of the Scripture book of Ecclesiastes. He has seen it all. There is nothing new under the sun. He gives my spirit no "lift" today. And yet he makes a strong point. God, be with me through it all.

Stocking Up on Gentleness

My dear friends, you should be quick to listen and slow to speak or to get angry. If you are angry, you cannot do any of the good things that God wants done. *James 1:19-20,* CEV

You will be better off if you discover a way to live entirely without anger. This is far better than trying to make even a little use of it. When we are pushed into anger, it is best to push it away immediately. Don't get involved with anger. Give it even a little attention and it will become the paramour of your soul. It is like a snake slithering into a hole.

With the first attack of anger, promptly call all your forces to battle stations. Don't be violent and noisy about it. Resist anger in all seriousness, but with gentleness. Don't be like the usher shouting, "Be quiet down there!" making even more noise than the offenders. If we agitate our heart, we will no longer be its master. Prayers said against anger should be said calmly and peaceably.

If your anger flares out at someone, correct it promptly with an act of gentleness toward the person who made you angry. Immediately repair the anger with an opposite act of gentleness. Fresh wounds heal most quickly. Saint Paul said, "Do not let the sun go down while you are still angry" (Ephesians 4:26).

Accumulate a stock of gentleness. Speak and act in the mildest way you can. Sweet words are not enough. They must come from a sweet soul.

—Francis de Sales: *The Devout Life*

 A Personal Response

Creator of us all, anger appears to be a quite natural response. You gave us the capacity for it. If you gave us the potential for being angry, you also provide the means to escape it. Help me, Lord. Control my anger. Help me to stock up on gentleness.

Everyone Is Indebted to God

For who makes you different from anyone else? What do you have that you did not receive? And if you did receive it, why do you boast as though you did not? *1 Corinthians 4:7*

Nonreligious persons may not admit that God is worthy of love. But even they are hard-pressed to ignore his goodness to them. Who provides them with food, eyesight, and air? It would be ridiculous to try to make a list of God's gifts to them. The very dignity which sets us apart from the beasts is a gift to us from him. The same is true of our rational minds and moral virtue. We are made what we are by a power not our own. It is a gift. "The person who wishes to boast should boast only of what the Lord has done" (1 Corinthians 1:31, NLT).

While we should be cautious of holding too low an opinion of ourselves, we should be even more afraid of thinking we are better than we are. It is dangerous to presume that any good in us is the result of our own efforts. We become arrogant. Not only do we fail to give God the credit due him, we actually despise him.

Everyone, believer and unbeliever alike, has a responsibility to respond to God's providential care with total love. That this is not ordinarily the case is affirmed by Scripture. "They are all wrapped up in their own affairs and do not really care for the cause of Jesus Christ" (Philippians 2:21, PHILLIPS). "All of them have evil thoughts from the time they are young" (Genesis 8:21, CEV).

—Bernard of Clairvaux: *On Loving God*

A Personal Response

There is no doubt in my mind, O Lord, that you love all of your creation. Why don't we all love you? Whatever others may do, let me lift my heart to you in praise and thanksgiving.

August 3 ## The Right Stuff

In your struggle against sin, you have not yet resisted to the point of shedding your blood
Hebrews 12:4

Y ou have suffered very little in comparison with others. Think about the heavy burdens others carry, and you will easily bear your own small troubles. And if you do not think yours are small, perhaps it is only because you are impatient. Whether they are small or great, try to bear your burdens without complaint.

Do not say, "I can't take it! I'm not required to take it! This person has hurt me deeply and accused me of things that are not true." That is foolish. It fails to take the crowning virtue of patience into account. It focuses on the offending person and the injury.

You are not patient if you are willing to accept difficulty only up to a certain point and from a few selected people. Genuine patience cares nothing about the source of the problem, whether it is from a superior, an equal, or an inferior; whether it is from a good and holy person or a villain. You must take it all thankfully, as though God gave it. Consider it your gain. It is impossible that anything, however small, can be suffered for God's sake without some reward.

Be ready for battle if you want to win. Without struggling you cannot gain patience, and if you will not suffer, you refuse to be crowned.

—Thomas à Kempis: *The Imitation of Christ*

A Personal Response

Lord, let this become possible for me, even though it seems out of reach. You know I can endure so very little and I am quickly defeated. Please let every difficulty become a desirable thing, for to suffer and to be harassed for your sake is beneficial to my soul.—Thomas à Kempis

August 4   # Pulled in Two Directions

Simon, Simon, Satan has asked to sift you as wheat. But I have prayed for you, Simon, that your faith may not fail. *Luke 22:31-32*

As sinful creatures we are shaken like wheat in a sieve. We are pulled this way and that by a seductive world. We can't settle down.

Christ can make a difference. A Christian's mind and heart can be centered on the divine. Over a period of time this can free us from being sifted. It will bring us peace. We will live balanced lives.

You can easily determine your preferences. If your interest is in money, honors, power, or violence you will quickly give yourself to such things. This shows that you love them. What absorbs your interest? Is it clothes? Gossip? Dirty jokes? Maybe you sleep too much. Many different kinds of chains bind you to the earth. If you do not resist these objects of your affection, you are hindered in your ability to direct your thoughts to God.

Imagine a burning house. A few occupants run naked from the house. They abandon everything else to save their lives. Others in that house attempt to save some furniture and other precious possessions. They return into the blazing structure several times in order to bring things out. Ultimately they die in the smoke and flames. This is misplaced attachment. The same thing happens to people in shipwrecks. Those who attempt to cling to their possessions often perish. Those who swim away unencumbered live.

—Pseudo-Macarius: *Homilies*

A Personal Response

You did not create an evil world, Lord God. There is beauty here, love and laughter. You have provided for us. The things of this world are in your stockroom. *Balance.* That is the word to remember. Help me to know when enough is enough, and when to let go of things that aren't important.

August 5 Offending and Offended

Oh, the depth of the riches of the wisdom and
knowledge of God! How unsearchable his
judgments, and his paths beyond tracing out!
Romans 11:33

Don't be too hasty to judge or condemn another person.
Love is not quickly offended.

Yes, the world is full of offenses, and quite ready to be
offended. I think that if our Savior were here upon earth again and
should talk with a woman at the well as he once did, I think there
would be some among us who would be offended with him. We
would think ill of both him and her.

Beware of rash offenses and rash judgments. If my neighbor does
something that upsets me, let me go to that neighbor and speak about
it. But to judge a person instantly without knowledge is a mistake.
Follow this rule: seek your neighbor's good and not your own. I must
use my liberty so that my neighbor will not be hurt by it.

How is it that God allows such offenses in the world? The answer
is: "How unsearchable his judgments." God can use them to good
purposes.

—Hugh Latimer: *Fruitful Sermons*

 A Personal Response

Lord, teach me the way of love: to seek my neighbor's good
and not my own. Teach me to hold out on judgment and to
avoid being easily offended.

Morning

Because of the Lord's great love we are not consumed, for his compassions never fail. They are new every morning; great is your faithfulness. *Lamentations 3:22-23*

Morning is the best part of the day.

It is worthwhile to go to bed soon enough to allow yourself to wake up early in the morning. It is the brightest, most pleasant, and least troubled part of the day.

In the morning, birds invite us to sing praise to God.

Early rising is good for health and holiness.

—Francis de Sales: *The Devout Life*

A Personal Response

We wake differently. Some are quickly up and running, others start more slowly. A few find becoming fully awake something of an ordeal. And yet, O Lord, there is little doubt that what has been said about the qualities of morning is true.

A Special Prayer

Hasten, O God, to save me; O Lord, come quickly to help me. *Psalm 70:1*

This verse from Psalm 70 fits every mood and disposition of human nature. It covers every temptation and every situation. It contains an appeal to God, a plain disclosure of faith, a reverent anticipation, a contemplation on our weakness, a trusting in God's answer, and an assurance of God's providence.

This verse is an unbeatable defense. It is a shield, a suit of armor. Souls drowning in a sea of anxiety will find it to be the cure for despair. It reminds us of God's constant watchfulness. If life is sweet and one is happy, it warns against complacency. It reminds everyone that we keep what we have won only with God's protection.

Whatever the condition of our spiritual life, we need to use this verse. It reminds us that we need God to help us in both prosperity and suffering, in happiness and sorrow. Our frail nature cannot survive in either state without God's help.

Suppose I lust after food. I am trying to deny myself, but I can smell a wonderful dish cooking. In spite of my better judgment, I cannot help hungering for it. Then I must say immediately: "Hasten, O God, to save me; O Lord, come quickly to help me!" I can quote this verse as an effective prayer.

This is true for every imaginable situation. Maybe I can't concentrate on my Bible reading. Perhaps I am suffering from insomnia. Or maybe I am tempted to anger, selfishness, sex, pride, egotism, or criticism. To stop these devilish suggestions I can cry aloud, "Hasten, O God, to save me; O Lord, come quickly to help me!"

Pray this prayer all the time. In adversity it asks for deliverance. In prosperity it seeks security without puffed-up pride. Meditate on it. Keep it turning over in your mind. Whatever your work, wherever you are going, keep praying it. Let sleep catch you thinking about this verse until at last you pray it in your dreams.

—John Cassian: *Conference Ten on Prayer*

A Personal Response

Whatever my situation, O Lord, let me seek your assistance. Whether I am desperate or comfortable, let me turn to you.

You Are What You Eat

Teach me knowledge and good judgment. *Psalm 119:66*

Think about what you eat and drink. Remember that it is God who provides food for you. Praise God with every bite. Focus more on God than on what is on your plate. This way not even mealtime will separate your spirit from God.

Many vacillate in their eating habits. One week they are on a crash diet. Another week they stuff themselves. They are not able to develop a sensible approach to food. They jump from one diet to another, thinking each one is best.

For the foolish and uneducated, who have never known anything of the love of Christ, thoughtless abstinence is considered holiness. They want others to notice what they are sacrificing. Abstaining from eating and drinking is not a religious act in itself. If it is done quietly it may help one to become more holy. If it is done for exhibition it is a hindrance to holiness.

If you want to abstain from food and drink in a radical way, do so in private. Avoid the praise of others. Take no pride in your achievement. Do not pretend to be religious. You can be sure that if one or two applaud your abstinence, others will call you a hypocrite or a phony.

Some are so hungry for silly honor they will starve themselves until others notice it and comment upon it. Sometimes they will restrict their diets so that they must have some different food brought to them when eating with others. May I be far from their madness and inflexibility!

I would rather see someone fail because of too much love than because of too much fasting.

—Richard Rolle: *The Mending of Life*

A Personal Response

I know, dear God, that eating and drinking are associated with health. It never occurred to me that it could also be a matter of spiritual health. My appetites and compulsions are beyond self-analysis. Be with me in my eating and drinking. Be with me if I abstain.

The Origin of Evil

Remember, no one who wants to do wrong should ever say, "God is tempting me." God is never tempted to do wrong, and he never tempts anyone else either. Temptation comes from the lure of our own evil desires. *James 1:13-14,* NLT

All qualities that are in God are good. If they are in God they are infinitely perfect. It is absolutely impossible that they could have any evil defect.

But the same qualities that are infinitely good and perfect in God may become evil and imperfect in the creature. The creature is limited and finite. The creature can make a mess of things. Strength and fire in the divine nature are the strength and fire of love. They can never be anything else as long as they are in God. But we can separate them from love. Then they become evil. They become wrath and darkness, and we do mischief with them.

Good things can be used in an evil way. There is only one explanation for the existence of evil, guilt, and deformity in the natural and moral world. These things have been separated from God.

Wrath in the soul is like poison in the body. It becomes poisonous because it is separated from other qualities. Strength and fire are valuable in themselves. They are a necessary part of every good life. But they become a problem when they are separated from other important qualities.

Don't blame God for evil. It would make more sense to blame the sun for darkness! We have free will. We make choices between right and wrong. Every quality is equally good. It becomes an evil when we, of our own free will, separate it from God. The same thing can be both evil and good depending upon whether it is used by a devil or an angel.

—William Law: *Mystical Writings*

 A Personal Response

Lord, keep me from the lure of twisting that which is good into something evil. Teach me how to keep the things that you created as good and pure, good and pure.

August 10　　Prayer for a Friend

If you fall, your friend can help you up. But if
you fall without having a friend nearby, you are
really in trouble. *Ecclesiastes 4:10*, CEV

A friend asked me to pray earnestly to God for him. He did
not need to ask. I was going to pray for him quite naturally.

I went to the place where I prefer to pray alone and began to talk
to the Lord in a foolish way. This often happens in spontaneous
prayer. It is love that is speaking. My soul is transported. It becomes
immersed in God. Love that understands it is in God forgets itself and
speaks absurdities.

I recall that after I begged God with many tears for my friend, I
said that even though I thought he was good, this wasn't enough. I
wanted him to be exceptionally good. I said, "Lord, don't let me
down. This man is able to be our friend."

O the goodness of God! You don't look at the words, but at the
desires and the will with which they are spoken! How can you bear
it when someone like me speaks so boldly to you? May you be blessed
forever!

—Teresa of Avila: *Life*

A Personal Response

O my Jesus, a soul inflamed in your love can accomplish
much!—Teresa of Avila

Fighting the Good Fight

This is what the Lord says to you: "Do not be afraid or discouraged because of this vast army. For the battle is not yours, but God's."
2 Chronicles 20:15

Fight with great determination. Don't excuse yourself by mentioning your weak human nature. If your strength fails you, ask for some more from God. He will not refuse your request. Even if your enemies are great in number, the love of God which holds you is infinitely greater. His angels are more numerous.

Don't lose heart. It might seem to you that you are cut off and doomed. You might think that this warfare will continue all your life. You feel threatened by inescapable dangers. Keep in mind that neither the power nor the trickery of your enemies can hurt you without the permission of him for whose honor you fight. God delights in this kind of spiritual battle. He encourages us to engage in it.

But he will not permit your spiritual enemies to accomplish their evil plans. He will fight on your side. Sooner or later he will crown you with victory even if the battle ends only with your life.

The only thing God asks of you is that you defend yourself courageously. In spite of any wounds you may receive, never lay down your arms or leave the battleground.

This spiritual war in unavoidable, and you must either fight or die. The enemies of the soul are obstinate, fierce. There is no chance of an arbitrated peace with them.

—Lawrence Scupoli: *The Spiritual Combat*

A Personal Response

Lord, I've just been given some armor and told to get onto that spiritual battlefield. Shells burst around me. Smoke fills the air. People cry out, wounded and dying. The dangers are many and great. I don't think I'm ready, but I know I need to be. Help me.

August 12   # Faith's Rough Road

The Lord disciplines those he loves. Hebrews 12:6

If God sends you to sea, promising to go with you and bring you back safely to land, he will bring a storm against you. He wants you to feel your faith and see his goodness. If it were always fair weather and you were never at risk, your faith would be a mere presumption. You would be unthankful to God and merciless toward your neighbor.

If God promises riches, on the way there will be poverty. The ones he loves, he chastens. The ones he saves, he condemns first. He brings us to heaven by way of hell. God is not a patcher. He does not build on another's foundation. He goes to work when things are beyond help. God delivered his own Son, his only Son, his dear Son, to death. He did that for the good of his enemies! To win his enemy. To overcome his enemy with love. To let his enemy see love, and love again.

The Holy Spirit uses tribulation to purge us, to kill our fleshly wit, our worldly understanding, our gut-level hunches (literally, "belly-wisdom"). Then we can be filled with the wisdom of God. Tribulation is a blessing according to Christ. "Blessed are those who are persecuted because of righteousness, for theirs is the kingdom of heaven" (Matthew 5:10).

—William Tyndale: *Preface to Obedience*

A Personal Response

Testing. Chastising. Discipline. These seem like negatives, Lord. There is an ugliness about them. And yet, there is no denying the great saints could affirm it is true. And I know I must learn to affirm it as true too. This is the way it works. This is the way it is.

August 13 ## Difficult Passages

Our dear brother Paul also wrote you with the wisdom that God gave him. He writes the same way in all his letters, speaking in them of these matters. His letters contain some things that are hard to understand. *2 Peter 3:15-16*

I f you find something when you are reading the Bible that is difficult to understand or seems repugnant, don't be too hasty to reject it. The problem may be your ignorance, and may have nothing to do with the Bible.

It will help a lot if you notice not only what is spoken or written, but also of whom, and to whom, it is being said. Consider the circumstances and the intentions. Read what comes before and after. Some things are written with the intent that we should "go and do likewise" (Luke 10:37). Other things are written to demonstrate what we should avoid, such as when David causes Uriah to be slain because David wanted his wife.

Read the Bible wisely and carefully. When you come across strange behaviors and cryptic statements, leave them with God. Let those who are better informed than you worry about them.

—Miles Coverdale: *A Prologue to the Bible*

A Personal Response

I remember something Abraham Lincoln said about the difficult passages of the Bible not troubling him. The things that did trouble him were those passages he easily understood!

I am troubled and challenged by the things I know, Lord. Don't allow me to dodge these things by exploring divine mysteries that are beyond my understanding.

August 14 ## An Important Detail

> We must go through many hardships to enter the
> kingdom of God. *Acts 14:22*

We read in the Bible about some people who pleased God. They are considered God's friends and favorites. We miss one important detail. They suffered for God. They had to survive tremendous struggles. They fought serious battles with all kinds of afflictions. We applaud them and wish we could be honored in a similar way, but we ignore the cost.

The best things of God are often hidden in ugly things. It is like a seed that falls on barnyard soil and grows into a beautiful plant, bearing much fruit. The afflictions and crucifixions are a necessary part of the process. Jesus says, "In this world you will have trouble" (John 16:33).

Joseph waited a long time and endured many trials before things worked out for him. Ultimately, he was in charge of Egypt and was able to take care of his family during a famine.

David was anointed king and immediately Saul began to try to kill him. Where was the anointing of God when David was afraid, hiding for his life? He had to go hungry in the desert. It was only after a long and dangerous waiting that God's will was accomplished.

Moses was tested severely as he became a leader of his people. Again, after a long period of time and travel, after many difficulties, God accomplished his will through him.

These, and many other illustrations from the Bible, teach us that God's gift to the faithful is the product of great difficulties and enduring patience. The spiritual blessings come at the end of trying times.

—Pseudo-Macarius: *Homilies*

A Personal Response

Lord, how often I have been told that becoming a Christian will end a person's troubles! But the evidence seems to point to something different: discipleship is a costly thing. Is there a meeting place between the two?

Prayer in a Time of Trouble

May the Lord answer you when you are in distress. *Psalm 20:1*

The only ones who understand the power of prayer are those who have learned from experience.

It is important to pray in a time of extreme need. I know about this. Whenever I have prayed with passion, I have been heard. I have received more than I prayed for. Sometimes there was a delay, but the answer always came.

Prayer is a potent thing! God welcomes our prayers. There is no reason for us to hesitate. Trusting Christ's promises, we can pray with the assurance that God hears and answers.

God wants us to pray when we are in trouble. He may hide himself a little. We will have to go looking for him. Christ says, "Ask and it will be given to you; seek and you will find; knock and the door will be opened to you" (Matthew 7:7). If we intend to come to God, we must knock and then knock some more. We need to continue with much knocking at God's door.

You will learn to pray when you need to pray. Formal prayer in public places may be nothing more than the croaking of frogs. Saint Bernard says that God doesn't hear the words we pray unless the one praying also hears them. "Pray for each other so that you may be healed. The earnest prayer of a righteous person has great power and wonderful results" (James 5:16, NLT). God has tied himself to prayer.

—Martin Luther: *Table Talk*

A Personal Response

I know I should pray all the time, giving you thanks for my blessings and remembering the needs of others. It often seems like prayer is hard work. But I am grateful to you, Lord, that when I am in difficulty, prayer comes naturally for me. It's clear I need balance in my prayer life. Give me equal fervor in every kind of prayer.

August 16 ## Tongue Diagnostics

By your words you will be acquitted, and by your words you will be condemned. *Matthew 12:37*

Doctors sometimes learn about a person's health by looking at his tongue. The tongue can also be a guide to diagnosing the condition of the soul. Our hand quickly moves to the location of pain, and our tongue goes for what we like. If we are truly in love with God, we will speak frequently of him in ordinary conversation. "The mouth of the righteous man utters wisdom, and his tongue speaks what is just" (Psalm 37:30).

In the same way that bees use their tiny tongues to extract nothing but honey, so your tongue should always be sweetened with God. There is no greater pleasure than to taste the praise of his holy name blossoming between your lips. It is reported that whenever Saint Francis would speak the name of Jesus, he would lick his lips as though he wanted to gather something sweet.

Be careful! Always speak of God with reverence and devotion. This is not for showing off your religiosity. Speak in a spirit of humility and love. Distill your devotion's honey a little drop at a time into the ears of others. In the secret depths of your soul, ask God to be pleased with this holy dew you are passing into the heart of your listener. Above all else, speak with meekness and gentleness. It is not to be done for correction, but for inspiration.

Never speak of God or devotion in an ordinary or careless way. Be reverent and attentive. I am telling you this so that you might escape the strange vanity found in some who talk about devotion. They speak pious words mechanically, as though they were not aware of what they were saying. When they speak like this, they think they are in harmony with their words, but they are not.

—Francis de Sales: *The Devout Life*

A Personal Response

When I try to talk about you, Lord, and the really important things like devotion and faith, I make a mess of it. Teach me how to talk about you in a way that is gentle and honest and inspiring.

Requests for Prayer

Jesus answered them, "It is not the healthy who need a doctor, but the sick." *Luke 5:31*

When people ask you to remember someone in prayer they will often say, "This is such a nice person!" That is like taking someone who is ill to the doctor and saying, "Make him well because he is so healthy!" Maybe what they mean by the "nice person" idea is that there may be a little hope for that individual's salvation.

Sometimes they will say, "Pray for so-and-so because this person has done good things on your behalf." I would prefer to pray for someone who has done me wrong. Such a person actually needs my prayers.

It is a good thing to pray for anyone who confesses and asks for forgiveness. It is even better to pray for someone who does not yet feel guilty about anything. Ask God to help them notice their sin. And pray also for those who know they are guilty but will not admit it. Maybe they are ashamed. Maybe they are actually enjoying their guilt. Ask God to help them.

—Guigo I: *Meditations*

A Personal Response

Lord Jesus, you instruct us to pray for our enemies. You tell us to forgive those who have sinned against us. You want us to pray for those who persecute us.

What a prayer list you give us! Here I am ready to ask for all the things I want for my loved ones. Help me to get my priorities straight. Let me deal with these others first. Then maybe I will be ready to love those who love me in a new light.

The Difference between Law and Gospel

> Once I was alive apart from law; but when the commandment came, sin sprang to life and I died. I found that the very commandment that was intended to bring life actually brought death. *Romans 7:9-10*

The law points to sin; the gospel remedies it.

The law condemns; the gospel redeems.

The law is a word of wrath; the gospel is a word of grace.

The law fills us with despair; the gospel comforts.

The law says, "Pay the debt!" The gospel says, "Christ has paid it."

The law says, "You are a sinner!" The gospel says, "Your sins are forgiven."

The law says, "Make amends!" The gospel says, "Christ has made amends for you."

The law says, "God is angry with you!" The gospel says, "God loves you."

—Patrick Hamilton: *Treatise on the Law and the Gospel*

A Personal Response

Sometimes I wonder if we will ever get this straight, Lord God. All too often, your Church proclaims law rather than gospel. Would Jesus be able to sit still while the angry shouting about the importance of the law goes on in his name?

Obedience and Understanding

Though his disease was severe, even in his illness [Asa the king] did not seek help from the Lord, but only from the physicians. *2 Chronicles 16:12*

We will be perfect when we are in complete cooperation with God. The way toward this perfection is slow and hidden from our observation. There are many books written about these things. There are many theories and theological explanations. If we want, we can go to school and learn about all of this. We might even become competent to teach and write about it ourselves. Maybe we will even begin to give others some spiritual direction. To have only an intellectual understanding of our faith is to be like a sick medical doctor living among healthy people.

You don't need to understand how medicine works in order to be cured. All you have to do is take it. You can be warmed and cheered by a fire without a knowledge of combustion and chemistry. If we are thirsty, we want a drink of water rather than a book that explains thirst. Holiness is not the result of study. If we have a thirst for holiness, reading about it will only make us thirstier!

Take it easy. Become like a child. Be willing to accept everything that God sends your way. This is the holiest thing you can do.

—Jean-Pierre de Caussade: *Abandonment to Divine Providence*

 A Personal Response

Great learning is not enough by itself. The knowledge I acquire must be accompanied by some living experience. Lord God, help me to apply the things I have learned about Christ to the living I do today.

A Careful Tongue

All of us do many wrong things. But if you can control your tongue, you are mature and able to control your whole body. *James 3:2,* CEV

Never let an indecent word slip from your mouth. Even if you don't mean it in an evil way, others may be offended. An evil word dropping into a weak person grows and spreads like a drop of oil on linen. It might spark a thousand unclean thoughts and temptations. If bodily poison enters through the mouth, spiritual poison enters through the ear. The tongue that speaks it is a murderer of a soul.

Don't try to tell me you speak without thinking. Our Lord who searches our hearts says, "Out of the overflow of the heart the mouth speaks" (Matthew 12:34). Those who eat an herb called *angelica* have sweet breath. Those who have angelic virtues within their hearts speak sweetly.

As for profanity and obscenity, the apostle doesn't even want us to be familiar with such language. "Among you there must not be even a hint of sexual immorality, or of any kind of impurity, or of greed, because these are improper for God's holy people" (Ephesians 5:3). He insists that "bad company corrupts good character" (1 Corinthians 15:33).

Immodest words that are interjected with subtlety are even more damaging. A sharp dart penetrates most easily. The sharper an obscenity, the deeper it penetrates the heart. Those who take pride in being sophisticated do not fully understand what conversation is when they use such words. Rather than being a bee gathering honey, they are wasps out to sting. Turn away from anyone who speaks to you in a bawdy manner.

—Francis de Sales: *The Devout Life*

 A Personal Response

Lord, the temptation is to prove that I am not "holier than thou" by using a few four-letter words. I'm trying to do the right thing in the wrong way. Teach me what speaking maturely means. Don't let me use my tongue as a stinger.

August 21   ✿   # Seeking What Is Good

> I want you to be wise about what is good, and innocent about what is evil. *Romans 16:19*

We labor, struggle, and even kill for things that do not last. We do this because these things are familiar. We are simply not aware of an alternative. When we are troubled by a moment of need or difficulty, we desire things that are not all that different from the source of our pain. We try to escape the troubles they cause either by calling a truce or by turning to things that are similar in nature.

We want to do the best we can for ourselves. We seek pleasure and avoid pain. But often we attempt to do this in ways that not only fail to achieve what we desire, but also make our goal more difficult to attain. We chase after happiness and find only misery.

You will not be hurt if someone cuts off all your hair. It will grow back. Real injury would come only if the roots of your hair were damaged. In the same way you will be harmed if someone ruins the things that have become important enough for you to crave. The more such things you have, and the more you love them, the more extreme will be the torments they will produce.

It is best if you do not desire something earthly, even if it is good that will itself require another good. Its need will increase your need. Ultimately, it will make you even more unhappy.

You have a choice. You can free yourself of passionate appetites, or you can get ready to be upset.

—Guigo I: *Meditations*

A Personal Response

How often I see it, my Lord. "Batteries not included." "Accessories sold separately." "Starter set." You do not ask me to ignore this world. You have not asked me to be unproductive or to avoid entertainment and recreation. But what is this good I need that is complete in itself? *Who?*

A Gift from Prison

The Law of the Lord makes them happy, and
they think about it day and night. *Psalm 1:2*, CEV

*The following was written on the last page of
her Greek New Testament, which Lady Jane
Grey sent to her sister the night before she herself was martyred:*

I have sent you a book. It is not rimmed with gold, but its contents are worth more than precious stones. It contains the laws
of the Lord. It is his last will and testament. It will lead you to
the path of eternal joy. If you will read it with an earnest desire to
follow it, it will bring you to immortal and everlasting life. It will
teach you to live and die. It will win more for you than you could
have gained from your deplorable father's real estate. In the same
way that you should have inherited his lands, you shall be an in-
heritor of riches that can never be lost or stolen.

Apply yourself diligently to this book. Direct your life after it.
Desire with David, good sister, to understand the law of the Lord God.
Your youth does not guarantee you a long life. If God calls, the young
go as quickly as the old. Learn to die. Deny the world, defy the devil,
despise the flesh, and delight yourself only in the Lord. Be penitent
for your sins, but don't despair. Be steady in faith, but not presumptuous.

Since you bear the name of a Christian, follow Christ's steps as
nearly as you can. Take up your cross. Lay your sins on his back.
Embrace him always.

Regarding my death, rejoice as I do, good sister. I shall be
delivered of this corruption and put on incorruption.

—Lady Jane Grey: *Letters*

 A Personal Response

It's hard for me to understand how this young woman should
be required to surrender her promising life because of her faith,
dear God. She lived in difficult and troubled times. Help me
to keep the advice she gave her sister. It comes from one who
can speak in authentic terms.

August 23 # Laziness

The soul of the sluggard desireth, and hath nothing: But the soul of the diligent shall be made fat. *Proverbs 13:4,* KJV

Laziness is a poison that will spread through all the faculties of the soul. It infects the will by making work undesirable. It blinds the understanding so that the best of resolutions has no effect. We put off doing anything about slothfulness.

On the other hand, simply being fast has little to commend it. Things must be done at the proper time, and in the best manner possible. Speedy carelessness is only an artful, refined laziness.

This disorder results from a failure to consider the value of something done at the right time and in the right way. God gradually withdraws his graces from those who neglect them.

God has granted you the morning, but he does not promise the evening. Spend each day as if it were your last.

—Lawrence Scupoli: *The Spiritual Combat*

A Personal Response

I have never considered the fact that laziness is an indicator of the condition of a soul. Let me understand, O God, the difference between being still in order to know you, and being still because I am not inclined to work.

The First Commandment

You shall have no other gods before me. *Exodus 20:3*

There are ways in which we worship false gods. It is possible to be so attached to a thing or a person as to turn it into an idol. Even though you don't say it with your mouth, you have an object of worship that is not God.

Another way to have a false god is to put your confidence in anything other than God. If you wish you were rich, or desire to have a certain friend or supporter, and think that this will bring you happiness and security, you may have taken a false god. The Lord is God alone. Our confidence is to be anchored in him alone.

Think about these false gods as weeds in your garden. Pull them out by the root. Set your heart on nothing that is not God. Love God with your whole heart. Do everything for his sake. And above all, *obey* God. For if we merely revere, love, and trust—but do not obey—God, we are making God into what we want; we are making him into a false god.

Some greatly fear and believe in the conjunctions and influences of the heavenly planets and bodies in the sky. Others stand in awe of tyrants. Some put their trust in money, and they scratch everywhere for money, not regarding whether they get it by right or by wrong.

There are those who are overly self-confident. They have their merits and good deeds to rely on instead of relying on God. This is the greatest idolatry of all.

Others are servants to their own bellies, forgetting God while they eat and drink. Their stomach is their god.

Some are even able to make an idol of the true and living God. When we *imagine* the form and shape of God, we have missed God. Be careful not to create an idol in your heart.

—Thomas Cranmer: *Catechismus*

A Personal Response

When I really love you with my whole heart, God, I will find peace. This is the peace of those who have no hindering thing, no false gods.

Putting Faith into Action

"You have answered correctly," Jesus replied. "Do this and you will live." *Luke 10:28*

Many who cry out against sin can live comfortably with it in their heart, home, and business. It is possible to learn all about the mysteries of the Bible and never be affected by it in one's soul. Great knowledge is not enough.

Christ told his disciples, "Now that you know these things, you will be blessed if you do them" (John 13:17). He did not bless their knowledge. The blessing is in the doing. A person may know like an angel and still not be a Christian.

Talkers and boasters enjoy knowing something. God is pleased when it is done.

But we do need this kind of knowledge: "Give me understanding, and I will keep your law and obey it with all my heart" (Psalm 119:34).

—John Bunyan: *The Pilgrim's Progress*

A Personal Response

I remember seeing a verse inscribed over a church altar: "Be doers of the word and not hearers only." That is a summary of the book of James. "Dear brothers and sisters, what's the use of saying you have faith if you don't prove it by your actions? That kind of faith can't save anyone. Suppose you see a brother or sister who needs food or clothing, and you say, 'Well, good-bye and God bless you; stay warm and eat well'—but then you don't give that person any food or clothing. What good does that do? So you see, it isn't enough just to have faith. Faith that doesn't show itself by good deeds is no faith at all—it's dead and useless" (James 2:14-17, NLT).

God's Humility and Ours

Unto us a child is born, unto us a son is given.
Isaiah 9:6, KJV

Jesus was born an infant, but he was at the same time "the Ancient of Days" (Daniel 7:9). The eternity of the Word is beyond our comprehension. But think of it! As the Ancient of Days he is not a child, and yet he is new. His newness can renew everything. We grow old when we slip away from him. We are renewed when we return to him.

In a manner that has no parallel, Christ's youth and age are one. His eternity did not begin when he was born and did not diminish as he matured. His newness is ancient and his antiquity is new.

In the birth of the Christ child, God "emptied himself" (Philippians 2:7) of his majesty and took on both an ordinary human body and the vulnerability and unimportance of a baby. This sacred childhood restored our innocence.

Are you an important person? Have you been successful? Are you proud of your status as a giant in this world? "Unless you change and become like little children, you will never enter the kingdom of heaven" (Matthew 18:3). Unless your proud head is bowed, you will not be able to enter through the door of humility. Let this shake your self-confidence. If we approach him haughtily, we will be cast out.

How can you still be proud, dust and ashes, after God has humbled himself? How can you still be great in your own eyes when you know God made himself a child? God emptied himself. Why are you puffed up? You are leading yourself astray.

If you want to be someone even greater than you are, gain more humility. The Greatest of All made himself Least of All. The holy and the humble see this and honor it. The secular and proud see it and are bewildered.

—Guerric of Igny: *Liturgical Sermons*

 A Personal Response

What loving kindness allows me to see the God who made me, make himself a child for my sake! You are everything that is good and desirable. You leave no room for anger or sadness. Childlike, we praise you.—Guerric of Igny

For the Committed

I have revealed you to those whom you gave me
out of the world. They were yours; you gave
them to me and they have obeyed your word.
John 17:6

L ove your enemies and pray for those who persecute you"
(Matthew 5:44). We must follow in the footsteps of our
Lord Jesus Christ, who called Judas—his betrayer—a friend
and freely laid down his life for him. Our friends are those who
bring suffering, shame, even death to us without provocation. We
must love them. We must love them passionately because they are
helping us to receive eternal life.

Our base nature, so prone to sin and vice, must be hated. As our
Lord says in the Gospel, "For from within, out of a person's heart, come
evil thoughts, sexual immorality, theft, murder, adultery, greed, wickedness, deceit, eagerness for lustful pleasure, envy, slander, pride, and
foolishness. All these vile things come from within; they are what defile
you and make you unacceptable to God" (Mark 7:21-23, NLT).

We have turned away from the world and must be careful to obey
God's will. We must keep our guard up. Satan will try to turn our
minds and hearts away from God by making us think we can have or
do something more valuable.

With God's love I urge all my friars to get rid of all attachments
and concerns for this world. Serve, love, honor, and adore our Lord
and God without any idea of looking out for your own interests. Let
us make room for God within ourselves that he may come and live
with us.

Stick to the words, the life, the teaching, and the Holy Gospel of
our Lord Jesus Christ. He has prayed to his Father for us and revealed
his name to us.

—Francis of Assisi: *Rule of 1221*

A Personal Response

I want that kind of dedication and commitment, Lord. I know
that the life of faith is not only for monks, people called to a
devout life. You desire it for me also.

Poking Fun

In the last days scoffers will come, scoffing and
following their own evil desires. *2 Peter 3:3*

Scoffing at others is a wretched practice. God detests this vice.
In the Old Testament he inflicts strange punishments on scoffers. There can be nothing more opposed to love and devotion than to despise and condemn your neighbor. Poking fun and
scoffing are the same thing. Derision, mockery, scorn, and contempt
are sins.

There are some good-humored words that can be spoken in modest jesting that are acceptable. This is innocent fun. The Greeks called
it *eutrapelia.* We call it pleasant conversation. With it we can have a
friendly, amusing discussion about human imperfections.

The trick is to avoid moving from light-hearted mirth to vicious
scoffing. Scoffing produces laughter through scorn and contempt of
another. Laughing banter comes from freedom and familiarity in clever
expression. Jokes and puns can be healthy.

—Francis de Sales: *The Devout Life*

 A Personal Response

This has been a hard lesson to learn. There is a huge difference
in laughing *with* someone and laughing *at* someone. Spare me,
Lord, from all manner of degrading jokes and stereotypes. Give
my generation more true wit.

Is It Real? Is It Good?

Take the helmet of salvation and the sword of the Spirit, which is the word of God. *Ephesians 6:17*

In your spiritual life, guard against *illusion*. Beginners in faith are extremely vulnerable. It is not surprising that they mistakenly accept illusion as truth. Many who seek God succumb to this.

Mental prayer is the highest of all, but an arrogant and shameless person who tries to capture God is easily led astray. If you are praying and "see" something—an image of Christ, an angel, light—do not accept it. Our minds have a way of dreaming that can easily create fantastic images. Beware of this. Do not allow yourself to believe something without asking rational questions and investigating thoroughly, even if it seems to be good or benign. Always have a distaste for these images. Try to keep them out of your mind. Challenge them if they come along. God is not disturbed by this carefulness on our part.

Find someone whose life shines with authentic faith and seek guidance regarding these things. Not everyone is able to help you. It will not be easy to find the right person. You are looking for someone who is guided by the Scriptures. Such a person will explain to you that excess leads to conceit, followed by illusion.

There are clear signs that identify the actions of God's grace. These cannot be produced by the devil even through the cleverest transformations. They are meekness, friendliness, humility, selflessness, and decency. Works from evil sources display arrogance, immodesty, intimidation, and corruption. With this as a guide you will be able to tell whether something is from God or from Satan.

Lettuce looks like the mustard plant, and vinegar has the color of wine, but your tongue can tell the difference. In the same way, the soul can discern differences in the taste of the gifts of the Holy Spirit and the illusions of Satan.

—Gregory of Sinai: *Instructions to Hesychasts*

 A Personal Response

Teach me the secret of serious prayer. Don't let me chase after spiritual spectaculars. Once I really learn to pray, that will be exciting enough.

Studying the Bible

We live by faith, not by sight. *2 Corinthians 5:7*

To be a student of the Bible you need to read it. Even if you can't understand all of it, you will do well to read all of it. Get to know these books. Memorize a few passages. Become familiar with Holy Scripture.

Once you know what is between the covers of the Bible, you can begin to study it more intelligently. Important teachings regarding faith and living are clear first lessons. This light will eventually help illuminate the more difficult parts. The things you are sure about will help you with the things that seem uncertain.

There are two causes of misunderstanding. Either something is unknown or it is an ambiguous sign. The only cure for ignorance is education. If you have a strong desire to understand the Scriptures more fully, learn the original languages. The multiplicity of translations creates questions and doubts because they do not all agree in the details. Some words defy translation.

Comparing various translations can make a difficult verse easier to understand. One may be explained by the other. Both may contain something valuable to a careful reader.

Faith is the most important ingredient in Bible study. Someone said, "If you don't believe, you won't understand."

—Augustine: *On Christian Doctrine*

A Personal Response

Give me a burning curiosity to know what is in the Bible. It contains what you think is important for me to know. Don't let me be put off by its size. Many have read it all several times. Guide me to the best translation for me. Let me read as one who is faithful.

A Good Way and a Better Way

> [Jesus] came to a village where a woman named Martha opened her home to him. She had a sister called Mary, who sat at the Lord's feet listening to what he said. But Martha was distracted by all the preparations that had to be made. She came to him and asked, "Lord, don't you care that my sister has left me to do the work by myself? Tell her to help me!" "Martha, Martha," the Lord answered, "you are worried and upset about many things, but only one thing is needed. Mary has chosen what is better, and it will not be taken away from her." *Luke 10:38-42*

There are two kinds of Christian living. One is a life of activity. The other is the contemplative life. These two lives are united. It is impossible to live the one without having some of the other. The active life begins and ends right here. The contemplative life begins here and continues into eternity. This is why the part that Mary chose will never be taken away from her. The active life has many irritations. The contemplative life is at peace because it is intent upon only one thing.

Those focused on activity complain about contemplatives. Those Christians who are active in the world should be excused for this. We must allow for their ignorance. They are like Martha, who could not comprehend what her sister was doing. She complained about Mary to our Lord.

Jesus answered her courteously. Notice how he called her name twice because he wanted her to pay special attention to his words. There are those who are always busy, active in acts of mercy. Our Lord does not deny Martha's business is good and profitable for her. He only indicates that Mary's choice is superior to Martha's. One is good and the other is better.

—Anonymous: *The Cloud of Unknowing*

 A Personal Response

Give me respect for the way other people live as Christians. Lord, teach me to look at my own life and ask, "I have my own particular gifts—am I using them in the best way?"

God's Point of View

The fear of the Lord is pure, enduring forever.
The ordinances of the Lord are sure and
altogether righteous. *Psalm 19:9*

It is best if we accept God's decisions without complaint. Do not ask him to defend his actions, or to explain why one person is favored and another seems slighted. The answers to these questions go far beyond our comprehension.

When you are tempted to object, say with the psalmist, "Righteous are you, O Lord, and your laws are right" (Psalm 119:137). God's decisions are to be respected. They are not to be debated.

Don't waste your time trying to determine which of the saints is the most saintly, or who shall be the greatest in the kingdom of heaven. This can cause arguments and dissension, and you may even form parties and admiration societies. The saints would be the first to tell you to stop it!

God does not reserve his favor for these saints. He loves everyone. If you look down on the least person, you fail to honor the greatest. God made both of them. Everyone in his kingdom is equal. They are bound together in God's love.

When the disciples asked who would be the greatest, this was Jesus' answer: "I assure you, unless you turn from your sins and become as little children, you will never get into the Kingdom of Heaven. Therefore, anyone who becomes as humble as this little child is the greatest in the Kingdom of Heaven" (Matthew 18:3-4, NLT).

—Thomas à Kempis: *The Imitation of Christ*

 A Personal Response

I look only to you, merciful Father, for help and comfort. My soul praises you and seeks to become your holy dwelling place. Let nothing in me offend you.—Thomas à Kempis

September 2 Slander

Let slanderers not be established in the land.
Psalm 140:11

I f you rob your neighbor of a good reputation, you have the obligation of making reparation. You can't enter heaven carrying
someone else's property. Of all external possessions, a good name
is most important. Slander is a form of murder.

With a single stroke of the tongue you can commit three murders.
You kill your own soul, the soul of anyone who hears your slanderous
comments, and the social life of your victim. It is spiritual homicide.
Saint Bernard says that the slanderer has the devil on the tongue, and
the one who listens to slander has the devil in the ear. A snake tongue
is forked with two points. So also is the slanderer's tongue: It poisons
the listener as well as the one being spoken against.

Beware of falsely accusing another person. It is not your business
to expose someone's secret sins or to exaggerate the ones already made
public. You are wrong to put an evil interpretation on a person's good
works, or to maliciously degrade those good works with your words.

People who preface slander with comments about doing "the
right thing" or who make little private jokes are the most vicious
slanderers of them all. "I really like him," they say. "In every other
regard he is a fine man, but the truth must be told." "She was a nice
girl, but she must have been caught at a weak moment." You can see
what they are up to with these little tricks. The archer pulls the arrow
back as near to himself as possible in order to put more force into the
shot. Slanderous joking is the most cruel of all. Hemlock is not a quick
poison by itself. There is time to take an antidote. When hemlock is
taken with wine, there is no antidote for it. In the same way slander
that might pass lightly in one ear and out the other, sticks in the mind
when it is told with a funny story.

—Francis de Sales: *The Devout Life*

 A Personal Response

If we do not pick on members of our own family or our neighbors across the street, we go after people who are in the public
eye. What motivates us to slander? Perhaps it is a way of
self-aggrandizement. Maybe it is simply vicious aggression.
Forgive us, Lord.

September 3 Offering Ourselves

Joseph and Mary took [Jesus] to Jerusalem to present him to the Lord . . . and to offer a sacrifice in keeping with what is said in the Law of the Lord: "a pair of doves or two young pigeons." *Luke 2:22-24*

It is only when we finally abandon ourselves to God that we realize that everything up to then was separation from God.

What will matter when I am no longer of any concern to myself? I will think less about what happens to me and more about God. His will be done. That is sufficient. If enough self-interest remains to complain about it, I have offered an incomplete sacrifice.

It isn't easy. Old ways of thinking and behaving do not vanish at once. Every now and then they spring back to life. I begin to mutter, "I didn't deserve such treatment! The charges are false and unfair! My friend is letting me down! I have lost everything! No one comforts me! God is punishing me too severely! I expected some help from those good people, but they are ignoring me! God has forsaken me!"

Weak and trembling soul, soul of little faith, do you want something other than what God wills? Do you belong to him or to yourself? Renounce the miserable self in you. Cut every string. Now you are getting down to the business of sacrifice. Anything less is child's play. There is no other way your two doves can be offered to God.

—François de Fénelon: *Meditations and Devotions*

A Personal Response

O Jesus, I offer myself to be with you. Give me the courage I need to completely renounce myself. Your doves did not spare you your cross. Your presentation in the temple was but the beginning of what ended at Calvary. None of the offerings I can make will ransom me. I must give myself even to the point of dying on a cross. It is nothing to lose luxury, fame, money, life. We must lose ourselves in you.

—François de Fénelon

Basic Instruction

God did not call us to be impure, but to live a holy life. *1 Thessalonians 4:7*

Saint Paul wrote: "God wants you to be holy, so you should keep clear of all sexual sin. Then each of you will control your body and live in holiness and honor—not in lustful passion as the pagans do, in the ignorance of God and his ways" (1 Thessalonians 4:3-5, NLT). This is God's will. We need to promise him that we will serve him in holiness all the days of our life.

A good and loving father, who sends his son on a dangerous journey, will instruct him with good advice. He will tell him how to avoid risks and perils. Watch out for this! Be careful of that! In such places many a good man's child has been cast away! Be careful my son!

If a father is that careful about worldly dangers, he must be even more careful of spiritual dangers. He should say to his child, based on words found in Psalms and Proverbs, "Understand what God has done for you. The world is strewn with snares. Be strong in the faith. The name of the Lord is a strong tower of defense. Call upon him in the day of trouble and he will deliver you."

—John Jewell: *Exposition on the Thessalonians*

 A Personal Response

Help me to understand, dear Lord, that every instruction, every rule, every command given me by the Bible is for my own best interest. It is not there to destroy fun. It is there to prevent great sadness.

The Advantage of Difficulty

Today I am giving you the choice between a blessing and a curse! *Deuteronomy 11:26,* NLT

Prosperity is a real curse. Christ says, "What sorrows await you who are rich, for you have only your happiness now. What sorrows await you who are satisfied and prosperous now, for a time of awful hunger is before you. What sorrows await you who laugh carelessly, for your laughing will turn to mourning and sorrow. What sorrows await you who are praised by the crowds, for their ancestors also praised false prophets" (Luke 6:24-26, NLT).

Suffering for good is not only a blessing but also a gift God gives to special friends. The apostles rejoiced that they were counted worthy to suffer for Christ's sake. Paul wrote, "Everyone who wants to live a godly life in Christ Jesus will be persecuted" (2 Timothy 3:12). "It has been granted to you on behalf of Christ not only to believe on him, but also to suffer for him" (Philippians 1:29). You can see that it is God's gift to suffer for his sake.

"Dear friends, do not be surprised at the painful trial you are suffering, as though something strange were happening to you. But rejoice that you participate in the sufferings of Christ, so that you may be overjoyed when his glory is revealed. If you are insulted because of the name of Christ, you are blessed, for the Spirit of glory and of God rests on you" (1 Peter 4:12-14). Christ is never strong in us until we are weak. As our strength diminishes, the strength of Christ grows in us. When we are entirely emptied of our own strength, then we are full of Christ's strength. As much as we retain of our own we lack of Christ's.

—William Tyndale: *Preface to Obedience*

 A Personal Response

Sometimes I bring troubles on myself. Sometimes it is a temptation to think that I am suffering for Christ when I am only paying for my own misjudgment. But, with the apostle Paul, I rejoice in my weakness, that the strength of Christ may dwell in me (2 Corinthians 12:9).

Knowing the Unknowable

Who among the gods is like you, O Lord?
Who is like you—majestic in holiness,
awesome in glory, working wonders? *Exodus
15:11*

I f we attempt to comprehend God, the God we think we understand is not God. The human mind is not large enough to investigate God. We will be led into errors. The deeper we dig, the farther we go away from God.

God's presence and activity are beyond our ability to comprehend. We can accept them with faith. We can be deeply thankful for them. But there is no way we can grasp them, describe them, and explain them. We are not even able to understand our own motives and behavior. How can we expect to know the mind of God?

We enjoy bread without understanding how the wheat grew. We drink our fill of water at a riverbank without having any idea of its source. We protect our eyes from brightness in order to see things in daylight, but we have no way to figure how much light there is in the sun. A baby drinks from its mother's breast but cannot think how the breast got there.

The closer we are to God, the less we know about God.

—Pseudo-Macarius: *Homilies*

 A Personal Response

You gave us intellects, dear God. We naturally go around classifying and cataloging things—we can't help ourselves. But I am learning that no matter how much I read or write about you, Lord, it is not enough. I cannot comprehend you.

A Daring Prayer

Let us then approach the throne of grace with confidence, so that we may receive mercy and find grace to help us in our time of need.
Hebrews 4:16

I had some fun with God today! I dared to complain to him. I said:

Explain to me, please, why you keep me in this miserable life. Why do I have to put up with it? Everything here interferes with my enjoyment of you. I have to eat and sleep and work and talk with everyone. I do it all for the love of you, but it torments me.

And how is it that when there is a little break and I can have some time with you, you hide from me? Is this the way you show me mercy? If you love me, how can you do this to me? I honestly believe, Lord, that if it were possible for me to hide from you the way you hide from me, you would not allow it. But you are with me and see me always. Stop this, Lord! It hurts me because I love you so much.

I said these and other things to God. Sometimes love becomes foolish and doesn't make a lot of sense. The Lord puts up with it. May so good a King be praised! We wouldn't dare say these things to earthly kings!

—Teresa of Avila: *Life*

A Personal Response

Lord, you respect an honest prayer. Help me to be straightforward with you rather than try to pray pretty little prayers with little life in them.

September 8 # Love Makes the Difference

God has poured out his love into our hearts
by the Holy Spirit, whom he has given us.
Romans 5:5

Fasting until your head aches is easy. You can walk to Rome
and Jerusalem on your bare feet if you want. It would not be
a struggle to preach fervently in order to convert everyone
with your sermons. It is not difficult to build churches and hospitals. You can feed the poor with little effort.

But it is extremely difficult to love a fellow Christian, to hate sin
while loving the person. The good works mentioned above are done
by both Christians and non-Christians. There is not much challenge
in doing what anyone can do. But to genuinely love a fellow Christian
is a gift from God.

Without God's love in our heart no good deed will make us good.
If you fast, go on pilgrimages, and forsake the pleasures of this world
for your own notoriety, the only reward you will receive is earthly.
In the same way, a true preacher is humble. The hypocrite looks for
rave reviews and for worldly fame.

Saint Paul expressed this idea in these words: "If I could speak in
any language in heaven or on earth but didn't love others, I would only
be making meaningless noise like a loud gong or a clanging cymbal. If
I had the gift of prophecy, and if I knew all the mysteries of the future
and knew everything about everything, but didn't love others, what
good would I be? And if I had the gift of faith so that I could speak to a
mountain and make it move, without love I would be no good to anybody. If I gave everything I have to the poor and even sacrificed my
body, I could boast about it; but if I didn't love others, I would be of no
value whatsoever" (1 Corinthians 13:1-3, NLT).

Whether another person is genuine or insincere is not for us to
say. Only our Lord knows. Therefore love everyone. Approve everything they do that has the appearance of goodness.

—Walter Hilton: *The Scale of Perfection*

 A Personal Response

If Christian love cannot become mine by the good things I
do, how do I get it? Give me a receptive spirit, O Lord. Prepare
me to receive your gift of love.

The Name of Jesus

Therefore God exalted him to the highest place and gave him the name that is above every name, that at the name of Jesus every knee should bow, in heaven and on earth and under the earth, and every tongue confess that Jesus Christ is Lord, to the glory of God the Father. *Philippians 2:9-11*

I became ill. While I was having chills and fevers, the sweet name of Jesus filled my being. I could not keep quiet. Everything I said began with "Jesus Christ." For me, this name is the sweetest thing in the world. With this name I can suffer lovingly with my Lord. This name fills me with the great joy. Bathed in this name I become stronger.

When I say the Lord's Prayer this name takes hold of me. There is something about it that goes beyond the ordinary. Sometimes I wonder if I can experience such grace and continue living until I have finished the prayer! I wonder if the joys of heaven could be superior to this.

There is no rational explanation for this kind of spiritual experience. Love and faith are given to me in a powerful way. There is no doubt that God is present with me. Even if I were in hell I believe I would still experience his presence within me.

—Margaret Ebner: *Revelations*

A Personal Response

There is no other name like yours, my Lord. Let your name take hold of me. For so many, *Jesus* and *Jesus Christ* are used as swear words. I want to reverently say your name. Use it to fill me with your divine presence.

It's All Yours!

[Lord,] you put us in charge of everything you made, giving us authority over all things—the sheep and the cattle and all the wild animals, the birds in the sky. the fish in the sea, and everything that swims the ocean currents.
Psalm 8:6-8, NLT

Some people see no value in human relationships beyond what can be advantageous or profitable. They love their friends the same way they love their cattle. They expect to get something.

But true friendship is not bought. Nothing but love is traded. Friendships among the poor are usually more lasting than those among the rich. There is no hope of gain. The friendship does not depend upon value received. One may flatter a wealthy person, but there is no pretense with someone who is poor. Whatever you give a poor person is a true gift because you expect nothing in return.

You may have a friend who is more interested in what you have than in you, always waiting for something you can give—contacts, position, money, freedom. You can easily spot such a person. Such a person will turn to someone else if you cannot produce what is desired.

Imagine that you are the only person left alive on earth. Everything is now yours. You own the gold, silver, jewels, cities full of buildings, sculptures, and paintings. Would you enjoy it without a companion?

If you had one other person to love as much as you love yourself, wouldn't all these meaningless possessions become enjoyable? Wouldn't you think you would be happier the more such companions you could find? Do you think there is any human being who does not want to be loved? The most fortunate person of all is the one who has loving friends.

—Aelred of Rievaulx: *Spiritual Friendship*

 A Personal Response

God, give us all good friends. Teach us to value the friendship that others offer us. Teach us to give of ourselves in friendship. This is true riches.

September 11   ## Misdirected Devotion

> A time is coming and has now come when the true worshipers will worship the Father in spirit and truth, for they are the kind of worshipers the Father seeks. *John 4:23*

God is truly worshiped when someone actually gives full attention to God with feelings of awe, love, devotion, respect, and wonder. Such a moment is genuine worship. It is idolatrous to think and feel this way about anything other than God. This is why the apostle Paul says that "their god is their stomach" (Philippians 3:19) and "such people are not serving our Lord Jesus Christ, but their own appetites" (Romans 16:18).

The one who attempts to attract this kind of worship and adulation is playing the very devil. "Being greedy, indecent, or immoral is just another way of worshiping idols. You can be sure that people who behave in this way will never be part of the kingdom that belongs to Christ and to God" (Ephesians 5:5, CEV).

If you tell idolaters the object of their devotion is not God, they will immediately disagree with you. Of course this idol is God!

Instead of wanting what is good for us, we desire what we *think* is good for us. If the outcome of these mistakes is pain, we console ourselves by imagining that we are suffering for our own good.

—Guigo I: *Meditations*

A Personal Response

Examine my heart, O God. Do I have other gods? Have I placed my allegiance somewhere other than in you?

September 12 Be Slow to Categorize

> When the Pharisee who had invited [Jesus]
> saw this, he said to himself, "If this man were
> a prophet, he would know who is touching
> him and what kind of woman she is—that she
> is a sinner." *Luke 7:39*

Do not report that someone is a drunkard even if you have seen
that person drunk. Refrain from saying that so and so is an
adulterer even if that person has been caught in the act. A
single experience is not enough to justify such a label. The sun stood
still once to help Joshua win a battle and it was darkened for our Savior's victory, yet we don't say that the sun is stationary or dark. Noah
got drunk once. Lot got drunk twice. Neither man was a drunkard. Saint
Peter once blasphemed, but that did not make him blasphemous. To
earn the title it must be habitual. It is not right to call someone quick-
tempered or a thief on the basis of one observation.

Even if someone is addicted to vice for a long time, we risk
falsehood if we label that person. Simon the leper called Mary Magdalene a sinner. She certainly had been a sinner not long before, but
she was not any longer. She was sincerely penitent. Jesus took up for
her. God's goodness is so vast that it can change character. How can
we be certain that someone who was a sinner yesterday is the same
today? Never draw conclusions based on yesterday.

Here is the rule to follow: when you must condemn a vice, spare
as far as possible the person in whom it is found.

We can speak openly of infamous, notorious public sinners if we
are compassionate rather than arrogant. We should take no pleasure
in the mistakes of others. It is our duty to denounce as sternly as
possible schismatic sects and their leaders. It is an act of love to cry
out against the wolf when it is among the sheep.

—Francis de Sales: *The Devout Life*

 A Personal Response

Like you, Lord, let me take up for the accused. If I can't
defend the accused, at least let me be silent.

September 13   # The Healing of a Soul

Night and day among the tombs and in the hills [a man possessed by an evil spirit] would cry out and cut himself with stones. *Mark 5:5*

My soul was like a broken vessel. It was driven by the winds. It was tossed headlong into despair. It was shattered to pieces on the rocks.

I gained one advantage. I realized that the Scriptures were the Word of God. I felt the steadiness of Jesus Christ, the rock of our salvation. What was done could not be undone, added to, or altered. Even when I thought I might have committed some unpardonable sin, the Word of God assured me I had not.

Greatly depressed, I walked to a neighboring town and sat down on a park bench. I sat still and thought about all of this for a long time. When I looked around, it seemed that the stones in the streets and the tiles on the houses were shunning me. I thought the sun gave its light begrudgingly. I felt unwelcomed in this world. Everyone else seemed much happier than I.

Then I sighed deeply within my soul and asked, "How can God comfort such a wretch as I am?" I had no sooner said it than I heard an answering echo-like voice, "This sin is not deadly."

I felt like I had crawled out of a grave! I cried out again, "Lord, how could you say such a thing as this?" I was impressed with the correctness of what I had heard. It was the right word at the right time. It came with power, sweetness, light, and glory. At last I felt I could actually be open to forgiveness. Only someone who has shared my experience can understand what I felt.

The next evening I sought the Lord. I prayed. I wept. I cried out to God with a strong voice, "O Lord, please! Show me that you love me with an everlasting love!" As soon as I said it, this sweet echo returned to me: "I have loved you with an everlasting love." Now I went to bed in quiet. When I awakened the next morning, it was fresh upon my soul, and I believed it.

—John Bunyan: *Grace Abounding*

A Personal Response

If you, O Lord, kept a record of sins, O Lord, who could stand? But with you there is forgiveness.—Psalm 130:3-4

September 14 **An Exchange in Troubled Times**

God is our refuge and strength, an ever-present help in trouble. *Psalm 46:1*

od speaks: My child, do not be worn out by the work you are doing for me. Let no setback discourage you. I will give you strength. Remember, you will not be working here forever. If you will wait a little while, things will change. Soon enough all labor and trouble will end.

Keep going, then. Work faithfully in my garden, and I will be your wages. Write, read, sing, mourn, be silent, and pray. Take all blows gladly. The kingdom of heaven is worth all this and much more.

A Christian responds: Heavenly Father, the time has come for me to be tested. It is proper that I should now suffer something for your sake. Before time began you knew this hour would come. Outwardly, I will be tormented; inwardly, I will be with you. For a little while, I will be a failure and an object of scorn. Go down with me Father, so I may rise with you in the dawning of a new light.

Such humbling is good for me, Lord. It helps me throw away haughtiness and pride. It is valuable that "I endure scorn for your sake, and shame covers my face" (Psalm 69:7). This makes me turn to you for comfort rather than to others. Thank you for this painful challenge. You know how troubled times can scour away the rust of sin. Do with me as you choose.

O Lord,
let me know what is worth knowing,
love what is worth loving,
praise what pleases you,
honor what is worthy in your sight,
and avoid all that is evil.

—Thomas à Kempis: *The Imitation of Christ*

 A Personal Response

Teach me who I am in your sight. As I work through painful challenges, help me understand that you are my worth.

September 15   # Facing the Day Ahead

He is like the light of morning at sunrise on a cloudless morning, like the brightness after rain that brings the grass from the earth.

2 Samuel 23:4

W hen you begin the day, think about your insensitivity to God. Remember that he is constantly calling you and that you need to respond.

Think about your forgetfulness of your high value to God and how "your body is a temple of the Holy Spirit" (1 Corinthians 6:19).

Say to your soul, "Let's get going! Follow God. Make good plans and pursue them. Live in a manner that will please God. Consider this day's work an assignment from God."

Pray for God's help. Ask him to give you the ability to make the most profitable use of your opportunities.

Begin well and go on to better.

Do everything for the glory of God and the benefit of others.

Consider time lost if you do not use it to at least think of the glory of God and seek for a way to do something for someone else's advantage.

—John Bradford: *Daily Meditations*

A Personal Response

Such a day would dawn beautifully for me, O Lord. Yet there are so many forces that pull at me! Distractions from such a plan for a day lie in wait all around me. And by the end of the day I am tired, sometimes battered, and always admitting that I have had a difficult time thinking of your glory and trying to help others. Lord, help me.

September 16 One Way Only

In everything, do to others what you would
have them do to you, for this sums up the
Law and the Prophets. *Matthew 7:12*

When another person says bad things about you, and it is
not true, you are not harmed. The one talking is the one
who is hurt. Suppose someone calls gold "dung." What
harm is that to the gold?

If the accusations against you are true, you can learn a lesson
from it. Here is something in yourself to be careful about.

The reverse is also true. When you are praised, you receive no
benefit.

Criticize another person only in love. Let love be the motive. If
you reprove or chastise someone for any other reason, you condemn
yourself. Apply the same attitude toward others that you want God to
have toward you.

—Guigo I: *Meditations*

A Personal Response

Nothing, Lord, is more revealing of my true self than admitting
the things I like and dislike. If I do not respond to a work of
art, I am saying more about myself than about the art. Broaden
my acceptance of others. Help me to see the best in them.

September 17   # The Loudest Speech

> It is true that some preach Christ out of envy
> and rivalry, but others out of good will.
> *Philippians 1:15*

A speaker's quality of life is more important than eloquence.
It is possible to teach others without gaining any benefit for
your own soul. Paul said, "[Some] preach Christ out of
selfish ambition, not sincerely, supposing that they can stir up
trouble for me while I am in chains. But what does it matter? The
important thing is that in every way, whether from false motives or
true, Christ is preached. And because of this I rejoice" (Philippians
1:17-18).

Someone may be proclaiming truth but not speaking authenti-
cally. Evil people may teach what is good. Our Lord gave us this
advice: "Obey [the Pharisees] and do everything they tell you. But do
not do what they do, for they do not practice what they preach"
(Matthew 23:3). While they may help many by teaching what they do
not observe, they would help many more if they would do as they say.

A Christian teacher offers an example to others. A manner of
living may be something like an eloquent speech. On the other hand,
it may cancel the best words. If we think about this carefully, we will
see that leaders do not always say the good things they attempt to say.
Their words are denied by their deeds. The apostle said of them,
"They claim to know God, but by their actions they deny him" (Titus
1:16).

—Augustine: *On Christian Doctrine*

A Personal Response

Help me, Lord, to be alert to authenticity. Let me neither mani-
pulate nor be manipulated. Above all, keep me honest in my
life of faith.

September 18 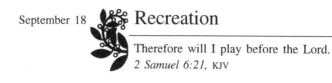 Recreation

Therefore will I play before the Lord.
2 Samuel 6:21, KJV

It is important to take a break now and then. Recreation relaxes both mind and body. Cassian tells us that a hunter found Saint John cradling a living bird in his hand and gently petting its neck. The hunter asked him why he was wasting his time like that. John asked him why he didn't keep his bow always taut. "It would lose its spring if I did," the hunter answered. The apostle replied, "Then don't be surprised if I relax sometimes. After a little recreation I can concentrate better."

It is a mistake to be so strict, driven, and austere that you can neither play a little yourself nor allow others a little diversion. Get out into the open air. Have some fun! Play the lute, sing, go hunting. Enjoy some innocent recreation. The only requirement is enough prudence to give it a proper time, place, and quantity.

—Francis de Sales: *The Devout Life*

 A Personal Response

Teach me how to play, how to enjoy, how to relax, Lord—and also what "a proper time, place, and quantity" truly means.

September 19 Beauty

Let the beauty of the Lord our God be upon us. *Psalm 90:17,* KJV

Regulate your senses carefully. Use them for creative purposes and not for mere pleasure.

When something pleasing stimulates your perception, try to understand what is happening. Remind yourself of the Creator of all things. When you admire something beautiful remember that, in itself, it is nothing. Let your thoughts soar to the great hand of God that produced it. Place all your delight in him. Say, "O my God, you are the universal source of all good things! The perfections of your creation are but a faint shadow of your glory!"

If you see lovely trees and beautiful flowers, remind yourself that they have life only through the design of God. The sight of animals can bring into your mind and heart the One who authored sensibility and motion.

When the beauty of other people impresses you, immediately distinguish between external and internal beauty. All physical beauty flows from the beauty of God. It is an almost imperceptible drop flowing from a source without limit, an immense ocean from which uncountable perfections keep coming. God is the source of everything beautiful!

When you meet people who are intelligent, kind, friendly, or gifted in any way, try to determine how much of that is their own and how much they have received from God. When you do something good, remember that God is the author of the act. You are but his instrument. When you taste something delicious, think how God gives food taste.

If you smell a pleasant scent, do not be satisfied with the fragrance alone. Let your spirit go to God. Ask the author of all sweetness to lift your soul to himself as a fragrant perfume.

When you hear beautiful music, give God the praise for harmony and melody.

—Lawrence Scupoli: *The Spiritual Combat*

 A Personal Response

Open my eyes, that I may see. Open my ears, that I may hear. Open my heart, that I may praise your name, O God!

September 20   ## Why We Work at It

When the plowman plows and the thresher threshes, they ought to do so in the hope of sharing in the harvest. *1 Corinthians 9:10*

We work because we want to achieve something. The point of the labor is making some money. When the farmer tills the soil and plants some seeds, that farmer expects to reap a harvest. One engaged in international commerce will face every hazard of the ocean, even life-threatening risks, in order to turn a profit.

It is the same way in the kingdom of Heaven. A person will turn away from the world and engage in serious prayer because there is a strong desire for the things of God. The things such a person wants are not totally dependent upon personal effort. The Spirit is also at work.

Once you have experienced the goodness of the Lord, when his light replaces the darkness of this world, there will be an indescribable joy. It will be even more pleasurable than what the merchant feels selling those goods at a profit.

If the rich person fears thieves, the religious person fears those attitudes and behaviors which will steal the fruit of the Spirit.

—Pseudo-Macarius: *Homilies*

A Personal Response

Is it enough, Lord, for me to earn your good favor? Do I seek other things for myself? Am I trying to be a Christian because I think it might increase my profits? Do I attend church because of the business contacts I can make? Bless me and my family, dear God, but let me be content to live as a child in your light with no ulterior motives.

Spiritual Pilgrimage

Jesus went through the towns and villages,
teaching as he made his way to Jerusalem.
Luke 13:22

There was a man who wanted to go to Jerusalem. He had no idea how to get there. He asked someone he considered to be an authority.

"You can't get there without a lot of hard work. It is a dangerous trip. There are many roads you can take, but people are getting robbed and killed on them all the time. No one ever gets there. There is only one safe way to travel to Jerusalem."

The would-be pilgrim was excited. "I don't care what troubles I suffer. Tell me the way. I will faithfully follow your instructions."

"Here is the right road. Be sure to follow my directions. Don't let anything hinder you. Allow no pleasurable distractions. Keep moving. Think only that you want to be in Jerusalem. Consider nothing else. If you are beaten and robbed, scorned, and despised, do not fight back. Bear the pain and continue your journey. Don't listen to questions or attempt to answer them. If you are offered gifts, don't accept them. Always keep your mind on Jerusalem. If you do this, you will reach your goal."

Jerusalem stands for the sight of Jesus, contemplation of the perfect love of God. If you are on your way to this Jerusalem, carry two things with you: humility and love. Humility says, "I am nothing. I have nothing." Love says, "I only desire one thing—Jesus." These two strings make good harmony on the harp of the soul when they are plucked by the talented finger of reason. They resonate. The more you are humble, the more you love.

—Walter Hilton: *The Scale of Perfection*

 A Personal Response

Help me to see that I have not already arrived. I am on my way on a journey toward you, Jesus. Bring yourself—my destination—into clear, sharp focus.

September 22 # Taking It As It Comes

> God blesses the people who patiently endure testing. Afterward they will receive the crown of life that God has promised to those who love him. *James 1:12*, NLT

Patience is a willing acceptance of things that are bitter. The one who is patient does not complain about adversity but praises God at all times. Persecution, worries, and illness are willingly endured.

If sinners place burdens upon our backs, we will not be weighed down if we bear them patiently. They may bring us a little pain, but they also bring us a crown. Holy people welcome tribulations. They use them as guides to eternity.

You simply will not know if you are strong or weak unless you are tempted. If you are at peace, there is no way you can know whether or not you are patient. It is only when your attention is grasped by an injury that you will determine your degree of patience. When not under attack, many seem to be patient. But even a mere whisper of trouble can stir them into resentfulness and rage. If they hear a single word of criticism, they return twice as much, using harsh words.

The only way to protect yourself against the darts of an enemy is to smother the darts with humility and the love of Christ. You can be sure you are on the road to perfection if scorn is like praise to you, poverty like wealth, and shortage like a feast. You can live with either extreme in the same spirit of contentment.

The praise of others will mislead you. The things your critics say will confound you even more. Give little value to either.

—Richard Rolle: *The Mending of Life*

A Personal Response

Are you asking me to "shrug it off," Lord? That seems inadequate, unreal, unhealthy. Where are you leading me? Humility? Love of Christ? I know I need to grow.

The Importance of Abstraction

You shall not make for yourself an idol in the form of anything in heaven above or on the earth beneath or in the waters below. *Exodus 20:4*

Don't mistake smoke for light. God is Spirit. God has no bodily form we can imagine. Your spirit will remain in a deep calm during a time of prayer if you can grasp the meaning of "immaterial knowledge."

God has compassion on the ignorant. He will visit even someone who is as insignificant as you. When he does, you will receive the most wonderful gift of prayer.

In the same way that bread nourishes the body and virtue feeds the soul, spiritual prayer is food for the intellect. Never try to conceive some image of God or to visualize his form when you pray. Suppress every desire to see angels or even Christ. This can dim your wits. You will be accepting a wolf for your shepherd.

Egotism is the source of the illusions in your mind. It attempts to wrap God in form and pattern. The healthiest spiritual goal is to achieve formlessness in a time of prayer.

If you want to pray in the spirit, take nothing from the flesh. It would be a dark cloud obscuring your vision.

I heard of a man who prayed often and was very dear to God. Two angels joined him in a walk across the desert, one on his right side and one on his left. He paid no attention to them. He did not want them to distract him from what Jesus called "the better part." He concentrated on what the apostle Paul said: "Neither angels nor principalities nor powers can separate us from the love of Christ" [Romans 8:35, quoted from Evagrius's memory].

—Evagrius Ponticus: *Chapters on Prayer*

 A Personal Response

I am an ordinary person, Lord. It is easy for me to conceive spiritual things in earthly terms. Abstractions seem dull, lifeless. I see there is a higher form of prayer that is without images. Give me the discipline to work on this.

A Time and Place to Pray

Arise, cry out in the night, as the watches of the night begin; pour out your heart like water in the presence of the Lord. *Lamentations 2:19*

If you want to pray, you must choose not only the right place but also the right time. Quiet time is best. The deep silence when others are asleep inspires natural prayer. Prayer is a secret thing at night. It is witnessed only by God. It is pleasing, untainted, modest prayer. There are no interruptions, no noise. It becomes pure prayer, sincere prayer. There is no trace of exhibitionism or human adulation.

—Bernard of Clairvaux: *On the Song of Songs*

A Personal Response

Lord, teach me what the modest and untainted prayer of the quiet hours is.

September 25 Freed to Give

Since God did not spare even his own Son but gave him up for us all, won't God, who gave us Christ, also give us everything else?
Romans 8:32, NLT

We are attached and subservient to worldly goods. We are anxious to get enough of them to satisfy our needs. This does not allow us to be free to help others because we imagine that certain things are indispensable, and we never think that we have enough.

Only the security of knowing that we are all God's children will allow us to think that we already possess enough for the present and the future. Only faith can put our heart at peace. What good could God withhold from us? His love is too great! Once we understand this, we will be ready to do good to all others. It is a blessed sense of security.

It is the nature of true goodness that it cannot hoard for itself. It pours out as far and wide as possible. A good tree bears good fruit.

—Martin Bucer: *Instruction in Christian Love*

 A Personal Response

I long for that kind of confidence, dear God. It not self-confidence. It is trust in you. It will be wonderful when my own self-image is formed by believing that I am your child. My worth is based not on what I can accumulate but on your great love for me. Once I have that superior security, I will begin to regard others more highly and be able to share with them more freely.

September 26 ## Misusing God's Name

You shall not misuse the name of the Lord
your God, for the Lord will not hold anyone
guiltless who misuses his name. *Exodus 20:7*

The name of God can be misused in several ways. The first is to give the title and name of God to those things which are not God. The heathen called the sun, the moon, and the stars gods. They have considered kings and emperors gods. Idols and statues have been considered gods.

A common way of misusing God's name today is by swearing deceitfully when we intend to deceive someone. Do as Christ teaches: "I tell you, Do not swear at all. . . . Simply let your 'Yes' be 'Yes,' and your 'No,' 'No'; anything beyond this comes from the evil one" (Matthew 5:34-37). If necessity or a public officer calls you to take an oath, then speak the truth. Be faithful to what you have sworn.

We also abuse the name of God with cursing and profanity. We damn by the name of God, a sin quite prevalent in our time. We can hear men, women, and children outrageously cursing in the name of God. God's name is to be respected. It is not to be used to wish miseries, plagues, and adversities on others. It is a great wickedness to wish evil things by the name of God.

The name of God is also misused when we make false interpretations of Holy Scripture, or when we make a trifle or a laughing sport of the words of Scripture. This abuse causes contempt for the Word of God and diminishes its authority.

This is a commandment of great importance. The right ways to use the name of God are by praying to him, by confessing his name and his Word, and by thanksgiving. Speak God's name reverently.

—Thomas Cranmer: *Catechismus*

A Personal Response

My manner of living is a speaking of your name, dear God.
Since I have let it be known that I am a Christian, everything
I think, do, and say, is thought, done, and said in your name.
Help me to live faithfully to your divine name.

September 27 **Discussing Illness**

The Lord nurses them when they are sick and eases their pain and discomfort. *Psalm 41:3,* NLT

Moaning and complaining when we have a little ailment is a sign of imperfection. If the sickness is bearable, don't talk about it. If the illness is serious, it will talk about itself with a distinctive kind of moaning.

If you are really sick, say so and take your medicine. If you have a minor ailment which comes and goes, don't make a habit of talking about it all the time. Our bodies have one fault: the more we cater to them, the more things they want.

There are many poor people with no one who will listen to them complain. Poverty and self-indulgence don't get along.

Learn to suffer a little for the love of God without needing to tell everyone about it. Keep your minor ailments a secret between you and God. Talking about them does nothing at all to mitigate them.

Serious illness is another matter. I am thinking, here, about ordinary ailments which you may have, but they are slight. You still can keep going. There is no need to bother everyone else.

Consider the holy hermits of past days. The endured tremendous sufferings in solitude. They were cold, hungry, and exposed to desert sun. They had no one to complain to except God. Do you think they were iron men? They were not. They were as frail as we are. When we start to subjugate these bodies of ours, they give us much less trouble. Our bodies mock us. Let's mock our bodies.

This is not a trifling matter. God will help us to gain mastery of our bodies.

—Teresa of Avila: *The Way of Perfection*

A Personal Response

I admit it, Lord. Sometimes it is extremely pleasant to know that someone cares about me and is willing to take care of me—even when I am not very sick. Let me vividly perceive *your interest in me.*

Spiritual Mushrooms

A good tree cannot bear bad fruit, and a bad tree cannot bear good fruit. *Matthew 7:18*

The object of devotion is not sighs, tears, and spiritual delight. Many experience some pleasant consolations and remain vicious people. They have neither the true love of God nor authentic devotion. When Saul chased David into the wilderness, he entered a cave where David and his men were hiding. David had opportunities to kill Saul, but he spared his life. As Saul was leaving in safety, David called out to Saul to prove his own innocence and to demonstrate his mercy. Saul was touched. He called David his child, wept, and thanked him. There could have been no greater display of sweetness and tenderness on Saul's part. Even so, Saul's heart had not changed and he did not cease from pursuing David with cruelty.

In the same way, some people think about God's goodness and our Savior's passion, and feel a great tenderness of heart. They may even utter sighs and tearful prayers. They seem to be filled with intense devotion. But when a test comes, what a difference! A passing shower in the hot summer sends down great drops of rain. They fall to earth but do not sink in. All they produce is mushrooms. Likewise, these tender tears fail to penetrate the heart. For all the display of devotion they will not contribute a penny of their ill-gotten wealth. They will not surrender one of their perversities. They will not endure the least inconvenience for the service of the suffering Christ they were just weeping over. Any good feelings they get from their moment of devotion are nothing but spiritual mushrooms.

These things play tricks on us. They keep us from looking for a more authentic devotion to God. True devotion is a constant, determined, prompt, and active will to do what we know is pleasing to God.
—Francis de Sales: *The Devout Life*

A Personal Response

Lord, how can I tell if such things are good or evil? I can know them by their fruits.

September 29 ## God Is Revealed—
Not Discovered

> Then the Lord reached out, touched my lips, and said to me, "Listen, I am giving you the words you must speak." *Jeremiah 1:9,* TEV

God is a Word. The Word that is God is unexpressed. The only one who can speak this word is God himself. God speaks or God does not speak.

If you think you know something about God and describe it in words, the God you have described is not God. God is greater than your terminology. God is far greater than your language. He is inexpressible.

My mouth may speak of God, but so does the presence of a stone.

Actions are often more clearly understood than words. We can reflect God in all we do. Even then, it is only a tidbit of God we have communicated.

—Meister Eckhart: *Sermons*

 A Personal Response

If I were able to climb beyond the angels and touch you, O God, I would still be inadequate. It is not in my power to tell anyone of more than a fraction of your glory.

September 30 Moodswing

Being in anguish, he prayed more earnestly.
Luke 22:44

S o you feel one way today! You will feel another way tomorrow. Like it or not, you will be somewhat manic-depressive
as long as you live.

Some days you will be happy and other days you will be sad,
some days calm and other days troubled,
some days faithful and other days faithless,
some days vigorous and other days sluggish,
some days solemn and other days lighthearted.

But if you are well taught by the Spirit, you will live above such
changes. You will pass through your various moods unshaken and
push on toward your goal of seeking God only.

The clearer your target, the better you will weather emotional
storms.

—Thomas à Kempis: *The Imitation of Christ*

A Personal Response

I love you, my God. You are all I could ask for. What more
can I desire? When you are present, I live in delight. You give
me a calm heart, a tranquil mind, and a festive spirit. With
your help I can rejoice in all circumstances and praise you at
all times.—Thomas à Kempis

God Is Not in the Details

> Don't get involved in foolish, ignorant arguments that only start fights. The Lord's servants must not quarrel but must be kind to everyone. They must be able to teach effectively and be patient with difficult people. *2 Timothy 2:23-24,* NLT

Avoid arguments about the trivial details of faith. You don't need a religion that is composed of opinions. People who dispute violently about the fine points of religion are usually the least acquainted with God. If your religion is all in your firmly held opinions, you will be loud and obnoxious. If your religion rests in the knowledge and love of God, you will communicate pleasantly and be an attractive representative.

It is a rare thing to improve on a truth that is already well-known. My advice to you is not to spend too much time, thought, energy, and speech on disputes that have little to do with spiritual health. When you find hypocrites trying to nourish themselves with husks and shells, feed them on God's joys.

I wish you could defend every one of God's truths. But concentrate on the important things. The least controversial points are the ones that are most valuable to the soul. Study texts like this:

> Anyone who teaches anything different, and does not keep to the sound teaching which is that of our Lord Jesus Christ, the doctrine which is in accordance with true religion, is simply arrogant and must be full of self-conceit—with a craze for questioning everything and arguing about words. All that can come of this is jealousy, contention, abuse and wicked mistrust of one another; and unending disputes by people who are neither rational nor informed and imagine that religion is a way of making a profit. (1 Timothy 6:3-5, JB)
>
> —Richard Baxter: *The Saints' Everlasting Rest*

A Personal Response

Lord, teach me that there are few arguments worth the time. Your truth doesn't need my defense. Show me how to focus on the important issues: how you love us, forgive us, change us.

October 2 Friends

This is my lover, this is my friend. *Song of Songs 5:16*

L
ove is the strongest passion of the soul. We become like
what we love. Guard against loving wrongly.

Friendship is the most dangerous of all loves. It is based
on communication. Like a communicable disease, we cannot communicate with another person without sharing the qualities of the
message.

All love is not friendship. We can love without being loved in
return. Friendship is mutual love. If it is not shared, it is not friendship.
But even this sharing is not enough. The people involved need to be
aware of this shared affection.

Young people tend to base their friendships on such things as a
fine mustache or head of hair, smiling glances, brand-name clothes,
and knowledge of what's in fashion. This is acceptable for those who
are still only in blossom and whose judgment is only in bud. These
friendships are passing things. They melt like snow in the sun.

There are some playful friendships between persons of the opposite
sex. There is no intention of marriage. These are merely phantoms of
friendship. They are not entitled to the name of either friendship or love.
People become entangled with these empty, foolish affections.

Some simply need to love or be loved. They give in to amorous
desires. As soon as they meet someone who appeals to them, they
begin fond communication. They do not even bother to examine the
other person's character. They are caught in sordid nets and have a
hard time getting themselves out of these entanglements. They are a
waste of time, a loss of honor, and satisfy nothing but an insatiable
curiosity. They think they have a right to expect something from it
all, but they are not sure what it is. In this game the one who catches
is also caught. Can you feel sorry for the snake charmer who is bitten
by a snake?

—Francis de Sales: *The Devout Life*

A Personal Response

O God, it is blindness to gamble away the greatest power of
the soul for such trivial stakes!—Francis de Sales

Waking Up to God

Great is the Lord, and most worthy of praise.
Psalm 48:1

We are only a fraction of your enormous creation, Lord, but we still want to praise you. You have made us for yourself and our hearts are restless until they rest in you. Which comes first, knowing you or praying to you? Surely no one can pray to you who does not know you. And yet, maybe we need to pray before we can really know you. The faith you infused in me, Lord, cries out to you.

O God, you are the greatest and the best,
the strongest,
the most merciful and just,
absolutely concealed and absolutely present,
beautiful,
mysterious,
never changing, but changing everything,
never new, yet never old,
always in action, yet always at rest,
attracting all things to yourself but needing none,
preserving and fulfilling and sheltering,
conceiving and nourishing and ripening,
continually seeking but lacking nothing,
you love without the confusion of emotion,
you are jealous, but without fear.
You owe us nothing and yet you give to us as though you were
    indebted to us.
You forgive what is due you, and yet lose nothing yourself.

After all of this, what have I said? What can anyone say when speaking of God?

—Augustine: *Confessions*

A Personal Response

My soul is too small to accommodate you. Enlarge it. It is in ruins. Repair it. I know there are things in it that are offensive to you. "Who can discern his errors? Forgive my hidden faults" (Psalm 19:12).—Augustine

October 4 · **God Is Busy Everywhere**

Then [Jesus] touched their eyes and said,
"According to your faith will it be done to you."
Matthew 9:29

Everything exists in God. All we can perceive is the activity of nature, but with faith we can see God at work. The tiniest particle of matter and the smallest moment of time contain something of God's concealed activity. God hides behind the curtain of his creation's business.

Jesus confused his disciples by his resurrection appearances. Sometimes he seemed disguised and they thought he was someone else. Then he would reveal himself clearly and they would know exactly who he was. This same Jesus, still living and active, continues to catch us by surprise if we do not have the eyes of faith.

There is hardly a moment when God does not approach us disguised as a challenge or responsibility. Our response to such opportunities includes and obscures his activity. Because his action is unobservable, we are taken by surprise and can interpret what happened only in retrospect. If we could lift the curtain and observe what is really happening, we would see God constantly at work. We would be rejoicing all the time, "It is the Lord!" (John 21:7). We would accept every experience that came our way as a gift from God.

Faith is God's interpreter. Without faith, all we hear is a noisy babbling. Faith identifies God at work. In the same way that Moses heard the voice of God in the burning bush, we, with faith to guide us, are able to perceive him in what appears to be clutter and confusion. Faith will transform our perception. In this life, faith is our light. With it we can know what we can't see, we can touch what we can't feel, we can strip the world of everything superficial. Faith is the combination to God's vault.

—Jean-Pierre de Caussade: *Abandonment to Divine Providence*

A Personal Response

Give me faith, dear God. Give me the kind of faith that will see the emptiness of the things most treasured in this world. Grant me a faith that will see you everywhere, all the time.

October 5 # A Taste for Goodness

The fear of the Lord is the beginning of wisdom; all who follow his precepts have good understanding. *Psalm 111:10*

Wisdom is a taste for goodness. We lost this taste almost from the time of creation. The serpent in the Garden of Eden poisoned our heart's palate. We lost our taste for goodness. A corrupt taste replaced it. "People's thoughts and actions are bent toward evil from childhood" (Genesis 8:21, NLT).

Wisdom is stronger than malice. It will drive away the taste for evil. It does this by introducing something better. Wisdom makes sensuality taste flat. It cleanses the palate of the heart. This clean palate tastes good wisdom, and nothing compares with it.

Many good deeds are done by people who have no taste for them. They are required to do them but find no joy in it. In the same way, many do evil without a taste for it. They are motivated by fear or need. They take no pleasure in evil.

That person is happy who has a taste for good and a distaste for evil. This is true wisdom.

"Wait for the Lord; be strong and take heart and wait for the Lord" (Psalm 27:14). That is *virtue.*

"Taste and see that the Lord is good" (Psalm 34:8). That is *wisdom.*

—Bernard of Clairvaux: *On the Song of Songs*

A Personal Response

Is this right, Lord? Is wisdom a taste for goodness? Then let more of us acquire that taste! Let reverence for you bless our world.

Divine Illumination

God, who said, "Let light shine out of darkness," made his light shine in our hearts to give us the light of the knowledge of the glory of God in the face of Christ. *2 Corinthians 4:6*

There is a spiritual sun that illumines the soul with an even greater intensity than the physical sun illumines a body on earth. This spiritual sun casts no shadows and never leaves half of the earth in darkness. It is as bright at night as it is in the day. It exists within us. No one can block any of its light. There is no place we can go to escape it. It never sets. The only clouds that can obscure it are our emotions. It is a glorious day. It shines on a primitive person in a dark cave. Even a blind person can walk in its light.

Human theories are plausible only in proportion to their agreement with this inner teacher, this inner light. This light within us is superior to us. We may deny it and ignore it, but if we pay attention to it there is no way we can contradict it. I appear to have two kinds of reasoning abilities. One is my own; the other is given. My own is flawed, rash, unpredictable, obstinate, ignorant, narrow. The other is perfect, constant, eternal, inexhaustible. How do I put my finger on this reason that is given from without? Where is it? It is so near and yet so far. It is God himself!

—François de Fénelon: *Meditations and Devotions*

A Personal Response

"Sun of my soul, Thou Savior dear, it is not night if Thou be near." Illumine me, my Lord. Be the light that brings insight and understanding.

October 7 # Usury

> After thinking about the situation, I spoke out against these nobles and officials. I told them, "You are oppressing your own relatives by charging them interest when they borrow money!" *Nehemiah 5:7,* NLT

Usury is an unhappy trade. This is the most miserable and shameful deception of all. Many simple people don't even know what it is. They have never heard the name of it. The world would be a happy place if no one knew of it. The more you learn to know it, the more you will abhor it.

Usury is lending money, corn, oil, wine, or any other thing with a written agreement to return it all plus a lot more. The nurses and breeders of usury are these: insatiable greediness, deceitfulness, unmercifulness, oppression, extortion, contempt of God, and hatred of others. It is watered, fed, and nourished by these cruel monsters.

Usury breeds misery. It consumes the rich and eats up the poor. It causes bankruptcies and destroys many households. Couples separate. Children are driven to beg for bread. These result from the unmerciful dealing of a covetous usurer. A usurer is worse than a thief. A thief is driven by extremity and need. The usurer is rich and has no needs. The thief steals in corners and dark places. The usurer steals openly and boldly in any place. The thief runs away. The usurer stays to steal another day. The thief understands he is doing wrong. The usurer thinks his gain is well gotten and never feels sorrowful about it.

—John Jewell: *Exposition on the Thessalonians*

A Personal Response

Lord, if usury is in any part of me—if I give to people only because I expect more back, if I oppress anyone for my gain, or if I admire anyone who delights in usury—forgive me. Cleanse me.

Fulfilling the Possible

Jesus looked at them intently and said,
"Humanly speaking, it is impossible. But with
God everything is possible." *Matthew 19:26*, NLT

First there is possibility. Then there is willingness. Ultimately, there is doing. They come in this order: our nature, our will, our action. God gives the possibility. The willing and the doing are our business. But even the possibility of willing and doing are a gift from God.

It is not possible to lack the possibility of good. This is inherent in me whether I want it or not. It is not an option.

—Pelagius: *Pro Libero Arbitrio*

 A Personal Response

You are omnipotent, God, but you allow me to wish what I will. You limit your own power. You give me freedom of choice. But it is only you in me, you who are infinitely good, who gives me the possibility—and the strength—to choose.

A Variety of Ways to God

Then Peter replied, "I see very clearly that God doesn't show partiality. In every nation he accepts those who fear him and do what is right." *Acts 10:34-35*, NLT

God does not put us all on the same road. If you think you are on the lowest path of all, you may actually be on the highest in the Lord's view.

For me, contemplation and meditation are important. But these are God's gifts to me and are not necessary for salvation. It is not something God demands of us.

Don't be discouraged, then, and stop praying or participating in the community of faith. The Lord is not in a hurry. He gives to others now. He will give to you later.

Personally, I endured fourteen years without ever meditating satisfactorily unless I was reading something. I am not alone in this. Many Christians can't meditate even when they are reading. The best they can do is recite vocal prayers. Some have a problem with a short attention span. Unable to concentrate, they restlessly try to focus on God while fending off a thousand silly thoughts about religion.

I know a very old woman who is living an excellent life. I wish I were more like her. She is a penitent and a great servant of God. For years she has been praying the classic prayers aloud. Mental prayer is an impossibility for her. Many people are like this. This does not make them second-class Christians.

Unfortunately, many such people think they must be at fault. They think they are backward or handicapped. Those who are called to an active ministry should not murmur against others who are absorbed in prayer. It is all in the same package. Whether your specialty is meditation and prayers or caring for the sick and sweeping the floors in service to Christ, what should it matter? We are to do our best at whatever we do.

—Teresa of Avila: *The Way of Perfection*

A Personal Response

Lord, we don't all travel the same path to you. Why, then, do we want everyone to have a religious experience and a religious form of expression that is just like ours?

October 10 # Listening to Authority

Your servants are ready to do whatever our lord the king chooses. *2 Samuel 15:15*

When an Epistle, or Psalm, or Gospel is read in your hearing, remember whose words you hear. Remind yourself that these are the words of a gracious God. God is speaking to you for your benefit.

Why do so many have little regard for the Word of God? Why do they doubt it and suspect it? Why are they so quickly weary of it? Why do they give it no reverence?

It is because they don't think about where it comes from and for whose best interests it is written.

Let us not be ashamed to give a valued place to the Bible. Let it awaken our senses.

—John Jewell: *Of the Holy Scriptures*

A Personal Response

I will not go wrong if I allow the Bible to be authoritative for my faith. Spare me, Lord God, from twisting and distorting and doubting what you are telling me in the sacred book. Help me to listen as a child.

October 11 Adolescent Faith

When your words came, I ate them; they were
my joy and my heart's delight, for I bear your
name, O Lord God Almighty. *Jeremiah 15:16*

The sermons of Ambrose convinced me that all those deceptive knots others had tied around the Scriptures could be untied. As I listened to him, I was ashamed that I had been barking all those years, not against the Church but against imaginary doctrines. I had impulsively spoken against things I should first have learned more about. The Church never taught the things I accused her of teaching. It was refreshing to hear Ambrose repeat so often to his congregation, "The letter kills, but the Spirit gives life" (2 Corinthians 3:6).

He drew aside the veil of mystery and made clear the spiritual meaning of things which could not be accepted literally. I disagreed with nothing he said, but there were some things I still could not understand. I resisted because I wanted to be as sure of spiritual things as that seven and three equal ten.

Lord, with a gentle and merciful touch you worked on my heart. I thought of the many things I believed which I had not seen, or which happened when I was not present—so much history, so many facts about places I had never visited, so many things mentioned by others. Daily living requires belief in these things. Most of all, I was impressed with the fact that I believed I was the child of particular parents on no other authority than that I had been told it. What is so different about accepting the authority of the Bible? Since we are not able to discover the truth by reasoning, we need the Scriptures. The Bible speaks to all in clear language, and yet it also demands the close attention of scholarly minds.

I thought about these things and you were near me. I sighed and you listened. I wandered along the broad road of the world, but you did not forsake me.

—Augustine: *Confessions*

 A Personal Response
Lord, let your Spirit and your Word teach me truth.

October 12 Desperate Times

I am worn out from groaning; all night long I flood my bed with weeping and drench my couch with tears. *Psalm 6:6*

With his complaints, David speaks to God in the Psalms as though he were talking to someone who is ignorant of what he is suffering. It seems as though David thinks God is not taking care of him and knows nothing of his problems.

But no matter how deep and dark the dungeon of desperation is, the eyes of faith can find plenty of goodness in God. The storm may not cease at once. It is enough to cast out this anchor of faith. God will surely preserve your ship.

—John Knox: *Exposition of the Sixth Psalm*

A Personal Response

Assure me that I am not alone in any difficulty. Teach me there is no place so far away that it is beyond your sight. Give me the faith to turn to you for help.

October 13 Praise

Let another praise you, and not your own
mouth; someone else, and not your own lips.
Proverbs 27:2

When you enjoy praise you destroy it. If you delight in
being praised you cease being worthy of it. It is impossible to praise the person who seeks praise.

The one who is praised has done something worthwhile. The one who wants to be praised is merely arrogant.

Quietly and humbly accept any rebuke that comes to you as being your own opinion of yourself. Reject all praises as being the opposite of your own opinion.

Try to be the kind of person you would praise. Don't want to be praised. Want to be good.

—Guigo I: *Meditations*

A Personal Response

Applause is a heady drug, Lord. Let me pass on to you the kudos I receive. You are the vine. I am a twig.

Recovery

> The Lord is good, a refuge in times of trouble.
> He cares for those who trust in him. *Nahum 1:7*

Take your problems promptly to God. He could help you much faster if you were not so slow in turning to prayer, but you try everything else first.

Now that you have caught your breath and your trouble has passed, recuperate in God's mercies. God is near you to repair all damage and to make things better than before. Is anything too hard for God? Where is your faith? Stand strong in God. Have patience and courage. Comfort will come in time. Wait. He will come to you with healing.

Are you anxious about the future? What will that gain you but sorrow? "Do not worry about tomorrow, for tomorrow will worry about itself. Each day has enough trouble of its own" (Matthew 6:34).

What a waste to be disturbed or joyful about future events which may never materialize! When you think you are far from God, he is really quite near. When you feel that all is lost, sometimes the greatest gain is ready to be yours. Don't judge everything by the way you feel right now. If, for a while, you feel no comfort from God, he has not rejected you. He has set you on the road to the kingdom of heaven.

It is better for you to experience a little adversity than to have everything exactly as you choose. Otherwise, you may become mistakenly self-satisfied. What God has given, he can take away. He can return it again when he pleases. When God gives something to you, it is on loan. When he takes it back, he is not asking for anything that is yours. "Every good and perfect gift is from above, coming down from the Father of the heavenly lights, who does not change like shifting shadows" (James 1:17).

—Thomas à Kempis: *The Imitation of Christ*

A Personal Response

Lord Jesus, you did not send your disciples out into the world to enjoy earthly pleasures, but to do battle; not to receive honor, but to receive contempt; not to be idle, but to work; not to rest, but, in patience, to reap a harvest. —Thomas à Kempis

October 15 **False Devotion**

He will die for lack of discipline, led astray by
his own great folly. *Proverbs 5:23*

God is a spirit. Anyone who wishes to become one with God must live in a depth of spirit. The more refined your spirit becomes, the less it will be contaminated by physical things. It is natural for us to think of spiritual things in physical ways. Other people may need to see your posture to understand that you are praying, but God does not.

It is not my intention to separate what God has joined together. We are both body and spirit. God desires to be served in both. I am asking you to be careful not to think in a material way about what can only be understood spiritually.

Let me give you a simple example. What if novices read or hear about the necessity of drawing understanding into the inner self, or perhaps the importance of rising above the self. All too often this is taken literally. Abandoning humble prayer, the novices plunge into what they consider to be true spiritual exercises within their soul. This is the quickest way to physical and spiritual death. It is madness and not wisdom.

Such people do unnatural things. They put themselves into stressful situations. They ask too much of their imagination. The devil has the ability to put together false lights and sounds, trick smells and tastes, weird sensations and perceptions. Some consider this kind of illusion a serene awareness of God. They are more like sheep suffering from brain disease.

—Anonymous: *The Cloud of Unknowing*

A Personal Response
Spare me, Lord, from the traps of my own understanding.

No One Is Perfect

> Do not judge, or you too will be judged. For in the same way you judge others, you will be judged, and with the measure you use, it will be measured to you. *Matthew 7:1-2*

A sick person is not necessarily sick all over. Certain organs may be perfectly healthy. One may be desperately ill and still have good eyesight. While some bodily members may be weak, others are very strong.

It is the same way in the spiritual life. One may be healthy in this and that area, but not in another. There is always some imperfection.

For this reason Christians are instructed by their Lord not to be judgmental of others. Regardless of who or what they are, the rule applies. They could be outcasts of society, bad people. But we are to consider everyone the same way. Never judge, despise, and classify another person. Regard everyone as flawless. If someone is crippled, see that person as not crippled. It is an indicator of purity of heart when you can look at a sinner and have mercy, notice a weak person and feel compassion.

Christians will have an attitude that is simply different from secular people. Their minds work another way. They belong to another world.

—Pseudo-Macarius: *Homilies*

A Personal Response

Please help me to understand that you see all of the weaknesses of others—and all my weaknesses too, Lord. Even so, you love us all. Give me divine patience with the weaknesses of others. Give me your eye that I may look upon people's flaws with Christ's compassion.

A Little Effort—A Big Reward

The Lord is near to all who call on him, to all who call on him in truth. *Psalm 145:18*

God does not lay a great burden on us—
a little thinking of him,
a little adoration,
sometimes to pray for grace,
sometimes to offer him your sorrows,
sometimes to thank him for the good things he does.

Lift up your heart to him even at meals and when you are in company. The least little remembrance will always be acceptable to him. You don't have to be loud. He is nearer to us than you think.

You don't have to be in church all the time in order to be with God. We can make a chapel in our heart where we can withdraw from time to time and converse with him in meekness, humility, and love. Everyone has the capacity for such intimate conversation with God, some more, some less. He knows what we can do. Get started. Maybe he is just waiting for one strong resolution on your part. Have courage.

I don't know what is to become of me. Peace of soul descends on me even in my sleep. I can't imagine what God has in mind for me, or for what purpose he keeps me. I am in such a profound calm that I fear nothing. What can frighten me when I am with God? I try to stay with him, in his presence, as much as possible.

—Brother Lawrence: *The Practice of the Presence of God*

A Personal Response

Can it be that if I will make a little effort, my awareness of your nearness will grow? How will I know unless I try? Help me, Lord, to try.

Solitude and Society

Rejoice in the Lord always. I will say it again:
Rejoice! Let your gentleness be evident to all.
The Lord is near. *Philippians 4:4-5*

If you are not under an obligation to mingle socially or entertain others in your home, remain within yourself. Entertain yourself. If visitors arrive or you are called out to someone for a good reason, go as one who is sent by God. Visit your neighbor with a loving heart and a good intention.

There is great risk in visiting mean and vicious people. It is something like exposure to rabies. As for ordinary social gatherings, we need to be neither too careful to participate in them nor impolite in condemning them. We can modestly do our duty.

A vine planted among olive trees produces oily grapes with tainted taste. In the same way a soul that is often a companion with virtuous people will absorb their good qualities.

In all of your mixing with others, be natural, sincere, and modest. Some people annoy others with their affectations. Some don't speak: they sing instead. Some take steps and must count every one out loud to you! This becomes irritating. Artificiality in social life is very disagreeable.

In addition to a mental solitude to which you can retreat even in the middle of a crowd, learn to love actual physical solitude. There is no need to go out into the desert. Simply spend some quiet time alone in your room, or in a garden, or some other place. There you can think some holy thoughts or do a little spiritual reading. One of the great bishops said, "I walk alone on the beach at sunset. I use such recreation to refresh myself and shake off a little of my ordinary troubles."

Our Lord received a glowing report from his apostles about how they had preached and what a great ministry they had done. Then he said to them, "Come with me by yourselves to a quiet place and get some rest" (Mark 6:31).

—Francis de Sales: *The Devout Life*

 A Personal Response

In good company or alone, Lord God, let me be with you.

October 19 Fraud

No one should wrong his brother or take advantage of him. *1 Thessalonians 4:6*

L et no one defraud another with false weights or false measure, or by lying words. Let your weights, measures, and words be true. "The Lord detests differing weights, and dishonest scales do not please him" (Proverbs 20:23). Let your profits be just. God's blessing will make you rich. What God does not bless will waste and consume you. It will do you no good. "Do to others what you would have them do to you" (Matthew 7:12). This is true business.

If you say more than the truth, if you take more than your product is worth, your conscience will know it is not yours. The mouth that is familiar with lying kills the soul. "The buyer haggles over the price, saying, 'It's worthless,' then brags about getting a bargain" (Proverbs 20:14, NLT).

Don't defraud your brother. He is your brother, whether he is rich or poor. He is your brother and a child of God. Will you wrong your brother? Will you oppress a child of God, and do that in the sight of God? If he is simple and unskilled, don't abuse his simplicity. Deal fairly. Don't allow your conscience to accuse you.

Be careful not to teach your children and servants to deceive others. After they have learned to deceive others, they will also deceive you. "Food gained by fraud tastes sweet to a man, but he ends up with a mouth full of gravel" (Proverbs 20:17). Ill-gotten goods have an ill end. I have seen great heaps of wealth suddenly blown away, and great houses decay.

—John Jewell: *Exposition on the Thessalonians*

 A Personal Response

Lord, if someone has taken advantage of me, let me pray for that person. And let me surrender my loss to the cost of education of us both.

October 20 **Weeds and Wheat**

When the wheat sprouted and formed heads,
then the weeds also appeared. *Matthew 13:26*

I f your faith is tried, examine yourself concerning your enemy.
You are being harmed and slandered. Perhaps you will lose
your job. How should you conduct yourself against such people?

If you can find it in your heart to pray for your accusers, to love
them with all your heart, and forgive everything they have done
against you, then you are one of those who has faith. You will want
them to be saved as well as yourself.

No one can compel you to do this. Jesus told a parable about a
man who sowed some good seed in his field. "But while everyone
was sleeping, his enemy came and sowed weeds among the wheat,
and went away" (Matthew 13:25). Rather than attempt to remove the
weeds that sprouted, Jesus said it is best to let them grow together
until the harvest. Otherwise, damage could be done to the good wheat
while tearing out the weeds. The preachers and ministers of the Word
of God do not have the authority to force people to goodness with
violence.

We can admonish all people. But we are not able to pull the
wicked out by the throat. This is not our duty. All things must be done
God's way. "Let them grow together."

If you live in a place where some bad people will not be reformed
or amend their lives in any way, don't run them out of town. Be
patient with them. Every town has such people. When you get a
chance, tell them of about Jesus.

—Hugh Latimer: *Fruitful Sermons*

 A Personal Response

Again, the best way is the most difficult, Lord. It is much
easier to get rid of the scoundrels than to wait for an unlikely
change of behavior.

Hidden Treasure

All the Law and the Prophets hang on these two commandments. Matthew 22:40

Here are two ideas given to us in the written Word of God. "Love the Lord your God with all your heart and with all your soul and with all your mind" (Matthew 22:37). "Love your neighbor as yourself" (Matthew 22:39). This is a description of the perfect life. It is the life God intends for us. It is possible for us. We would not be asked to do something that is beyond our ability. The seed of this unity remains in us. It waits for a perfect renewal.

This is the hidden treasure of every human soul. To call us to love God with all our hearts, to put on Christ, to walk according to the Spirit proves that these things are rooted in us. It would be pointless to give such a command if we could not do it.

This mystery of an inward life hidden in us is our most precious treasure. It would be a miserable mistake therefore to place religious goodness in outward observances, in ideas and opinions anyone can receive and practice. It would be a tragedy to treat the real power and operation of an inward life of God in our souls as fanaticism and enthusiasm. Everything taught us by Scripture demonstrates that the kingdom of heaven must be within us.

The Holy Spirit of God can tune and strike our souls like a musical instrument. This increases the harmony of divine praise, thanksgiving, and adoration which arises from a symphony of instruments and voices. To condemn this variety in the servants of God, or to be angry with those who play a different instrument, is a clear sign that we are spiritually undeveloped.

—William Law: *Mystical Writings*

A Personal Response

Lord, developing that inner life! What freedom and independence that would give me! It would allow me to rise above any circumstance. I could participate in all of life. This is truly a hidden treasure, a gift from you.

October 22 A Sermon for the Birds

Look at the birds of the air; they do not sow or reap or store away in barns, and yet your heavenly Father feeds them. Are you not much more valuable than they? *Matthew 6:26*

While walking near Cannara and Bevegna, Saint Francis saw an unusual flocking of various birds in the trees along the road. It was such an impressive gathering of birds he told his companions to wait for him on the road while he went into the field to speak to "our sisters, the birds."

When he began to preach, the birds came closer to him, exhibiting no sign of fear. Brother James of Massa, a trustworthy man of God, said that he heard this from Brother Masseo, who was there.

In essence, this is what Saint Francis said to the birds: "My little sisters, remember to praise God because you are indebted to him. You are free to fly wherever you please. He has given you beautiful clothes. He provides you with food and teaches you how to sing. He saved you with Noah's ark and helped you to be fruitful and multiply. Thank him for the air you fly in. Thank him for the water you drink from rivers and springs. Thank him for the high cliffs and trees where you can build your nests. Thank him that you are not required to sow or reap, spin or weave. God gives you and your children everything you need. Such things can only mean that God loves you very much. Therefore, my little sisters, remember to thank and praise God."

The birds responded visibly to his preaching. When he dismissed them with the sign of the cross, they flew into the air singing a lovely song.

—Ugolino: *The Little Flowers of St. Francis*

A Personal Response

Is it possible, Creator of us all, that I can move into such harmony with your creation that I will discover a basic kinship? A beautiful thought!

October 23 Lending

Love your enemies, do good to them, and lend
to them without expecting to get anything back.
Luke 6:35

If you see someone in need, open your heart. Be merciful. Lend
in the spirit of mercy. Sometimes people in great need are
ashamed to beg. They will promise to pay you back. Instead of
lending, give. Say to them, "Here is as much as you need, or as
much as I can give you now. If you can return it, that will be good.
Then I can give it to someone else another time. But if you can't
pay it back, don't worry about it. Accept it as a gift. We are all
God's children. God wants us to help each other."

If you lend to someone who uses poor business judgment and
loses it all, be restrained. Don't rush to sue. Remember how God has
promised to bless the patient and the meek. Nevertheless, because
such persons corrupt society, corrective steps may be taken. If you
have lent to a fox who uses subterfuge to keep what is rightfully yours,
and the law is no help, be content to let it go. Don't let the wickedness
of others pluck you away from God.

Liberality is mercifulness that binds God to be merciful. Covetousness, the root of all evil, is merciless. Christ urges all his followers
to freely give and to beware of all covetousness.

—William Tyndale: *Exposition on the Sermon on the Mount*

A Personal Response

Lord, teach me how to open my heart to others.

October 24   Meddling

Jesus answered, "If I want [John] to remain alive until I return, what is that to you? You must follow me." *John 21:22*

Some things are not worth thinking about.

What difference does it make to you what someone else becomes, or says, or does? You do not need to answer for others, only for yourself.

Why get mixed up in such things?

God knows everyone and sees everything that is done under the sun. God understands the dynamics of every situation. He knows each person's thoughts, attitudes, and intentions.

All of this is God's business, not yours.

Don't worry about it.

—Thomas à Kempis: *The Imitation of Christ*

A Personal Response

For some reason, Lord, it is easier to evaluate the behavior of others than my own. It must surely be unfair when I project my own motives and point of view on others. Help me to work on myself.

A Gentle Touch

Blessed are the meek, for they will inherit the earth. *Matthew 5:5*

B e still and have your will. Much rest comes from little meddling. A patient person will wear out many enemies. Psalm 37 explains it this way:

> Be still in the presence of the Lord, and wait patiently for him to act. Don't worry about evil people who prosper or fret about their wicked schemes. Stop your anger! Turn from your rage! Do not envy others—it only leads to harm. For the wicked will be destroyed, but those who trust in the Lord will possess the land. (Psalm 37:7-9, NLT)

It is not possible to live any place where nothing will displease you. If it is an accident, as when your neighbor's animal breaks into your property, then you have every reason to be gentle and forgiving. If it is done with malicious intent, revenge will only fan the flames and bring more evil upon you.

When someone speaks to you harshly, make no response. This will help the heat to diminish. It's like not putting any more wood on the fire. If the wrong that is done is outlandish, trust in God and complain to the authorities.

God supports the meek. The furiously impatient are on their own.

Remember, however, there is an important difference between being good, kind, and merciful, and being a negligent milksop. If you are in a position of responsibility, you need to be in charge. Use sharpness if softness will not be heard.

—William Tyndale: *Exposition on the Sermon on the Mount*

 A Personal Response

Whether they intend to do it or not, people sometimes hurt me, Lord. Give me the gentle touch. Teach me mercy.

October 26   # Alternatives

> I have set before you life and death, blessings and curses. Now choose life, so that you and your children may live. *Deuteronomy 30:19*

You have a choice. You can be evil or good. Both are possible for you. If you decide to curse God, brew poison, and kill another person, you can do it. If you want to live for God, control your emotions, and be a valuable member of the community, that can be yours as well. The capacity for either extreme is in you.

Young men and women work as servants in a great mansion. They are surrounded with valuable things made of gold and silver. The natural desire of these poorer servants is to have such things for themselves. Sometimes they steal, but ordinarily they keep themselves in check. Because of fear of the consequences, they resist strong impulses to do the wrong thing.

An awareness of God is an even greater help in making better choices. It is entirely possible to keep God's commandments. They are not beyond you. Other animals have little choice. Their behavior is fixed. Snakes bite. The wolf is ordinarily a hunter. All wolves are like this. Lambs and doves are harmless and do not engage in deception. It is different with us. One individual may be predatory like a wolf. Another, lamblike, is victimized. Both belong to the same race of humans.

You will hear of a man who is unfaithful to his wife. You will hear of another who is a devoted husband. One person steals. Another person, touched by the love of God, gives generously to help others. Our human nature is pulled in two directions with more or less equal force. Whether it is for evil or for good, our actions are made with our consent. Neither choice is forced on us.

—Pseudo-Macarius: *Homilies*

A Personal Response

It is easier to blame someone else for my poor choices: childhood experiences, overwhelming temptations, an untrustworthy partner. If I take the wrong path it is because I desired it. You understand, dear Lord, that I will protest my helplessness, my innocence, even when I am completely at fault.

October 27 # Why Pray?

Do not worry, saying, "What shall we eat?" or "What shall we drink?" or "What shall we wear?" For the pagans run after all these things, and your heavenly Father knows that you need them. *Matthew 6:31-32*

S ome ask if God needs us as advisers. After all, if he already knows about our problems and is wise enough to know what we need, why bother to pray? Has he nodded off to sleep so that we need to wake him by calling loudly?

Anyone who asks such questions does not understand why the Lord taught us to pray. It is not so much for his sake as for ours.

Faithful people in the Bible were certain that God was merciful and kind. But the more they realized this, the more fervently they prayed. Elijah is one such example. He was confident that God would break a drought and send desperately needed rain. In his confidence he prayed anxiously with his face between his knees. Seven times he told his servant, "Go and look toward the sea" (1 Kings 18:43). He was eager for a report of a cloud beginning to form. In no way did he doubt God would send rain. He understood that it was his duty to lay his desires before God. His faith had to burn in a lively way within him.

It is true that God is awake and watches over us continuously. Sometimes he will assist us even when we do not ask. But it is in our own best interests to pray constantly. When we do, we will begin to understand that it is God who is in charge. It will keep us free of evil desires because we will learn to place all our wishes in his sight. Most importantly, it will prepare us to understand that God is the giver, and we will be filled with genuine gratitude and thanksgiving. Our prayers remind us that all things flow from his hand.

There is no better thing than to pray for what God already wants to give.

—John Calvin: *Institutes*

A Personal Response

The eyes of the Lord are on the righteous and his ears are attentive to their cry.—Psalm 34:15

Stewardship

Then the King will say to those on his right,
"Come, you who are blessed by my Father; take
your inheritance, the kingdom prepared for you
since the creation of the world." *Matthew 25:34*

The gardeners who maintain royal estates take better care of
them than they would their own property. Why? Because
they want to please their bosses.

Our possessions are not our own. God has put them in our care.
He wants us to cultivate them and make them fruitful enough to turn
a profit. Our job is to take good care of what has been entrusted to
us.

Those who do not realize this, labor only out of selfishness. This
ignorance can cause a violent struggle. There is always a sense of
uneasiness and impending danger. If we are working for God, life is
much more calm and peaceful.

Let's be careful to remember this as we preserve and increase our
material possessions.

Be on the lookout for avarice. Make it a habit to give away some
of what you have. Give it with a generous heart. Nothing makes us
more prosperous than to give alms to the poor. Any poverty brought
on by giving alms is holy and rich.

Don't stop with merely giving possessions away. Make yourself
the servant of the poor. Go to them and wait on them when they are
sick in bed. Wait on them with your own hands. Prepare their food
for them at your own expense. Do their laundry. Such service is more
glorious than working for a king.

—Francis de Sales: *The Devout Life*

 A Personal Response

Let me learn your lessons about this, Lord God. It doesn't
come naturally.

Stop a Wandering Mind

Then came Jesus forth, wearing the crown of thorns, and the purple robe. And Pilate saith unto them, Behold the man! *John 19:5,* KJV

I f your mind wanders during prayer, here is a technique that will certainly help. If you are a beginner at prayer, there is no need now for subtle meditation with many mental conceptions of Jesus. Simply look at him.

If you are in trouble, or sad, look at Jesus on his way to the Garden of Gethsemane. Imagine the struggle going on inside his soul. See him bending under the weight of the cross. Look at him persecuted, suffering, and deserted by his friends.

Let your prayer begin to take shape. "Lord, if you are willing to suffer such things for me, what am I suffering for you? Why should I complain? Let me imitate your way. I will suffer whatever I must and consider it a blessing. Where you go, I will go. We will suffer together."

Consider how much more difficult his troubles are than yours. As painful as your own struggles may be, they will become a source of comfort for you.

You ask me how you can possibly do this, protesting that Jesus is not physically present in the world today. Listen! Anyone can make the little effort it takes to look at the Lord within. You can do this without any risk and with very little bother. If you refuse to try this, it is not likely that you would have remained at the foot of the cross either.

—Teresa of Avila: *The Way of Perfection*

 A Personal Response

If I must remain a beginner at prayer, Lord God, let me be an *experienced* beginner. Help me to follow the guidance of those who know the way.

Seeking Perfection

Be perfect, therefore, as your heavenly Father is perfect. *Matthew 5:48*

Christian perfection is nothing to dread. There is pleasure in giving ourselves to one we love. There is a contentment which you will never discover by giving in to your passions, but which will certainly be yours if you give yourself up to God. It is not the satisfaction of the world, but it is nonetheless genuine. It is a quiet, calm peace. The world can neither give it nor take it away. If you have any doubt about it, try it yourself. "O, taste and see that the Lord is good" (Psalm 34:8, KJV).

Organize your time so that you can find a period every day for reading, meditation, and prayer. This will become easy when you truly love him. We never wonder what we will talk about. He is our friend. Our heart is open to him. We must be completely candid with him, holding nothing back. Even if there is nothing we care to say to him, it is a joy just to be in his presence.

Love is a far better sustainer than fear. Fear enslaves, but love persuades. Love takes possession of our soul, and we begin to want goodness for itself. God is a kind and faithful friend to those who sincerely become his friend.

—François de Fénelon: *Meditations and Devotions*

A Personal Response

Dear God, let me seek that perfection of faith that is found in giving of myself to you. You are a faithful friend to me. Let me be your friend.

Things to Ponder

Meditate on it day and night. *Joshua 1:8*

It has been my practice for some time now to meditate upon six things.

First, how God descended from heaven to earth, entering a woman's womb and living there for nine months.

Second, how Christ had a normal birth and actually lived among us for thirty-three years.

Third, how he was motivated by love and was even willing to die on the cross.

Fourth, how he gave himself to us and continues to give himself sacramentally.

Fifth, how he gives himself daily.

Sixth, how his love is not exclusive.

—Margaret Ebner: *Revelations*

A Personal Response

Lord, feed me with your sweet grace. Let your pure love strengthen me. Wrap me in your mercy. May your truth embrace me.—Margaret Ebner

November 1 An Important Difference

Do not be overcome by evil, but overcome evil with good. *Romans 12:21*

There is an art to overcoming evil with good!

This is a struggle in which opposites are attempting to beat each other. But you will make a serious mistake if you strike down someone who is wicked because you hate the wickedness. If someone dies full of iniquity, that iniquity continues forever. If you disapprove of wickedness, try to correct the wicked person. If you are successful, the iniquity will die.

—Guigo I: *Meditations*

A Personal Response

I heard someone say it the other day. "Hate the sin; love the sinner." How many have I ever seen change, dear God? Precious few. What's that, Lord? Concentrate on the few? Yes, I can think of some lives you touched in a remarkable way. Total reversals. Undeniable.

The Light in Darkness

Though I sit in darkness, the Lord will be my light. *Micah 7:8*

The one who loves God remains entirely in light. However, if someone begins to perceive that the love of this world is false and temporary, and therefore prefers the love of God, that person will not instantly be brought into that light. There will be night for a while. It is not possible to move quickly from one light to another, from the love of the world to perfect love of God.

This spiritual night is a dividing line. It separates the two loves. It is a *good* night, a luminous darkness. It has turned away from the false love of this world and is coming closer to the true day of the love of Jesus. The passage through this night means your soul is almost there. This is what the prophet Micah means in chapter 7. When my soul is protected from the stirrings of sin, the Lord is our light.

Even so, this night of the soul can be distressing as well as comforting. The greater the change taking place, the greater the pain. The world is near and God seems far away. If this should happen for you, don't be discouraged. There is no need to struggle. Wait for God's grace. Live through the night quietly. Focus your attention on Jesus. Think only of him.

When your soul is truly free and desires only Christ, it is then in a good darkness. It is a darkness against false light. Jesus, who is both love and light, is in this darkness. It does not matter whether it is pleasant or unpleasant. Understand that it is a darkness before dawn.

—Walter Hilton: *The Scale of Perfection*

 A Personal Response

When the trip is long, children ask, "Are we there yet?" Child-like, I wonder the same thing. Have I arrived, Lord? Am I just getting started? Have I even packed my bags?

November 3 Little Foxes

Catch for us the foxes, the little foxes, that ruin the vineyards, our vineyards that are in bloom. *Song of Songs 2:15*

A vineyard is never free from pests. It is important to guard the vineyard of your soul as well as to cultivate it. Do not allow it to become prey to foxes.

The worst fox of all is the secret slanderer. Equally bad is the flatterer with a slick tongue. Beware of these. Try your best to catch these foxes. Catch them with kindness and courtesy, by wholesome counsel, and by praying for them. Eventually, they may be rid of their envy and sanctimony.

Catch the little foxes that destroy the vines. See them blush. Catch them and either restore them to Christ or lead them to Christ. Let me catch the foxes, not for me, but for him.

—Bernard of Clairvaux: *On the Song of Songs*

A Personal Response

Help me, O Lord, to identify the pests in the garden of my soul. Many are of my own making. A few are invaders, uninvited. Many are carefully camouflaged. Help me to find them and, when possible, turn a problem into a blessing.

Rich by Invitation

A certain man was preparing a great banquet and invited many guests. At the time of the banquet he sent his servant to tell those who had been invited, "Come, for everything is now ready." *Luke 14:16*

A king puts a poor man in charge of his treasury. The individual who receives this responsibility does not think that the wealth belongs to him. It remains the king's. Because he needs this job, he is careful to protect the royal treasury. He wastes nothing. He oversees it carefully.

Anyone who has been given God's grace is in a similar situation. With humility we can admit our poverty. We can understand that we have been given responsibility for something valuable by our king. If we begin to think of it as our own and become arrogant and proud, the king may take it away from us. We will remain spiritually poor.

Remember, then, what God is doing for you. Let's continue to think through our illustration. What if the king finds a very sick poor person by the roadside? He would be glad to treat his injuries with the best royal medicines available. He might bring the person to his castle, dress him in royal clothing, and feed him at his own table. This is exactly the way Christ came to us, found us sick, and healed us. He invites us to be companions at his table. He does not twist our arms in order to force this upon us. He invites us with great dignity and appeal.

Many have declined the offer. They refuse to come to Christ's banquet.

—Pseudo-Macarius: *Homilies*

A Personal Response

Who would prefer to be poor? Who would choose to be sick? What hungry person could possibly walk from a banquet table? O Lord, help me to respond warmly to your gracious invitation.

November 5   ## Seniority

The last will be first, and the first will be last.
Matthew 20:16

Beware of thinking about your seniority. May God help us to avoid thoughts such as these: "But I have been here the longest." "I have worked harder." "Someone else is being favored."

If these kinds of thoughts come into your head, be quick to hold them in check. If you allow yourself to dwell on these ideas or include them in your conversation, they will spread like a plague. In church they will result in serious problems.

God deliver us from Christian servants who care about their own honor. Think how little they gain from it. The very act of wanting to be honored robs us of honor. This is particularly true in matters of seniority. There is no poison in the world more fatal to a life of faith.

You may reply that these are little human foibles that we don't need to worry about. I tell you it is not a trifling matter. In churches they spread like foam on water. This kind of sensitivity is extremely dangerous. There are many reasons why this is so. It may be rooted in some trivial thing, but it will grow.

Suppose someone thinks it's an act of love to report an offense to you. You are asked how you can allow yourself to be insulted like this. The reporter assures you of her prayers because even a saint could not take more. The devil is putting his poisonous words in another's mouth. You may be willing to bear the slight, but now you are tempted by egotism.

Our human nature is terribly weak. Even while we are protesting that there is nothing to make a fuss about, we imagine we are doing something good. We begin to feel sorry for ourselves. If others say they are sorry for us, that makes it worse.

For the love of God, never show pity to another person for anything that has to do with imagined insults.

—Teresa of Avila: *The Way of Perfection*

A Personal Response

When I seek honor, when I seek esteem, when I listen to the poisonous flattery of others, forgive me, Lord. Change me.

Finite Love for the Infinite

Love the Lord your God with all your heart and with all your soul and with all your strength. *Deuteronomy 6:5*

Faithful people understand how fully they need Jesus and his death on the cross. Seeing his love, they desire to return what little they can. Those who know they are loved are better able to love. The one who is forgiven more loves more. Seeing the wounds of Christ, the believer says, "I am faint with love" (Song of Songs 2:5).

Who is it that remembers God? It certainly is not "a stubborn and rebellious generation" (Psalm 78:8). Christ says to them, "Woe to you who are rich, for you have already received your comfort" (Luke 6:24).

The ones who remember God are those who can say, "I remembered God, and was troubled: I complained, and my spirit was overwhelmed" (Psalm 77:3, KJV). Our soul is Christ's bride and loves him ardently. But even when she thinks she is completely in love, she feels that her love is inadequate because she is loved so much. And that is true. How could she love as much in return? God loves with all his being.

—Bernard of Clairvaux: *On Loving God*

 A Personal Response

Even if my devotion were pure and absolute, it would still be inadequate. You love me with an infinite, unlimited love. I am a finite, limited creature. Let me begin to love you, O God, with all my being.

Value Calmness

They cried out to the Lord in their trouble, and he brought them out of their distress. He stilled the storm to a whisper; the waves of the sea were hushed. They were glad when it grew calm, and he guided them to their desired haven. *Psalm 107:28-30*

A calm mind is a great asset in this life. Without it your devotional life will not bear much fruit. If your heart is troubled, you are vulnerable to the enemy of the soul. When you are agitated, you are not able to make good decisions. You will stumble into snares.

The enemy detests this peace in you. He knows that is the place where the Spirit of God dwells. That's why he devises such devilish ways to destroy this peace.

Avoid rash acts. Even if you are sure the Holy Spirit wants you to do something, wait. Put off doing it until your eagerness has declined. Introduced with that kind of self-control, a good work is more pleasing to God than if it were done too hastily.

It is also necessary to overcome a certain inner regret. Sometimes we think our bad conscience is being generated by God when in fact it is the work of the devil. Here is the way to tell: if your regret results in greater humility and increases your desire to serve God, receive it with gratitude as a gift from heaven. If it creates anxiety, makes you sad, depressed, fearful, and slow to do your duty, then we can be sure it has been suggested by the enemy. Disregard it.

—Lawrence Scupoli: *The Spiritual Combat*

 A Personal Response

Lord, I can get so excitable. I enjoy the liveliness. All the more reason, I am sure, to turn aside regularly for some calming rest.

Genuine Peace

Peace I leave with you; my peace I give you.
I do not give to you as the world gives. *John
14:27*

Everyone wants peace, but very few care for the things that produce it. God's peace is with the humble and the gentle, and especially with the patient. If you will listen to God, and act accordingly, you will enjoy much peace.

Here is what to do. Care for nothing other than pleasing God. Do not judge others or meddle in things which do not concern you. Following this advice will spare you needless trouble. But remember that it is impossible to be entirely free of trouble and fatigue in this life.

Don't think that you have found true peace just because you feel no pain or have no enemies. Never think that life is perfect when you receive everything you want. Never consider yourself God's favorite child because you enjoy a great devotional life. That is not the way to true peace and spiritual growth.

Peace can be found in offering your whole heart to God. Forget your own will in great things and small things, thanking God equally for the pleasant and the unpleasant. Weigh everything in the same balance.

If you are strong enough to willingly suffer more and more without praising yourself, but always praising God's name, then you will be on the road to true peace. You will have the hope of seeing him in the everlasting joy of heaven.

—Thomas à Kempis: *The Imitation of Christ*

 A Personal Response

Lord, you have taught me the way of peace:

Do what pleases another rather than myself. Choose to have less rather than more. Seek the lowest place and be the servant of all. Pray that your will may be accomplished in me always.

If I do these four things, I will surely find peace and inward rest. Whenever I am upset and burdened, it is because I have not practiced these simple rules. I cannot attain it on my own. Help me.—Thomas à Kempis

November 9 The Territory of the Heart

Above all else, guard your heart, for it is the wellspring of life. *Proverbs 4:23*

O God! We don't know who you are! "The light shines in the darkness" (John 1:5) but we don't see it. Universal light! It is only because of you that we can see anything at all. Sun of the soul! You shine more brightly than the sun in the sky. You rule over everything. All I see is you. Everything else vanishes like a shadow. The one who has never seen you has seen nothing. That person lives a make-believe life, lives a dream.

But I always find you within me. You work through me in all the good I accomplish. How many times I was unable to check my emotions, resist my habits, subdue my pride, follow my reason, or stick to my plan! Without you I am "a reed swayed by the wind" (Matthew 11:7). You give me courage and everything decent which I experience. You have given me a new heart that wants nothing except what you want. I am in your hands. It is enough for me to do what you want me to do. For this purpose I was created.

—François de Fénelon: *Meditations and Devotions*

A Personal Response

My Creator, I close my eyes and shut out all exterior things. They are nothing but pointless irritations to the spirit. In the depths of my heart, I can enjoy an intimacy with you through Jesus, your Son.—François de Fénelon

Serving Others

Whenever you did it for any of my people, no matter how unimportant they seemed, you did it for me. *Matthew 25:40,* CEV

Christ took the form of a servant. "Being found in appearance as a man, he humbled himself and became obedient to death—even death on a cross!" (Philippians 2:8). If a believing heart meditates upon that, it will be kindled to love not only for our Savior but also for others.

Faith takes us away from love for the present with its honors, fortunes, and pleasures. These things hinder true love and service. They are a burden. "If you try to keep your life for yourself, you will lose it. But if you give up your life for me, you will find true life. And how do you benefit if you gain the whole world but lose or forfeit your own soul in the process?" (Luke 9:24-25, NLT).

In Christ we will become new creatures who will no longer be able to live selfishly. God has ordered us to serve others. "I desire mercy, not sacrifice" (Hosea 6:6). Creatures do what they were intended to do. A bird flies, a fish swims, a human speaks. "If I could speak in any language in heaven or on earth but didn't love others, I would only be making meaningless noise like a loud gong or a clanging cymbal" (1 Corinthians 13:1, NLT). If we do nothing but grab things for ourselves, it is clear we have no faith in God. We shall hear him say, "I never knew you. Away from me, you evildoers!" (Matthew 7:23).

Only the Word of God makes us wholesome and blessed. The divine Word brings faith. Faith brings love. Love results in good deeds.

—Martin Bucer: *Instruction in Christian Love*

A Personal Response

All I have is through you, my Lord. I will keep nothing for myself. With joy I will put everything I own at the service of others. With you, I will accept suffering and disgrace. I will take up my cross and follow you.—Martin Bucer

November 11   Subtle Theft

You shall not steal. *Exodus 20:15*

Stealing is not confined to open robbery, extortion, and plun-
der. There are also many crafty and subtle ways to take
things from others while continuing to appear virtuous and
honest. To help you understand this, here are some examples.

It is understood that we are supposed to pay princes and gover-
nors, services, customs, toll, subsidies, and taxes in order for them to
administer civic responsibilities. When they overcharge their subjects,
they are stealing. When they wring money out of their subjects' hands
unjustly and against their wills, wasting everyone's money on parties
and the like, God will judge them thieves.

Bishops, pastors, and preachers are thieves when they hide God's
truth in order to win favor. This uttering of false ideas is theft before
God.

Likewise lawyers, advocates, and attorneys are thieves when they
make money for themselves by counseling someone to wage the law,
making that person believe that his case is good, when they actually
know it is not. The same is true when for money they will cleverly
plead a matter, shifting and coloring the truth in order to hide it.

Merchants, brokers, and people in sales are thieves when they
take too large a profit. Forged letters and feigned testimonials that
persuade others to sell at a discount what will be valuable in the near
future is stealing. The same is true of retailers who tell craftsmen they
really don't need their wares at that time, and by such means compel
them to sell at a low price.

Craftsmen and laborers steal when they do not work faithfully
and carefully or are paid more than they are worth. Farmers are thieves
when they are not diligent in their plowing and cultivating. Those who
do not pay their workers on time are stealing. Those who will not pay
their debts or sell things they have found without looking for the true
owner are thieves. Anyone who does not return what has been borrowed is stealing.

—Thomas Cranmer: *Catechismus*

A Personal Response

Am I a secret thief, O God? Is my stealing even known to
myself?

November 12 Busybodies

Make it your ambition to lead a quiet life, to
mind your own business and to work with
your hands, just as we told you.
1 Thessalonians 4:11

Don't meddle in the business of others. Don't be an eaves-
dropper, attempting to overhear what is being said or done
in your neighbor's house. Wide ears and long tongues
come together. Those who love to hear everything that may be told
them also love to blab it out.

When everyone is busy looking into the affairs of others, trouble
is near. Busybodies will forever find fault with their neighbors, their
families, with the government, and with the church. They are an
unquiet kind of people. They are forever looking for something they
can dislike. They are never content.

From such people come private whispering, slander, backbiting,
mutiny, conspiracy, treason, and the utter decay of society.

—John Jewell: *Exposition on the Thessalonians*

 A Personal Response

I never thought of quietly minding my own business as an act
of Christian devotion. No doubt about it, Lord. Clearly it is.

November 13 The Loved Love Best

Love the Lord, all his saints! *Psalm 31:23*

It is the faithful who understand how fully they need Jesus and his death on the cross. Seeing his love, they desire to return what little they can. Those who know they are loved are better able to love. The one who is forgiven more loves more.

Who is it that remembers God? It is certainly not "a stubborn and rebellious generation" (Psalm 78:8) to whom Christ says, "But woe to you who are rich, for you have already received your comfort" (Luke 6:24).

Our soul, Christ's bride, loves ardently. But even when she thinks she is completely in love she feels that her love is inadequate because she is loved so much. And that is true. How could she love as much in return? God loves with all his being. The complete Trinity loves, if "complete" is not a misnomer for the infinite and incomprehensible.

—Bernard of Clairvaux: *On Loving God*

A Personal Response

How could I ever doubt, Lord God, that you are worthy of my love?

Interpretation of Scripture

Do not interpretations belong to God? *Genesis 40:8*

One says, "Moses meant what I say."

Another disagrees, "No, he meant what I say."

It seems to me that it is nearer to the truth to ask, "Why can't he have meant both? And if someone would see a third or a fourth or any number of meanings in the same language, why can't we believe that Moses meant them all?" God has adapted the Bible to many interpretations.

Without a doubt—and I do not hesitate to speak from my heart—if I had to write with such great authority I would attempt to write in a way that my words would communicate as much truth as possible to each reader. I would not write down one true meaning so obvious that it would prohibit any other meaning, even though there was nothing offensive in the alternate interpretations.

—Augustine: *Confessions*

A Personal Response

Sometimes, dear God, I get excited. I think I have finally understood what you are trying to tell me. I want others to share my discovery. They confound me by reporting they understand you in a different way. Because I am convinced of the truth I have discovered, it seems necessary to debate with them. I must not be very good at this because I have not persuaded anyone to think differently. Is the great saint right? Could several of us have a different hold on the same truth? Can we do that without invalidating each other? Is it possible that the great truth I possess is only a fragment of it all?

November 15 Power

"Do you refuse to speak to me?" Pilate said. "Don't you realize I have power either to free you or to crucify you?" Jesus answered, "You would have no power over me if it were not given to you from above." *John 19:10-11*

Power is ignoble. God demonstrated this by giving Pontius Pilate the power to kill his son, and Nero a worldwide empire. This is something God rarely gives his saints. When a saint is given power over others, it is for their good. It does nothing for the saint. The saint does not need subjects, but people need a good ruler.

Power can be a useful thing in this world. It is not for ourselves, but for our neighbors. It can be used to protect them in the orderly conduct of business, or to restrain them from doing harmful things.

Most complaints come down to a question of power. People complain that they can't do what they want. They never complain that they don't want what is good for them or that they want what will hurt them. They are bothered only because they do not have the power to accomplish what they desire. They do not ask if it is good for them.

Long ago people said, "Come, let us build ourselves a city, with a tower that reaches to the heavens, so that we may make a name for ourselves and not be scattered over the face of the earth" (Genesis 11:4). There is no security in pride. Nothing can be as high as God. We do what they did, building a tower in order to sin without submitting to a higher authority.

—Guigo I: *Meditations*

A Personal Response

Lord, that hunger for power is everywhere. It may be in me. Show me the better way. Show me how to hunger for you.

November 16 **Avoid Pride**

Though the Lord is on high, he looks upon
the lowly, but the proud he knows from afar.
Psalm 138:6

Beware of a proud and haughty spirit. This sin puts a great barrier between an individual and God. You will have a hard time being aware of God as long as you are filled with pride. If it gets angels cast out of heaven, it will certainly keep your heart out of heaven. It was the downfall of Adam and Eve. It increases our separation from God and expels us from paradise.

It is after a soul-humbling day—or a time of trouble when the soul is lowest—that we have free access to God. The delight of God is in "those who have humble and contrite hearts, who tremble at [God's] word" (Isaiah 66:2, NLT). And God is the delight of such souls! Where the pleasure is mutual there will be free admittance, warm welcome, and easy conversation.

God denies access to a proud soul. "God opposes the proud but gives grace to the humble" (1 Peter 5:5; Proverbs 3:34). A proud mind is conceited. A humble mind finds self-esteem in God and holy aspirations. These two forms of high-mindedness are at opposite poles.

Most wars are between prince and prince, and not between prince and plowman. Are you puffed up with pride? Do you welcome the praise of others? Do you seek the highest honors? Do you become angry when your word or will is crossed? Can you not serve God in a low place as well as high? Do you enjoy celebrity? Are you unaware of the deceitfulness and wickedness of your heart? Are you more ready to defend your innocence than to confess your fault?

If these things describe your heart, you are a proud person. It is not likely you will have any familiarity with God. You make yourself a god. You are your own idol. How could you possibly have your heart in heaven? You might speak a few proper words, but your heart does not understand what you are saying.

—Richard Baxter: *The Saints' Everlasting Rest*

A Personal Response

Jesus, you told me to humble myself like a little child. I can't
do it. Please do it for me.

November 17 ## Spiritual Poverty for the Rich

Whoever loves money never has money enough; whoever loves wealth is never satisfied with his income. *Ecclesiastes 5:10*

If Jesus said the poor in spirit are blessed because they will inherit the kingdom of heaven, does that mean the rich in spirit are cursed? One who is rich in spirit has a mind that is completely occupied with riches. Our hearts are to be open to heaven alone and impervious to things that decay.

There is a big difference between having poison and taking poison. Pharmacists keep all kinds of poisons on their shelves. They are not harmed because it is only in their shop and not in themselves. You can have great wealth without being harmed by it. All you have to do is keep it in your home and your purse rather than in your heart. Being rich in affect and poor in affection, you can have the advantages of both wealth for this world and poverty for the world to come.

We do not easily admit that we are greedy. Most people would deny this. Perhaps we excuse ourselves by saying we have to take care of our children. Prudence is an obligation. But then we can never have too much. We always need more. Greed is extremely hard to detect, but it is insatiable.

Try this test for yourself. Do you really crave something you don't have enough to do something crooked to get it? Will your desires deprive another of his possessions? It is soon enough to desire your neighbor's property when he is ready to get rid of it.

If you are strongly attached to the things you own, you will worry a lot about losing them. When people who are feverish are given a glass of water, they drink it with an eagerness and satisfaction that you don't often see in a healthy person. If you find yourself destroyed by a loss of property, you love it too much. The clearest proof of love for a lost object is suffering because it is lost.

Don't desire wealth you do not have. Don't attach your heart too closely to what you already have.

—Francis de Sales: *The Devout Life*

A Personal Response

Lord, help me to judge my own worth by who I am, and not by what I have.

November 18 # Forgiveness for Everything

If we confess our sins, [Jesus] is faithful and just and will forgive us our sins and purify us from all unrighteousness. 1 John 1:9

There are none so wicked that they cannot have a remedy. What is that? Enter into your own heart and search its secrets. Consider your own life. How have you spent your days? If you find some ugliness in yourself, what will you do? Ask God to forgive you. You will surely be heard. Your sins will be forgiven. God will be true to his promise. He sent his only Son into this world to save sinners like you.

Consider the great love of God the Father. Amend your life. Avoid temptation. If you will do this, you may be sure that though you have done all the sins in the book they will neither hurt nor condemn you. The mercy of God is greater than all the sins in the world.

—Hugh Latimer: *Fruitful Sermons*

 A Personal Response

Lord, how free you are with me, to give and to forgive.

November 19 ## Waving the Flag

For those who fear you, you have raised a banner to be unfurled against the bow. *Psalm 60:4*

In combat, the standard-bearer is not armed. He is exposed to no less danger than the other soldiers, but it is not his job to fight. He will suffer as much as anyone else, but he cannot defend himself. He is carrying the flag and must not allow it to leave his hands even if he is getting cut to pieces.

Christians need to hold the cross of Jesus high. It is our duty to suffer with Christ. This is a duty with high honor. Think about it! If the standard bearer lets the flag fall, the battle will be lost. The other soldiers can retreat if they must and no one will notice. They have no loss of honor. But everyone is looking at the flag for inspiration. It must hold its ground. This is a noble assignment. The King gives great honor to anyone who accepts it. It is a serious obligation.

True humility consists in being satisfied with what we are asked to do. Do your assigned task with good cheer. Let others do their jobs. Some of us want to ask God for favors. Do you call *that* humility?

Spiritual progress has nothing to do with having the most answers to prayer, or with raptures, visions, and favors from the Lord. We won't know the value of those things until we die. The thing I have been describing is for right now.

The Lord knows us as we really are. He gives each of us work to do. He understands what is most appropriate for us, what will be helpful to him, and what will be good for others. Unless you fail to prepare yourself for your assignment, you can be sure it will be successful.

—Teresa of Avila: *The Way of Perfection*

A Personal Response

I admit it, Lord. I have not been pleased with everything you have asked me to do. Sometimes I have looked for ways to get out of it.

November 20 Forgiveness As Giving Alms

If you forgive those who sin against you, your heavenly Father will forgive you. But if you refuse to forgive others, your Father will not forgive your sins. *Matthew 6:14-15,* NLT

There are passing and trivial sins of everyday life that all of us commit. No one is free of them. The Lord's Prayer completely blots out our minor and everyday sins. It also takes care of those sins of one's youth.

There is only one condition. We must truly pray, "Forgive us our debts, as we also have forgiven our debtors" (Matthew 6:12). What is said is also done. To forgive someone who is looking for forgiveness is the same thing as giving alms. It is an act of mercy.

We give alms whenever we feed the hungry, give a drink of water to the thirsty, clothe the naked, extend hospitality to a traveler, visit the ill and the imprisoned, bail someone out of jail, bear the burdens of the weak, lead the blind, comfort the sorrowful, heal the sick, give directions to the lost, provide advice to the perplexed, and do whatever is needful for the needy. We also give alms when we forgive someone who has trespassed against us. We are almsgivers when we correct and restrain those under our responsibility, if at the same time we forgive from the heart.

It is a small thing to wish well and do well to one who has done you no evil. It is far greater—a magnificent goodness—to love your enemy, and to wish and do well to one who is trying to harm you. Our Lord says, "Love your enemies and pray for those who persecute you" (Matthew 5:44). Such a high degree of goodness is not possible for most people who pray the Lord's Prayer.

If we do not forgive those who ask for forgiveness and are repentant of their sins, we should not imagine that our own sins are forgiven. If you can sleep through the thunder of that statement, you must be dead! And yet, this truth has the power to wake the dead.

—Augustine: *Enchiridion*

A Personal Response

Lord, I know forgiveness is key to a life of faith. Will I ever learn what it means? Will I ever learn to give it out like alms? Give it from the heart?

November 21 ## Almost Blind

Without faith it is impossible to please God, because anyone who comes to him must believe that he exists and that he rewards those who earnestly seek him. *Hebrews 11:6*

If someone is almost blind, that person has little desire for a guide. Seeing a little bit, we figure it is best to travel in the direction that is most appealing. The alternatives are dimly perceived and uninviting. We can even lead a guide astray by insisting that we take a particular route.

This is the way it is when the soul leans upon its own knowledge. Perhaps there was a little feeling or experience of God. That may be an important blessing, but no matter how great it may have been, it is still very much different from what God is. Continue down that path and you may either be lead astray or bump into a dead end. *Faith* is the true guide of the soul.

Union with God is not the result of understanding, experience, feeling, or imagination. Isaiah and Paul both say, "No eye has seen, no ear has heard, no mind conceived what God has prepared for those who love him" (1 Corinthians 2:9; Isaiah 64:4). A soul is hampered from attaining this high state of union with God when it clings to any mental or emotional process of its own.

—John of the Cross: *Ascent of Mount Carmel*

A Personal Response

My perception is so dull I am like that man who was not yet completely cured of his blindness. "I see people; they look like trees walking around" (Mark 8:24). I am sure that I am more than a little blind in this union with God business. Make me willing to let another show me the way beyond where I am today.

 # Regarding Love

God is love. 1 *John 4:8*

We welcome the obvious signs of love, such as a cheerful expression, in other people. Why do we not want them for ourselves?

It is good for you to have the love of others. It helps *them.* By loving you, they experience God, who is love. Love is its own compensation.

Be a good companion and friend of others, not their egotistical master. Do everything with love, not with overbearing pomposity.

Love belongs to everyone. Each of us is to love everyone. Anyone who desires exclusive love is a robber, and steals from everyone.

Ultimately, there will be no regret for having considered gold to be gold or soil to be soil. These thoughts are true. But if we give our love to something unworthy of it, or hope in something that is unable to help us, then we will regret it. Loving something that is not worth loving is as mistaken as thinking that soil is gold. The first mistake can be deadly. The second is not all that harmful. And yet many worry more about the second than the first!

You can look at a tender shoot on a vine and anticipate the harvest. In the same way, love those who are not yet good.

If you simply love those who love you, or love someone in order to be loved, you are not really loving. You are reciprocating. You are paying love for love. You are nothing more than a moneychanger. You already have your reward.

—Guigo I: *Meditations*

 A Personal Response

Others need my love, Lord Jesus. Let the love in me be your love. Love them through me.

November 23 Mercy

Blessed are the merciful, for they will be shown mercy. *Matthew 5:7*

To be merciful is to have compassion, to feel another's sickness, to mourn with those who are in grief, to suffer with someone in trouble, to help in any way we can, and to comfort with loving words.

To be merciful is lovingly to forgive someone who has offended you when they admit their behavior and ask you for mercy.

To be merciful is to be patient with sinners, praying that God will ultimately convert them.

To be merciful is to see the best in everything, to look through the fingers at many things and not make a grievous sin of every small trifle.

—William Tyndale: *Exposition on the Sermon on the Mount*

A Personal Response

With a few examples the point is made clear. Mercy is the product of a mature spirit. It comes with confidence and self-esteem. Those who are unmerciful are usually somewhere near the beginning of their spiritual development. Where, O Lord, am I?

November 24  Desiring Popularity

They loved human praise more than the praise of God. *John 12:43,* NLT

I have always desired to impress others. I want their approval. I need to feel loved. I crave popularity. I attempt to win my neighbors' hearts. It would be better to steal the incense that is glowing on God's altar than to try to capture what belongs only to God.

O God, when will I stop wanting to be loved? When will I cease being too eager for applause? All love and glory belong to you. I am ashamed of my desire for appreciation. Lord, punish my pride. I stand with you against myself. I take the side of your glory as opposed to my vanity.

Selfish man! In love with yourself! How could you be worthy of any tenderness or affection apart from God?

Lord, I no longer need to be loved. The more sensitive I am in demanding the love of others, the less I deserve their love. As for the applause of others, you can give it or take it away as it pleases you. I want to become indifferent to such things. If there is anything in my reputation that will bring you glory, that is all right. But let me care nothing about it. As long as any secret need to be approved and respected remains in me, I am not dead with Christ and will not be able to enter his resurrected life.

The errors of the old man must be buried. Everything must die. Everything must be sacrificed. It will be returned with interest. When we have lost all that is in us, we shall recover it all in God. Our love will grow until it becomes like the love of God.

—François de Fénelon: *Meditations and Devotions*

 A Personal Response

Lord Jesus, you died to help me die. Take my life. Don't let me hesitate. I draw no protective line around anything that needs to go.—François de Fénelon

Steadiness

Look to the Lord and his strength; seek his
face always. *1 Chronicles 16:11*

If we permit the love of God to replace our cares in this world,
and if we give ourselves over to steady prayer and meditation,
we will soon find our attitude and behavior changing. We will
stop racing from one thing to another. We will rest in tranquility
and peace.

A stable spiritual life requires much prayer and devout singing
of psalms. Evil is only conquered by continual prayer.

Prayer can become habitual. Whether praying or meditating, it is
possible to focus our attention on God. In this kind of prayer we do
not think of anything in particular. Our whole will is directed toward
God. The Holy Spirit burns in our soul. God is at the very heart of
our being. Our prayers are made with affection and they become
effective. If our prayers require words, we do not rush. We can offer
almost every syllable as a prayer in itself. The love burning in us will
give fiery life to our prayers.

Prayer of this kind is a delight.

—Richard Rolle: *The Mending of Life*

A Personal Response

Spiritual stability. That's an interesting concept, Lord. You have
given us distinctive personalities. Some of us are more excitable
than others. There is a place in your creation for the tortoise
and the hare, the sloth and the leopard. It is clear you do not
want us all to be alike. Then what does this stableness of spirit
mean for me?

November 26 # Really Praying the Lord's Prayer

When you pray, do not keep on babbling like pagans, for they think they will be heard because of their many words. *Matthew 6:7*

W hen I repeat the Lord's Prayer, my love causes me to desire to understand who this Father is, and who this Master is that taught us the prayer.

You are wrong if you think you already know who he is. We should think of him every time we say his prayer. Human frailty may interfere with this. When we are sick or our heads are tired, no matter how hard we try we may not be able to concentrate. If we are going through some stormy times we may be too distressed to pay attention to what we are saying. As hard as we try, we just can't do it.

Imagine that Jesus taught this prayer to each one of us individually and that he continues to explain it to us. He is always close enough to hear us. To pray the Lord's Prayer well there is one thing you need to do. Stay near the side of the Master who taught it to you.

"Ah!" you say, "This is meditation! I am not able to meditate. I have no desire to meditate. I am content to pray this prayer out loud." Maybe you are one of those impatient people who don't like to be bothered. Yes, it is a little troublesome to begin to consider Jesus when you pray the Lord's Prayer until it becomes habitual. You are right. This step turns vocal prayer into mental prayer. In my view, it is faithful vocal prayer. We need to think about who is listening to our prayers.

—Teresa of Avila: *The Way of Perfection*

 A Personal Response

Am I afraid of deeper water? I am always aware that there is an edge of prayer. I come up to it, hang onto something, and peer into the unknown. But I draw back. But, reading this, I am taken by the hand and shown the way.

November 27 # Eyes of Faith

Because you have seen me, you have believed; blessed are those who have not seen and yet have believed. John 20:29

There is a supernatural dimension to everything. The most ordinary object and the most commonplace event have a divine quality. Everything in life is a stone that builds a heavenly structure. If we are blind to this and live only according to what we can see and touch, we will stumble stupidly through a dark maze.

When we live by faith we see things another way. Those who trust only their physical senses will not perceive the riches that hide beneath outward appearances. If you realize that the man in front of you is really your king in disguise as a commoner, you will still treat him as a king. If you see the hand of God in ordinary events, even in disasters, you will accept whatever comes your way with respect and pleasure. You will welcome things that terrify others. They may be clothed in rags, but you will respect the majesty hidden beneath those rags.

Think of God's poverty as he lay crying and trembling on some hay in a manger! If you were to ask the citizens of Bethlehem their opinions of the baby Jesus, you would get ordinary responses. If he had been born in a palace among all the splendor of a prince, people would have been eager to honor him. Not so with a child in a stable.

Now go ask Mary, Joseph, the shepherds, and the magi. They will tell you that in this absolute poverty they see something beyond words that is the glory of God. It is the very things which cannot be perceived by our senses that nourish and enlarge faith. Seeing less, we believe more.

—Jean-Pierre de Caussade: *Abandonment to Divine Providence*

A Personal Response

Faith will place me in a minority group. That's troubling, Lord. But if I feel your Spirit stirring within me, give me the courage to respond. Open my eyes that I may see.

November 28 ## Tough Talk about Love

Having loved his own who were in the world, [Jesus] now showed them the full extent of his love. *John 13:1*

The only reason you "love" God and your neighbor is for what it might get you. "God has poured out his love into our hearts by the Holy Spirit" (Romans 5:5). But if you love in order to receive something, it is not love through the Holy Spirit. It is worldly love. It is not love that is pouring out. It is avarice.

You do someone a lot of good when you correct him. That person will not think it was good unless you truly correct for good out of love. It is one thing to want to hurt someone, and another thing to offer positive correction. The first is cruelty. The second is love.

It is a vice to worry about another's sin. It is also a vice *not* to worry about another's sin. The important thing is to have a genuine desire to help in a beneficial way. Remove love, and vice is all that remains.

Misery results from a lack of love of God. Misery comes from loving the perishing things of this world. This misery is what makes us do harm to others.

—Guigo I: *Meditations*

 A Personal Response

It appears to me, heavenly Father, that love is at the root of it all. It is the only definition the Bible gives me of you, other than to remind me you are spirit. It is the essence of the Gospel. Love is the unmistakable character of Christ. According to Saint Paul, love gives meaning to everything, and without it even the best actions are empty. Please, give me love to give.

November 29   In God's Presence

> In him we live and move and have our being.
> *Acts 17:28*

I will speak of my personal experience. It may not sound like much when you hear it, but I won't mind that. A spiritual person will not object, and one who is not spiritual simply won't understand a thing I say.

I speak foolishly. God often comes even to me. I never notice the precise moment when he arrives. I feel his presence and then I remember that he was with me. Sometimes I have a premonition that he is coming to me. But I have never been able to put my finger on the exact instant when he arrived or departed. What path he uses to enter or leave my soul is a mystery to me. "[His] footsteps are not known" (Psalm 77:19, KJV).

He could not enter through my eyes, because he has no color. Neither could it be through my ears, since he makes no sound. It was not my nose that detected his presence, because his sweetness blends with the mind, not the air. It could not have been my tongue that noticed him, for one does not taste him. And the sense of touch is of no value for discerning a presence that is not physical. How did he enter my soul?

Perhaps he did not enter at all. Maybe he was never outside. But how can I say that he exists within me when I know there is nothing good in me? When I am at my best the Word still towers high above me.

How, then, did I know he was in me? I couldn't miss it! It affected me in an undeniable way. My heart was softened and my soul roused from its slumber. He went to work in me. He cleared and cultivated the soil of my soul. He planted and watered and brought light to dark places. He opened what was closed, and warmed what was cold. I have seen a fraction of his glory and it is awesome.

—Bernard of Clairvaux: *On the Song of Songs*

A Personal Response

I am familiar with your gentle kindness. The small improvements I have made, the renewal of my mind and spirit, convince me of your love.—Bernard of Clairvaux

November 30 Knowing and Speaking

The kingdom of God is not a matter of talk
but of power. *1 Corinthians 4:20*

Telling me that bread is made of wheat is not a difficult task. But can you tell me how to mix and bake a loaf of bread? The Christian gospel tells us about being freed of our passions. Jesus clearly tells us, "Do not resist an evil person. If someone strikes you on the right cheek, turn to him the other also. And if someone wants to sue you and take your tunic, let him have your cloak as well. If someone forces you to go one mile, go with him two miles" (Matthew 5:39-41). Can you tell me how to do that if you have not done it yourself?

Anyone who talks about spiritual things without any experience in them is like a person who is lost in the desert, dying with thirst. With a dry, parched throat and burning lips, she draws a picture of a water fountain. You can't tell me about the sweetness of honey until you have tasted some honey. If you try to tell me about the Christian life without any personal involvement in it, you will mislead me. You will tell me fictional things, mistaken things. The faith you have tried to sell me is nothing more than words. Your religion is just talk.

It is impossible to understand and serve truth unless you have that truth.

——Pseudo-Macarius: *Homilies*

 A Personal Response

Let my faith be more than something to be noisy about. Grant, O God, that I do not teach what I do not know. Keep me from attempting to give what I do not have.

December 1 # The Face in the Mirror

We humans are merely grass, and we last no longer than wild flowers. At the Lord's command, flowers and grass disappear, and so do we. Flowers and grass fade away, but what our God has said will never change. *Isaiah 40:6-8*, CEV

God inspired certain sparkles of truth in the classic philosophers. They knew the importance of truly knowing yourself.

What do you have, vain one, that is worth praise? The Scripture tells us, "Every good and perfect gift is from above, coming down from the Father of the heavenly lights, who does not change like shifting shadows" (James 1:17). Whether they are outward gifts or inward, relating to body or soul, they come from above yourself. Christ reminds us that there is nothing we can do about these things (Matthew 7:25-27). Even our intelligence is a gift from God.

The most glorious gifts concerning our souls have their source in God. "It is by grace you have been saved, through faith—and this not from yourselves, it is the gift of God—not by works, so that no one can boast. For we are God's workmanship" (Ephesians 2:8-10).

Therefore let not the wise rejoice in wisdom, neither the strong in strength, nor the rich in riches. If you rejoice, rejoice in the Lord, to whom be all honor and praise without end.

—John Frith: *A Mirror, or Glass to Know Thyself*

 A Personal Response

I am told, my Lord, that I am the product of my genes. The DNA I inherited from my parents has shaped me. But with conscious awareness, help me to realize that everything good about me is a gift, O Lord, from you.

When You Stumble

"Come now, let us reason together," says the Lord. "Though your sins are like scarlet, they shall be as white as snow; though they are red as crimson, they shall be like wool." *Isaiah 1:18*

You have committed a sin. It may have been from weakness or with malice. Don't panic. Go to God with humility and confidence. "Look what I can do, O Master. When I trust my own strength, I sin."

Let the Lord know you are sorry. Admit it may have been worse if he had not stopped you. Thank God. Love God. He will be generous toward you. Even though what you have done is offensive to him, he will reach out to help you.

Once you have asked God's pardon, don't begin to wonder whether or not he has actually forgiven you. This is a total waste of time, a sickness of the soul. It may seem like a good and reasonable question, but it is not. Fall into the mercy of God and return to your regular life as though the sin had not occurred.

Maybe you sin again in a short time. Don't let that shake your confidence in God. Return to him again and again. Each defeat will teach you to trust your own strength less and less.

If you have really messed up, first try to regain your peace and calmness. Lift up your heart to heaven. Ask yourself whether you are really sorry for having sinned, or simply afraid of being punished.

To recover the peace you have lost, forget your sin for a while and think about the love of God. He does everything possible to call sinners back to himself and to make them happy.

After this has restored peace to your soul, then you examine the motive behind your sin. Wake up your sorrow in the presence of God's love and promise to do better next time.

—Lawrence Scupoli: *The Spiritual Combat*

A Personal Response

Kicking myself has never been very productive, Lord. Let me find rest and peace in your support, your forgiveness.

December 3 # Ignorance and Weakness

Forgive us our debts, as we also have forgiven our debtors. *Matthew 6:12*

There are two causes of sin. Either we don't know what we ought to do or we refuse to do what we know we should. The first cause is ignorance. The second is weakness.

While we can fight against both, we will certainly be defeated unless God helps us. God can teach us what is right. As our knowledge of good and evil grows, God can help us to desire the better.

When we pray for forgiveness, we need to pray also that God will lead us away from sin. The psalmist sings, "The Lord is my light and my salvation" (Psalm 27:1). With light he takes away our ignorance. With salvation he strengthens us in weakness.

—Augustine: *Enchiridion*

A Personal Response

O God. Teach me your law. Give me the strength to keep it.

December 4   # Real or Counterfeit?

You give a tenth of your spices—mint, dill and cumin. But you have neglected the more important matters of the law—justice, mercy and faithfulness. *Matthew 23:23*

True devotion must be sought out among its many counterfeits. People naturally think their way is best. Some who fast think this makes them very devout, even though they may harbor hatred in their hearts. Some who abstain totally from drink nevertheless trick and cheat their neighbors, drinking, as it were, their neighbors' blood. Others are sure they are devout because they say many prayers, and yet their language is arrogant and abrasive at home and at work. Others give liberally to the poor but are unable to forgive their enemies. Others forgive their enemies but don't pay their bills. All of these people could be thought of as devout, but they are not. They only hint at devotion.

Genuine devotion is simply honest love of God. When this love becomes so much a part of us that we automatically do deliberate good, then it can be labeled "devotion." Ostriches are not flying birds, chickens fly short distances with much effort, but eagles, doves, and swallows fly high and far. Sinners are like the ostrich and are earthbound. Good people who have not quite reached devotion are like the chicken; they fly in God's direction, but inefficiently and awkwardly. The devout soar to God with regularity. Devotion, then, is a natural agility of the spirit.

—Francis de Sales: *The Devout Life*

 A Personal Response

Give me genuine devotion, Lord. Let me see that what you require of me may not be what you require of someone else. And teach me that being devout demands integrity. Being true to you in one area of my life means being true to you in all areas of my life.

December 5   The Church Is Like A . . .

A furious squall came up, and the waves broke over the boat, so that it was nearly swamped. *Mark 4:37*

Sometimes our Savior compares the church to sheep. Sometimes the metaphor is children. Sometimes it is a vine. The early church fathers compared the church most often to a ship. A ship is at the mercy of the waves. It is tossed this way and that. It is in danger of sandbars and rocks and pirates. It may leak and sink.

If sheep were not inclined to stray, why would they need a shepherd? If little children could guide themselves, why would they need parents? If the vine did not hang down, and lie on the ground, what need would it have of props and pruning? If there were no fear for the passage of a ship, why would it need a captain?

Never think the church is safe forever and will never make a mistake. The church is not immune to decay. The church needs a Shepherd, a Father, a Vinedresser, and a Captain.

—John Jewell: *Exposition on the Thessalonians*

A Personal Response

Lord, the church seems full of ignorance, poor direction, and selfishness. Let me, in my small role in the church, seek your direction, your wisdom, and your selfless heart.

December 6 # Stealing at Its Worst

You shall not give false testimony against your neighbor. *Exodus 20:16*

Once we understand that we should never steal material things from anyone and to handle anything borrowed as if it were our own, we then need to apply this idea to another area. There is something more precious than gold, silver, and jewels. It is our neighbor's good name. Solomon says, "A good name is more desirable than great riches; to be esteemed is better than silver or gold" (Proverbs 22:1). You will preserve your own good name, as well as another's, if you will give no false testimony. Never defame anyone with lies and slanders.

This rule also applies to all evil suspicions. Do not think the worst about another person. There is nothing to be gained from interpreting what someone has said or done. It is wrong to repeat gossip. Anyone who tells evil tales and untrue reports that are based upon suspicion is giving false testimony. Utterly avoid this vice.

This is the very heart of Christian living. Saint Paul wrote, "Love does not delight in evil but rejoices with the truth" (1 Corinthians 13:6). God's commandment forbids us to speak any word that incorrectly harms another. Even if it is the truth, it is sin if it is not spoken in love. Jesus warned us, "You must give an account on judgment day of every idle word you speak" (Matthew 12:36, NLT). If we will be examined for our idle conversation, how much more shall we be held accountable for our slanderous words against others?

Keep the rule of Christ: "If another believer sins against you, go privately and point out the fault. If the other person listens and confesses it, you have won that person back" (Matthew 18:15, NLT). This is the best and most honest way to handle the faults of others. If you don't want to do this, at least hold your tongue.

—Thomas Cranmer: *Catechismus*

 A Personal Response

Help me to live according to your precepts, dear God.

December 7   # Faith and Beyond

> Dear friends, now we are children of God, and
> what we will be has not yet been made
> known. But we know that when he appears,
> we shall be like him, for we shall see him as
> he is. *1 John 3:2*

Imagine three people standing in sunlight. One of the three is blind. Another can see but has shut his eyes. The third looks out with full sight.

The first person, the one who is blind, has no way of experiencing light. This person believes there is such a thing as light because trustworthy people have described it. Many people have this kind of faith. They have been told about God by leaders of the church. This is enough for salvation.

The second person sees light through closed eyelids but does not really see anything other than a glow. The eyelids are in the way. This is like the Christian who has both faith and feeling. The Christian perceives something of the divinity of Jesus. It is an incomplete and imperfect vision, but it is enough to be convincing.

The third has full sight of the sun. There are no doubts remaining. That person fully perceives the glory of God. Acceptance of an idea, belief, is no longer a problem, for without any impediment of body or sin, we are face to face with Jesus. This way of knowing Jesus is the opening of heaven to a soul. But do not imagine that "the opening of heaven" means that the skies are parted and someone actually *sees* our Lord Jesus in his majesty. That's not the way it is. It is in our imagination that we "see" such things; we do not actually observe heaven. The kind of light we are thinking about is enough for simple souls.

—Walter Hilton: *The Scale of Perfection*

A Personal Response

I envy those who walked around with Jesus. That must have been the greatest adventure of all time. I believe in one whom I have not seen. Lord, have I perceived even a little of your glow in this dark world? Prepare me for a fuller vision, a deeper perception of Christ.

December 8 Prayer beyond Prayer

... That people may see and know, may consider and understand, that the hand of the Lord has done this. *Isaiah 41:20*

It is possible, while you are praying the Lord's Prayer (or some other vocal prayer), that the Lord will give you *perfect contemplation.* It turns the prayer into an actual conversation with God. This works beyond the understanding. Words become unimportant. Anyone who experiences this will know that the Divine Master is doing the teaching without the sound of words.

The soul is aroused to love without understanding how it loves. It understands how distinctly different this moment is from all others. This is a gift of God. It is not earned.

This is not the equivalent of mental prayer, which is silently thinking about what we are saying and to whom we are saying it.

Don't think of it as something esoteric with an unusual name. Don't let the technical term for it frighten you away.

It's like this: in regular prayer we are taking the lead with God's help. But in the perfect contemplation described above, God does everything. It is not easy to explain.

—Teresa of Avila: *The Way of Perfection*

 A Personal Response

With these words, I am left silent. God, be in the silence.

Peacemaking

Peacemakers who sow in peace raise a harvest of righteousness. *James 3:18*

S omething more is required than that you should be at peace in yourself. It is not enough to be difficult to offend and always ready to forgive. There is something missing even if you do not stir up trouble or avenge wrongs.

It is also required that you actively make peace, to be a mediator in situations where you know there is strife, malice, and envy. It is necessary, when you know of disruptive situations, that you leave nothing undone that will help resolve the crisis.

Attempt every diplomatic effort possible before you fight. When all fails, the prince is bound to defend his land and subjects. This is also peacemaking. The same is true when he punishes thieves and murderers and those who disturb the peace of others.

Peace breakers are cursed. Those who pick quarrels, the whisperers, backbiters, sowers of discord, slanderers, and faultfinders are cursed. So are those who place an evil interpretation upon that which is done for a good purpose.

Do not avenge yourself. Do not seek more than that such wrongs should be forbidden. Anything beyond this takes away the authority of God. God is Father over all. It is his right to judge his children. God alone takes care of the avenging.

—William Tyndale: *Exposition on the Sermon on the Mount*

A Personal Response

Help me, dear God, to determine the difference between being passive and being a peacemaker.

December 10　 Keeping Prayer on Track

Do not be quick with your mouth, do not be hasty in your heart to utter anything before God. God is in heaven and you are on earth, so let your words be few. *Ecclesiastes 5:2*

So you have difficulty with wandering thoughts in prayer! That's nothing new! You have a lot of company.

One way to remedy this is to tell God about it. Don't use a lot of fancy words or make your prayers too long. That in itself will destroy your attention. Pray like a poor, paralytic beggar before a rich man. Make it your *business* to keep your mind in the Presence of the Lord. If you have difficulty with that, don't fret about it. That will only make it worse. Bring your attention back to God in tranquility.

Another way to stay with a prayer is to keep your mind from wandering too far at other times of the day. Keep it strictly in the Presence of God. If you think of him a lot, you will find it easy to keep your mind calm in the time of prayer.

—Brother Lawrence: *The Practice of the Presence of God*

A Personal Response

If I am interested, O Lord, I pay attention. If I am bored, my mind wanders. How can your divine presence ever be a bore? The only possible answer is that I do not truly believe you are here at my side. Open my eyes that I may see.

Pointed Questions

Search me, O God, and know my heart; test me and know my anxious thoughts. *Psalm 139:23*

If you can enjoy violent and dishonest experiences, how will you respond to the highest good?

Why do you fail to see in yourself the same fault you censure in others?

If being called good is such a sweet thing, how much sweeter is it to actually be good?

Do you like being angry? Isn't it actually misery?

All misery is the result of loving something you have set your heart on. What is it for you?

If you put up with yourself, why not put up with everyone else?

Everyone wants to accomplish what they want. But how do they know that what they want is good or beneficial? How will they determine this?

How does God reward the angels? Why do they serve him?

—Guigo I: *Meditations*

A Personal Response

Lord Jesus, you were the great asker of questions. "What does it profit you to gain the whole world and lose your own soul?" "Who do you say I am?" "Whose image do you see on this coin?" "Which one was neighbor to him?" "Do you want to be well?" "Where is your faith?" The list is a long one. . . .

December 12 # Filling an Emptiness

While he was blessing them, he left them and was taken up into heaven. *Luke 24:51*

Lord, you began to perfect your apostles by taking away from them the very thing they didn't think they could do without—the actual presence of Jesus. You destroy in order to build. You take away everything in order to restore it many times over. This is the way you work. You do it differently than we would do it.

Once Christ was gone, you sent the Holy Spirit. Sometimes lacking is more powerful than having. Blessed are those who are deprived of everything. Blessed are those from whom Jesus is removed. The Holy Spirit, the Comforter, will come to them. He will comfort their sorrows and wipe away their tears.

But Lord, why isn't my life filled with this Spirit? It ought to be the soul of my soul, but it isn't. I feel nothing. I see nothing. I am both physically and spiritually lazy. My feeble will is torn between you and a thousand meaningless pleasures. Where is your Spirit? Will it ever arrive and "create in me a pure heart, O God" (Psalm 51:10)? Now I understand! Your Holy Spirit desires to live in an impoverished soul.

Come, Holy Spirit! There is no place emptier than my heart. Come. Bring peace.

The Holy Spirit floods the soul with light, recalling in our memory the things Jesus taught when he was on earth. We find strength and inspiration. We become one with Truth. It is no longer outside of us, but a part of our being.

The Spirit of love teaches without using any words. There is neither sound nor gesture, but all becomes light. There are no demands, but the soul is prepared in silence for every sacrifice. Once we have experienced holy love, we are no longer satisfied with any other love. Unspeakable joy becomes ours without any effort on our part! Love is now a fountain that flows through us.

—François de Fénelon: *Meditations and Devotions*

A Personal Response

O my Love, my God! Glorify yourself in me. My only joy in life is in you. You are everything to me.—François de Fénelon

December 13 Idleness

Laziness lets the roof leak, and soon the
rafters begin to rot. *Ecclesiastes 10:18,* NLT

Idleness is the root of all mischief. Paul wrote to the Thessalonians, "We gave you this rule: 'Whoever does not work should not eat.' Yet we hear that some of you are living idle lives, refusing to work and wasting time meddling in other people's business. In the name of the Lord Jesus Christ, we appeal to such people—no, we command them: Settle down and get to work. Earn your own living" (2 Thessalonians 3:10-12, NLT).

Water is clear and fresh. If it stagnates in a hole or is kept too long in a container, it will rot and smell. It becomes unwholesome. It is the same with us. If we have nothing to do, no way to use our minds constructively, we will decay into mischief.

Idleness fills prisons and causes many parents to grieve for their children. Many diseases begin with idleness. Ask the doctors. They will tell you that a lack of exercise is dangerous to your health.

You protest, saying that kings and all sorts of well-educated people neither plow nor sow nor dig ditches nor do anything strenuous. They sit at rest and live idly. You are wrong. The toil and great cares of people in such positions pass all other cares in the world. Those who master a ship seem to be doing nothing. They sit still. They are not working the pump or driving the oars or sounding the depth. They do not climb the rope or scale the shrouds. You will not see them running this way and that, forward and backward, under the hatches or above. They sit still. They hold their peace. They appear to be doing nothing. But their labor surpasses all the rest. Without this labor, all the efforts of the other mariners are futile. It is the same way with those in positions of responsibility. They may seem to be idle, but they are quite active.

—John Jewell: *Exposition on the Thessalonians*

 A Personal Response

The truth is, Lord, if we are not idle, we are probably way too busy. Either way, we are promoting a way of life that is not a life you want for us. Show us the *true* way to work.

December 14 # Natural Outcome

By their fruit you will recognize them. Do people pick grapes from thornbushes, or figs from thistles? *Matthew 7:16*

Where there is love and wisdom, there is neither fear nor ignorance.

Where there is patience and humility, there is neither anxiety nor anger.

Where there is poverty and joy, there is neither greed nor covetousness.

Where there is quiet and meditation, there is neither care nor waste.

Where there is compassion and discretion, there is neither excess nor indifference.

Where the fear of the Lord guards the door, the enemy cannot enter.

—Francis of Assisi: *Admonitions*

 A Personal Response

It seems obvious: certain behaviors produce inevitable results. Knowing this, why don't I make better choices? O God, guide my actions, guide my understanding, guide my spirit into truth.

Unequal but Fair

"These men who were hired last worked only one hour," they said, "while we put up with a whole day's work in the hot sun—yet you paid them the same as you paid us!" Matthew 20:12, TEV

God is the giver of all we have and are.

If one has received more, and another less, both are God's. Without God there is no blessing at all.

The one who has received the most cannot say that it is deserved or think it shows any sort of superiority. The greatest and the best person, after all, is the one who thinks the least of himself and is humbly grateful.

If someone has received less, that person must not be disturbed about it— and certainly shouldn't envy anyone else. Instead, the one who gets less should turn to God and praise him for his goodness and his gifts.

God knows what is suitable for everyone. God has a reason for giving one less and another more. This is not for us to figure out.

Those who have received less can take special comfort because "God chose the foolish things of the world to shame the wise; God chose the weak things of the world to shame the strong. He chose the lowly things of this world and the despised things—and the things that are not—to nullify the things that are, so that no one may boast before him" (1 Corinthians 1:27-29).

—Thomas à Kempis: *The Imitation of Christ*

A Personal Response

Some people get less. Some people get more. Forgive me, Lord, when I am jealous of others. Forgive me when I envy them. Forgive me when I covet what they have. You know my special needs and know what is suitable for me.

Spiritual Showoffs

When you fast, do not look somber as the
hypocrites do, for they disfigure their faces to
show [others] they are fasting. I tell you the
truth, they have received their reward in full.
Matthew 6:16

S ome faithful people behave in odd ways. When they listen
they waggle their heads. Their mouths gape open as though
their ears were inside. Others, when speaking, use their fingers and poke their own and their listeners' chests. They can neither
sit, stand, nor lie still. They tap their feet, flex their fingers, and
make rowing motions with their arms as though they were swim-
ming instead of talking. Some laugh or smile with every other
word, like off-balance amateur jugglers.

Look at them staring like demented people. Some of them have
their eyes set in their heads as though they were dying. They hold
their heads to one side as though they had a worm in their ear. Some
squeak instead of speaking normally. Some are so eager to speak that
they gurgle and splutter. Hypocrites tend to behave like this.

I suppose they will go on loving God in these peculiar ways until
they go stark raving mad. Perhaps God will show them mercy and put
an end to this put-on behavior. It is no great sin in itself. It is simply
not necessary. It can take control of an individual. It can become a
sign of pride. It can be a form of outlandish exhibitionism.

The proper thing is for our words and outward gestures to reflect
an inner humility. Speak in a normal, natural voice. If the words are
true, utter them in a truthful way.

—Anonymous: *The Cloud of Unknowing*

A Personal Response

Sometimes I enjoy being the center of attention, Lord. Help
me to understand that my job, like the Holy Spirit's, is to put
the spotlight on you and not on myself.

December 17   Taking the Right Medicine

Is there no balm in Gilead? Is there no physician there? Why then is there no healing for the wound of my people? Jeremiah 8:22

Physicians do not wrap injuries carelessly. There is an art to binding wounds. The bandages have beauty as well as function.

In the same way that a cure can lead to health, Christ received sinners in order to heal and strengthen them. In Christ, God took on our humanness, accommodating himself to our wounds.

Doctors sometimes apply the opposite of our condition—ice on a burn, moisture on dryness. At other times similar things may be applied—a round wound gets a round bandage, a long cut gets a long bandage. The same dressing is not applied to every area of the body. Similar things fit together.

Now see God's wisdom. Determined to cure us, he applied himself. He is both the doctor and the medicine. We fell by pride. He applies humility as the cure. We threw away our immortality in the Garden of Eden. God uses his mortality to save us. This is the doctor's practice of contraries. Christ's virtues cure our vices.

We can also see similarities in God's spiritual medicine. As a human, he freed humans. As one capable of dying, he rescued the dying.

If we thought about it, we could come up with many more illustrations of Christian medicine working by contrary and similar properties. The diligent will discover them, but those who must hurry away to finish something they have started will not.

—Augustine: *On Christian Doctrine*

A Personal Response

Opposites. Fast and slow. Deep and shallow. Bright and dark. Health and sickness. Love and hate. Joy and sorrow. Rich and poor. The list is endless, Lord. Am I to understand that your healing touch to my spirit could be at either *extreme?*

December 18   ## Grab It and Growl

Some of the Lord's followers think one day is more important than another. Others think all days are the same. But each of you should make up your own mind. *Romans 14:5,* CEV

People will claim a piece of the world and think they have discovered a treasure. Then they will see something else they like. They become torn between the two pieces like a dog placed between two pieces of meat. It doesn't want to lose one piece while going for the other.

Most of us think we are living well. We convince ourselves that what we are doing is good for us, or we fret over the fact that we aren't. Sometimes we think our fretting is good for us. We are all mistaken.

The one who finds a secure place to work is blessed. Here is what makes a secure choice of worthwhile work: the desire to do something good for others. The more concerned you are with your own interests, the less good you may be doing.

All of us really want to be secure. The more things we love, the more easily we can be insecure. Suppose someone says to you, "I am going to hurt you. I am going to destroy your peace of mind. I am going to tell some bad things about you." That person will be as upset and disturbed as you are. Your spirit is exposed to as many hazards as are the things you love.

Because of physical needs and anxieties, you let the world in. Now you are anxious because you have the world.

—Guigo I: *Meditations*

A Personal Response

Lord, I know what's essential: making secure choices. I must choose the security of your love, the security of giving of myself to others. Teach me how to choose you even when I don't know how.

December 19 ## Our Rights

Create in me a clean heart, O God; and renew a right spirit within me. *Psalm 51:10,* KJV

There are many statements you need to avoid. "I was right." "They did not have the right to do this to me."

God deliver us from such false notions of what is right! Do you think it was right for Jesus to suffer all those insults? Did the people who did those bad things to a good man have the right to do so? Why do we think we should only bear crosses we think we have a right to expect?

Do you think that you have to put up with so much now that you have the right not to bear any more? How does the question of rightness even enter this discussion? It has nothing to do with it.

When we are offended and hurt, there is nothing to complain about. We can share the dishonor with Christ. Consider yourself fortunate to have such an opportunity, and you will lack honor neither in this life nor the next.

—Teresa of Avila: *The Way of Perfection*

 A Personal Response

This advice isn't easy to take, Lord. But the strong sense of it remains reasonable. Help me to bear personal injustice with strength, and to work for true justice for others.

December 20 # The Power of God

As the mountains surround Jerusalem, so the Lord surrounds his people both now and forevermore. *Psalm 125:2*

God can accomplish anything. He can speak a word and grant desires. He said, "'Let there be light,' and there was light" (Genesis 1:3). God can give me peace with a glance. When a tumult of thoughts stir a storm within me, God can declare my soul to be still. All its tempests obey him.

If God smiles, let the world frown! When God works with me, I will fear no obstacle that earth or hell can put in my way.

—Elizabeth Singer Rowe: *Devout Exercises of the Heart*

A Personal Response

Let nothing hide you from my sight. Let me look through everything and see you. Don't let me so much as glance in love or hope at anything below you. Let me understand that all of creation rests in the hollow of your hand. Let your hand be with me to keep me from evil. Let me live in your shadow. Then I will be secure. Then I will be sheltered.

—Elizabeth Singer Rowe

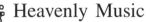 Heavenly Music

> Shout for joy to the Lord, all the earth, burst into jubilant song with music; make music to the Lord with the harp ... and the sound of singing, with trumpets and the blast of the ram's horn—shout for joy before the Lord.
> *Psalm 98:4-6*

Nothing less than God can fill our soul. Its capacity is designed for God alone. If we try to fill it with earthly things, we will never be satisfied. Lovers of God will be at peace when they are filled with God through desire and meditation.

Singing is a delightful way in which our spirits can ascend to the pleasures of heaven. We are swept away by a beautiful hymn flowing with joy.

Once I was sitting in a chapel, singing the Psalms as well as I could in the evening before supper. It seemed as though I could hear stringed instruments playing above me. With my prayers I reached out to these heavenly sounds. I experienced a blending of the internal melodies I was improvising with the heavenly harmonies. My meditation was transformed into music.

I am not saying that this is for everyone. If the gift is given, let the one receiving it enjoy it.

—Richard Rolle: *The Fire of Love*

 A Personal Response

O good Jesus, let me experience you. Since I cannot see you, let me know you. Pour yourself into the deepest places of my soul. Fill me with your brightness. Intoxicate me with your love.—Richard Rolle

December 22 # Gung-Ho for God

Ignorant are those who carry about idols of wood, who pray to gods that cannot save.
Isaiah 45:20

Beginners in the faith often develop a kind of spiritual avarice. They can't get enough of God. They can't attend enough services to satisfy them. They join study groups. They read book after book. They spend much time on these things rather than on getting down to the basics of living a spiritual life.

Moreover, they encumber themselves with images and spiritual gadgets. If they put down a rosary, they take up a prayer cloth. They change from one religious object to another.

True devotion comes from the heart.

—John of the Cross: *Dark Night of the Soul*

A Personal Response

He is not telling me that these things are not useful. Neither is he saying they are bad in themselves. It is the attachment to them that is the spiritual problem. Dear Lord, thank you for every reminder of your love in Jesus Christ. But always help me to look beyond the reminder itself to Christ himself.

December 23 ## Spiritual Inventory

Know this love that surpasses
knowledge—that you may be filled to the
measure of all the fullness of God. *Ephesians
3:19*

When wealthy people throw a party, there is lavish spending. There is no question of not having enough money. Guests are treated to the best food, music, and entertainment available.

It is not this way with those who are poor. They may have a desire to invite some friends to a meal, but they own nothing. They have to obtain the use of things that belong to others. They borrow plates, bowls, and tablecloths. When the meal is over, everything must be returned. They continue to be without possessions.

This is the way it is with anyone who is rich in the Holy Spirit. They are actually in fellowship with the Spirit. They can share what they have. When they speak, their words have firsthand authority. They can give away spiritual food freely because they have a full supply.

On the other hand there are many who try to help others without ever finding the riches of Christ for themselves. They can pour out a torrent of words. They can do some good deeds. They can even hint at mysterious knowledge and understanding. It is all without foundation. They are pumping a dry well. They can memorize things and spout them back. They can quote sentences they have read. They can pass along ideas they have heard from other speakers. They can organize and systematize the spiritual insights of others. A few can repeat these things in an entertaining, witty manner. No doubt, someone will be the better for having listened to them.

The problem is that when that kind of speech is finished, the words return to their source. The speakers are as indigent and unclothed as ever. They have no spiritual treasure within themselves.

—Pseudo-Macarius: *Homilies*

A Personal Response

Do I want to care for the souls of others? Lord, please help me care for my own soul first.

December 24 # Moderation

Keep falsehood and lies far from me; give me
neither poverty nor riches, but give me only
my daily bread. *Proverbs 30:8*

Not everyone can live like a saint, and yet we can follow
many of their ways. We can prize heaven more than the
world. We can be silent and humble. We can love people.
We can endure trouble patiently. We can return good for evil.
These things are pleasing to God. When it comes to attempting
saintly penances, it is better to start slowly.

Some are very concerned about their health. They are careful
about what they eat. Sometimes they actually harm themselves by
always eating what they consider to be the best food. They have a
hidden sensuality. They think they can combine the flesh and the
spirit, but they are wrong. They end up damaging both their health
and their devotion.

Devotional progress comes best to those who live a plain, simple
life.

—Lawrence Scupoli: *The Spiritual Combat*

 A Personal Response

Extremism seems commendable when one is intent upon being
good. And yet health is infrequently found at any extreme.
Thank you, Lord, for this levelheaded encouragement from the
past. Teach me how to live a plain, simple life.

An Abbreviated Word

[God] made himself nothing, taking the very nature of a servant, being made in human likeness. *Philippians 2:7*

D o you want to see the humility of God? Look in the manger and see him lying there. "Surely this is our God" (Isaiah 25:9). Seeing an infant, I wonder how this could be the one who says, "Do not I fill heaven and earth?" (Jeremiah 23:24). I see a baby wrapped in swaddling clothes. Is this the one who is clothed in the beautiful glory of unapproachable light?

Listen! He is crying. Is this the one who thunders in the heaven making the angels lower their wings? Yes, but he has emptied himself in order to fill us.

God understands that we are not able to see invisible things. It is not easy to teach us heavenly lessons. Faith comes slowly. If you are struggling to believe, don't listen to me. Go to Bethlehem and see the Word of God in a manger. Visible. Abbreviated. In heaven this Word fills angelic hosts with awe. In the manger he communicates with ordinary, simple people. "And the glory of the Lord will be revealed, and all mankind together will see it. For the mouth of the Lord has spoken" (Isaiah 40:5).

Simple shepherds were blessed with faith. They came in from their fields and saw a baby, wrapped in swaddling clothes, lying in a manger. This was not a disgrace for them. They thought no less of God. With love and affection they praised him.

—Guerric of Igny: *Liturgical Sermons*

 A Personal Response

I've never thought about Christmas this way, Lord. Holiness in miniature. Spiritual bonsai. An abbreviated Word. Charming! And isn't that what it is supposed to be?

A Prayer for the Earth

My job was to plant the seed in your hearts, and Apollos watered it, but it was God, not we, who made it grow. The ones who do the planting or watering aren't important, but God is important because he is the one who makes the seed grow. *1 Corinthians 3:6-7,* NLT

In the beginning you commanded the earth, O Lord, to yield green grass, herbs, and trees. Their seeds and fruits were food for your creatures living on the earth. To humans you gave dominion over everything, vegetable, animal, and mineral. We are to receive them with thanksgiving.

Because you alone are the Creator and Maker of all things, we seek your blessing. We may plant and water, but you give the increase. We pray that the earth may give her fruit abundantly. Bless the labors of our hands. We know we do not feed ourselves. We are the sheep of your pasture (Psalm 100:3).

You feed us. You give food to the hungry. You provide the earth. You water our gardens. You break up the clods and make them soft with rain. You make things multiply. You crown the year with your bountifulness. Your footsteps drop nourishment. You make the wilderness lush. You make the valleys to stand so thick with corn that they laugh and sing.

You cause wells to spring up in the valleys and rivers to run among the hills. All the beasts of the field may have a drink, quenching their thirst. The earth is filled with the fruits of your works. You make "grass to grow for the cattle. You cause plants to grow for people to use. You allow them to produce food from the earth—wine to make them glad, olive oil as lotion for their skin, and bread to give them strength" (Psalm 104:14-15, NLT).

If our barns are full, it is because you have blessed us. You have opened your hand.

—Thomas Becon: The Flower of Godly Prayers

A Personal Response

Thank you, God. Thank you.

December 27 God in the Commonplace

Where can I go from your Spirit? Where can I flee from your presence? *Psalm 139:7*

Here are the secrets of intimacy with God:

- Renounce everything that does not lead to God.
- Become accustomed to a continual conversation with him in freedom and simplicity.
- Speak to him every moment.
- Ask him to tell you what to do when you are not sure.
- Get busy with it when you plainly see what he requires of you.
- Offer your activity to him even before you do it.
- Give God thanks when you accomplish something.

The depth of your spirituality does not depend upon *changing* the things you do but in doing for God what you ordinarily do for yourself.

The biggest mistake is to think that a time of prayer is different from any other time. It is all one. Prayer is experiencing the presence of God. There should be no change when a time of formal prayer ends. Continue with God. Praise and bless him with all your energy.

—Brother Lawrence: *The Practice of the Presence of God*

A Personal Response

O my God, since you are with me, and I must now obey your command and apply my mind to these outward things, I pray that you will continue to be with me. Assist me. Receive all my labor. Possess all my affections.—Brother Lawrence

The Wisdom of Guigo

Let the wise listen and add to their learning, and let the discerning get guidance—for understanding proverbs and parables, the sayings and riddles of the wise. *Proverbs 1:5-6*

Affluence conceals and increases wretchedness. It does not take it away.

Don't let your intellectual pleasure exceed your fear of misusing it.

Rather than be a presumptuous controller of others, be a good companion.

Prefer to be taught rather than to teach.

Your burden is not nearly as heavy as the Lord's.

Flee from your own faults. The flaws in others will not hurt you.

Be angry with a sinner only if you think it will do him good.

It is your lack of interior pleasures that makes you go looking for exterior ones.

Your purpose is not to be seen or known or loved or admired or praised. Your purpose is to see, know, love, admire, and praise God.

We quickly accept an obtuse thought when an important person speaks it.

Never rejoice if you are better than others. Be sorry they are not better, and accept responsibility for it.

If you need to hate someone, hate yourself. No one else has hurt you more.

It is a mistake to love things that will inevitably decay, and to be annoyed when they do.

If it is for your own advantage that you do something for someone else, you are doing it for yourself.

—Guigo I: *Meditations*

A Personal Response

Dynamite comes in small packages. Lord, let me take these truths and work them, test them, prove them.

December 29 A Final Word

He has taken me to the banquet hall, and his banner over me is love. *Song of Songs 2:4*

In spite of our poor choices and spiritual blindness in this life, our courteous Lord continues to love us. We will bring him the most pleasure if we rejoice with him and in him.

When the end comes and we are taken for judgment above, we will then clearly understand in God the mysteries that puzzle us now. Not one of us will think to say, "Lord, if it had been some other way, all would be well."

We shall all say in unison, "Lord, bless you because it is all the way it is. It is well. Now we can honestly see that everything is done as you intended; you planned it before anything was ever made."

What is the meaning of it all? Listen carefully. Love is the Lord's meaning. Who reveals it? Love. Why does he reveal it? For love.

This is the only lesson there is. You will never learn another. Never. We began in love, and we shall see all of this in God forever.

—Julian of Norwich: *Showings*

A Personal Response

I trust you for this one, Lord. When it's all over and we meet face to face, I will trace through this life of mine, shared with others, and see in it all your love. Tears of happiness and tears of grief. Love. Achievement and discouragement. Love. Sickness and health. Love. Good and evil. Love.

December 30 Through the Eyes of a Child

I tell you the truth, unless you change and
become like little children, you will never
enter the kingdom of heaven. *Matthew 18:3*

I could see the divine light better when I was a child. I still remember how it was. It is the greatest of all gifts.

I was a little stranger who was surrounded by innumerable
joys when I arrived here. My knowledge was divine. I knew by
intuition things which I now attain by the highest reasoning. My
ignorance was an advantage. I was innocent. All things were spotless and pure and glorious. I knew nothing of sins or complaints or
laws. Everything was at rest, free, and immortal. I knew nothing of
sickness or death. In the absence of these I was entertained like an
angel with the works of God. Heaven and earth sang my Creator's
praise. Time was eternity. An infant is able to perceive mysteries
that the books of the learned never unfold.

Wheat was never reaped and never sown. I thought it had stood
in the field from everlasting to everlasting. Trees transported and
ravished me. Their unusual beauty made my heart leap ecstatically.
They were such strange and wonderful things.

Eternity was in the daylight. There was something infinite behind
everything I saw. The city seemed to be built in heaven. Everything
belonged to me. The skies were mine, and so were the sun and moon
and stars. All the world and everything in it was my possession. I was
the only spectator and enjoyer of it. I knew nothing of boundaries and
divisions. All treasures and the possessors of them were mine.

Then I was corrupted and was taught the dirty devices of this
world. Now I will unlearn them. I will become, as it were, a little child
again that I may enter into the kingdom of God.

—Thomas Traherne: *Centuries of Meditation*

A Personal Response

The childlikeness in me grows. There is an opening and increasing of everything about me that wants to observe, consider,
collate, create.

I will see you one day, Father. I will welcome the comfort
and security of your presence. Childlike, I will trust your love.

December 31 A Final Charge

You have made known to me the path of life;
you will fill me with joy in your presence,
with eternal pleasures at your right hand.
Psalm 16:11

If birds stop beating their wings, they quickly fall to the ground. Unless your soul works at holding itself up, your flesh will drag it down.

You must renew your determination regularly.

Oddly, a spiritual crash leaves us lower than when we began.

Clocks need winding, cleaning, and oiling. Sometimes they need repair. Similarly, we must care for our spiritual life by examining and servicing our hearts at least annually.

There is plenty of time for other things. You do not have to do it all every day.

Stay with it. Time flies away. Keep your eyes on heaven. Don't throw it away for earthly things. Look at Jesus Christ and be faithful to him.

Live, Jesus! To whom, with the Father and the Holy Spirit, be all honor and glory, now and forevermore. Amen.

—Francis De Sales: *The Devout Life*

A Personal Response

I will not say that I am devout, Lord God. But I desire to be.

Appendix A: Biographical Index

Aelred of Rievaulx (c. 1110–1167). Scottish monk. Met Bernard of Clairvaux who noticed his spiritual depth and literary skills and encouraged him to write. *1/27, 3/5, 5/3, 7/5, 9/10*

Anonymous (13th century). Well-educated Augustinian monks. Authors of *A Guide for Anchoresses,* written in a simple style of English. *7/1*

Anonymous (14th century). Hermit and author of *The Cloud of Unknowing.* His book is a down-to-earth guide to mystical prayer. *3/1, 5/4, 8/31, 10/15, 12/16*

Anonymous (19th century). Russian peasant and author of *The Way of a Pilgrim,* a book which explores the true meaning of the scriptural phrase "praying without ceasing." *6/8*

Thomas Aquinas (1225–1274). Italian philosopher who taught theology in Paris. Called "Dumb Ox" because he was slow and heavy. He was extraordinarily brilliant, however, and his religious thought is careful, rational, and systematic. He worked to reconcile science and theology. A prolific writer, his major work is *Summa Theologica.*

Anne Askew (d. 1546). Attendant to England's Queen Catherine Parr. Accused of heresy. Imprisoned in the Tower of London and burned at the stake. *3/24*

Augustine (354–430). Born in Tagaste, North Africa. Studied at the University of Carthage. The most influential theologian of his time. Became Bishop of Hippo in 396. He is best known for his spiritual autobiography, *Confessions. 1/24, 5/12, 5/30, 7/19, 7/29, 8/30, 9/17, 10/3, 10/11, 11/14, 11/20, 12/3, 12/17*

Richard Baxter (1615–1691). British Puritan minister. Exhausted his energy in the political struggles of his time and place. Persecuted and sometimes imprisoned for his beliefs. *2/5, 2/9, 2/19, 5/6, 10/1, 11/16*

Thomas Becon (c. 1510–c. 1567). English pastor. Jailed in the Tower of London. Wrote profusely, but very little remains in circulation today. *2/23, 12/26*

Bernard of Clairvaux (1090–1153). Considered the most influential individual in twelfth-century Western Christianity. His writings ushered in the "golden age of medieval spirituality." *1/6, 1/23, 2/20, 3/12, 4/7, 5/11, 5/29, 6/18, 7/17, 8/2, 9/24, 10/5, 11/3, 11/6,* 11/13, 11/29

1

Pierre de Berulle (1575–1629). Founder of the French Oratory (later known as the Sulpicians). *6/19*

Bonaventure (c. 1217–1274). The successor and official biographer of Saint Francis of Assisi. His masterpiece is *The Soul's Journey into God.* An Italian friar, he taught at the University of Paris. *3/25, 4/29*

John Bradford (c. 1510–1535). Youthful British reformer. Imprisoned in the Tower of London. Wrote extensively while incarcerated. Burned at the stake in Smithfield. *1/26, 3/6, 4/13, 7/12, 9/15*

Thomas Browne (1605–1682). British physician and writer. His personal confession of faith is expressed in *Religio Medici,* written about 1635. *2/29, 5/17, 7/18*

Martin Bucer (1491–1551). German monk. Present at Martin Luther's defense of his ideas to Rome, ideas that began the Reformation. Became a friend and supporter of Luther. Died in England, in exile and poverty. Queen Mary exhumed his remains and burned them at the stake. *1/28, 3/18, 5/21, 7/21, 9/25, 11/10*

John Bunyan (1628–1688). English. Jailed for his beliefs 1660–1672. Wrote *The Pilgrim's Progress,* an allegory that has captured the imagination of many generations. *2/11, 6/20, 7/16, 8/15, 9/13*

John Calvin (1509–1564). French. He was eleven years old and on his way to becoming a priest, when Martin Luther broke with Rome and started the Reformation. He wrote *Institutes of the Christian Religion,* a large and comprehensive work. *1/18, 3/3, 5/23, 6/12, 7/14, 10/27*

John Cassian (c. 360–433). Began as a youthful monk in Palestine and Egypt. He moved on to Gaul and founded monasteries near Marseilles about the year 415. In order to educate his new Gallic monks, Cassian gave a series of lectures and took part in conversations, many of which were preserved in book form. *1/25, 8/7*

Miles Coverdale (1488–1569). Bishop of Exeter. Published English translation of the Bible in 1535. A contributor to the first *Book of Common Prayer. 1/29, 5/26, 8/13*

Thomas Cranmer (1489–1556). Archbishop of Canterbury. Placed English versions of the Bible in British churches. Tried for treason, convicted of heresy, and burned at the stake. *3/21, 5/31, 8/24, 9/26, 11/11, 12/6*

Jean-Pierre de Caussade (1675–1751). French priest. Little biographical information is available about this man whose classic work on spirituality, *Abandonment to Divine Providence,* has been an important influence in the Christian church. *3/11, 4/26, 7/25, 8/19, 10/4, 11/27*

Francis de Sales (1567–1622). Bishop of Geneva. His *Introduction to the Devout Life* is one of the greatest devotional guides ever written. *1/2, 1/10, 1/20, 2/15, 3/2, 3/14, 3/22, 3/30, 4/10, 4/15, 4/17, 4/22, 4/27, 5/7, 5/16, 5/22, 6/2, 6/10, 6/22, 6/28, 7/7, 7/11, 7/20, 7/27, 8/1, 8/6, 8/16, 8/20, 8/28, 9/2, 9/12, 9/18, 9/28, 10/2, 10/18, 10/28, 11/13, 12/4, 12/31*

John Donne (1573–1631). Well-known seventeenth-century English poet. He was also an outstanding preacher of that era. Reared a Roman Catholic, he later became a member of the Church of England. *5/5*

Margaret Ebner (1291–1351). German Dominican nun. She lived and prayed with a profound awareness of the presence of God. She considered a personal relationship with Jesus Christ to be the major reference for answering life's difficult questions. *9/9, 10/31*

Meister Eckhart (c. 1260–c. 1329). German mystic. Prior, professor, and preacher at Strassburg. Condemned for his "radical" ideas. Profoundly influential in Christian thought and spirituality for centuries. *2/8, 5/13, 9/29*

François de Salignac de la Mothe Fénelon (1651–1715). French priest. Became Archbishop of Cambrai. His writings combine human warmth and spirituality with intelligence and erudition. *1/3, 2/25, 4/3, 4/18, 5/2, 5/28, 6/23*

John Fox (1517–1587). English. Preacher, reformer, and prolific writer. His son said of him, "Inured to hardness from his youth, what to others seems the greatest misery gave him no concern." *4/19*

Francis of Assisi (c. 1182–1226). Italian. Founder of the Franciscans. One of the most well-known characters among the Christian saints. *2/10, 6/1, 8/27, 12/14*

John Frith (c. 1503–1533). British reformer. Highly educated friend of William Tyndale. Burned at the stake in Smithfield. *12/1*

Gertrude of Helfta (1256–c. 1301). Entered the Benedictine abbey of Helfta (Saxony) when she was only four years old. At age twenty-five she experienced a religious conversion and gave all her energy to monastic life. *2/2*

Gregory of Sinai (c. 1295–1346). A monk who worked hard to guide and defend a particular way of monastic life at Mt. Athos and other Greek-speaking monastic centers. *1/7, 8/29*

Lady Jane Grey (1537–1554). Born to British royalty. A remarkably intelligent young woman and victim of her time and circumstances. She was imprisoned in the Tower of London and beheaded at age seventeen. *8/22*

Guerric of Igny (c. 1080–1157). Visited Clairvaux to meet its famous abbot, Bernard. There he was persuaded to become a monk. Remaining at Clairvaux for about thirteen years, he filled in administratively when Bernard was absent or ill. He became the abbot of a new monastery at Igny, between Rheims and Soissons, France. *7/30, 8/26, 12/25*

Guigo I, Prior of the Charterhouse (c. 1083–1136). A Carthusian monk. Other than the details of his correspondence with Bernard of Clairvaux, very little is known about his life. *1/17, 2/22, 3/23, 4/4, 4/11, 4/28, 6/11, 7/8, 7/31, 8/17, 8/21, 9/11, 9/16, 10/13, 11/1, 11/15, 11/22, 11/28, 12/11, 12/18, 12/28*

Patrick Hamilton (c. 1505–1528). English. The abbot of Fearn. The first person burned in Scotland during the British Reformation. *8/18*

Hermas (c. 96). Roman. His *Shepherd of Hermas* is written in simple Greek. It was accepted as a book of the New Testament by Clement, Origen, and others. *2/24*

Walter Hilton (c. 1343–1396). A monk of the Augustinian priory of Thurgarton in Yorkshire, England. His book, *The Scale of Perfection*, sometimes carries the title *The Reforming of Man's Soul*. This is the first book on the religious life in the English language. *1/15, 2/14, 2/27, 3/15, 3/26, 7/4, 9/8, 9/21, 11/2, 12/7*

John Hooper (1495–1555). English. Bishop of Gloucester. Wrote profusely on doctrine and theology. Burned at the stake. *4/9*

John Jewell (1522–1571). Bishop of Salisbury. Exiled under Queen Mary but returned to England after her death. Active in the British Reformation movement. *1/9, 2/12, 2/21, 3/9, 4/8, 6/5, 7/22, 9/4, 10/7, 10/10, 10/19, 11/12, 12/5, 12/13*

John of the Cross (1542–1591). Spanish mystic and poet. Founded the Discalced (shoeless) Carmelites. His *Ascent of Mount Carmel* and *Dark Night of the Soul* are enduring classics of spiritual literature. *3/8, 3/29, 4/24, 6/6, 11/21, 12/22*

Julian of Norwich (1342–c. 1420). One of the greatest English mystics. She became an anchoress who lived alone in a cell beside a Benedictine church. She was widely known as a spiritual counselor. Many came to talk with this woman who combined keen intellect with spiritual sensitivity. *2/15, 7/10, 12/29*

John Knox (c. 1505–1572). Reformer and founder of Presbyterianism in Scotland. Preached in England, where he helped revise the *Book of Common Prayer*. Consulted with Calvin in Geneva. Completed his ministry in Edinburgh. *6/9, 10/12*

Hugh Latimer (c. 1480–1555). Bishop of Worcester. Forceful and effective preacher. Burned at the stake with Ridley, to whom he said, "We shall this day light such a candle, by God's grace, in England, as I trust shall never be put out." *1/11, 2/26, 4/5, 6/13, 8/5, 10/20, 11/18*

William Law (1686–1761). English clergyman. His mystical and devotional writings were influential and sometimes controversial. *1/19, 6/17, 8/9, 10/21*

Brother Lawrence (1611–1691). French rustic. Uneducated and unordained. People came to him in droves in search of instruction on authentic devotional experience. Transcriptions of his conversations and some of his letters are gathered into *The Practice of the Presence of God. 1/5, 2/7, 3/10, 3/16, 4/6, 5/18, 6/7, 10/17, 12/10, 12/27*

Martin Luther (1483–1546). German leader of the Reformation who criticized the medieval church's abuses. His main theological focus was on the meaning of justification by grace through faith: Luther insisted we are saved by God's grace and not by our good works. *1/14, 3/27, 8/15*

Catherine Parr (1512–1548). Sixth wife of Henry VIII, surviving him to become queen of England, France, and Ireland. Published her *Prayers and Meditations* in 1546. *3/13, 6/21*

Pelagius (c. 255–c. 425). British monk and theologian. He engaged in heated theological debate with Augustine. Ultimately, Pelagianism was denounced as heresy. *10/8*

Evagrius Ponticus (345–399). Greek monk whose ideas influenced many well-known leaders in the church throughout the Middle Ages. His writings were misunderstood, criticized, attacked, condemned, lost, and destroyed. The recovery of his work is one of the great achievements of modern scholarship. *1/4, 2/1, 5/19, 9/23*

Pseudo-Macarius (c. 380). A Syrian monk who was *"not* Macarius of Egypt." Little is known of him apart from the charming little sermons (homilies) and letters he wrote. Taking his example from Jesus, he purposefully used illustrations for his messages. *1/13, 3/19, 3/31, 4/12, 4/20, 5/14, 6/3, 6/30, 7/28, 8/4, 8/14, 9/6, 9/20, 10/16, 10/26, 11/4, 11/30, 12/23*

Nicholas Ridley (c. 1500–1555). Bishop of London. Highly educated, receiving his training in England and France. Horribly and slowly burned at the stake, a victim of political-religious turmoil. *2/17*

Richard Rolle (c. 1300–1349). An English mystic. Studied at Oxford and possibly at the Sorbonne. He became a religious hermit, but the "solitary" experience was anything but unmolested and peaceful. Two of his books have remained in general circulation–*Emendatio vitae (The Mending of Life) and Incendium armoris (The Fire of Love)*. *2/16, 4/25, 5/20, 6/25, 7/24, 8/8, 9/22, 11/25, 12/21*

Elizabeth Singer Rowe (1647–1737). The first popular female English author. Isaac Watts published her religious material after her death. *12/20*

Lorenzo Scupoli (1529–1610). Italian priest widely presumed to be the author of *The Spiritual Combat*. Francis de Sales called this little book his "spiritual director." He carried it with him constantly for thirty years. *1/12, 2/4, 3/20, 4/21, 5/15, 5/24, 6/16, 7/26, 8/11, 8/23, 9/19, 11/7, 12/2, 12/24*

Heinrich Suso (c. 1296–1366). Swiss mystic. Entered a Dominican monastery at the age of fifteen. Was a friend and supporter of Meister Eckhart. *6/26*

Jeremy Taylor (1613–1667). English bishop, theologian, and devotional writer. Objected to religious intolerance and the ruthless persecution of heretics. *1/31*

Teresa of Avila (1515–1582). Spanish Carmelite nun. A busy, creative, determined administrator who was also one of the greatest contemplative spirits in history. Her *Interior Castle* is a unique study of Christian spirituality. *1/1, 1/21, 3/4, 3/28, 4/16, 4/30, 5/8, 5/25, 6/15, 7/2, 7/15, 8/10, 9/7, 9/27, 10/9, 10/29, 11/5, 11/9, 11/26, 12/8, 12/19*

Thomas à Kempis (1379–1471). Priest in Holland. Considered to be the principal author of *The Imitation of Christ. 1/8, 1/22, 2/6, 2/18, 3/7, 3/17, 4/2, 4/14, 4/23, 5/1, 5/9, 5/27, 6/4, 6/14, 6/24, 6/29, 7/9, 7/13, 8/3, 9/1, 9/14, 9/30, 10/14, 10/24, 11/8, 12/15*

Thomas Traherne (c. 1637–1674). English clergyman and metaphysical poet. Studied at Oxford. Relatively unknown until modern times. *12/30*

William Tyndale (d. 1536). British reformer. Translated the New Testament into English against much opposition. Visited Martin Luther while fleeing for his life. He was hunted down, returned to

England, and executed as a heretic. *1/30, 4/1, 5/10, 7/3, 7/23, 8/12, 9/15, 10/23, 101/25, 11/23, 12/9*

Ugolino di Monte Santa Maria (14th century). Italian. Gathered and published people's stories and comments about Saint Francis of Assisi. These are known as the *Fioretti* (Little Flowers). *1/16, 6/27, 10/22*

Peter Vermigli (1500–1562) Italian. Sympathetic with the Reformation, fled to Switzerland. Ultimately taught in England at Oxford. *2/13*

John Wycliffe (c. 1328–1384). English religious reformer. Responsible for the first translation of the Bible into English. Condemned as a heretic twice during the last four years of his life. *2/28*

Appendix B: Recommended Additional Reading

My introduction to the spiritual literature I have paraphrased in this volume began about forty years ago through an extensive set of paperback books published by Doubleday as Image Books. A few titles are listed below, but the entire series is worthwhile reading.

A carefully produced and highly respected series of books in this genre is published by Paulist Press under the heading The Classics of Western Spirituality: A Library of the Great Spiritual Masters. There is nothing else in print that is the equal of this magnificent collection. Again, only a few titles appear below.

Also, on the Internet you can find an amazing collection of the complete text to many books known as the Christian Classics Ethereal Library. The site is located at http://ccel.wheaton.edu/

Aelred of Rievaulx. *Spiritual Friendship.* Translated by Mary Eugenia Laker. Kalamazoo: Cistercian Publications, 1977.

Augustine. *On Christian Doctrine.* Translated by D.W. Robertson, Jr. New York: The Library of Liberal Arts, Macmillan Publishing Company, 1958.

Augustine. *The Confessions of St. Augustine.* Translated by Albert Outler. Philadelphia: Westminster, 1955.

Augustine. *The Confessions of St. Augustine.* Translated by John K. Ryan. Garden City: Doubleday, 1960.

Bernard of Clairvaux. *The Works of Bernard of Clairvaux.* Translated by Kilian Walsh, et al. Kalamazoo: Cistercian Publications, 1976.

Blakney, Raymond Bernard. *Meister Eckhart: A Modern Translation.* New York: Harper & Row, 1941.

Bucer, Martin. *Instruction in Christian Love.* Translated by Paul Traugott Fuhrmann. Richmond: John Knox Press, 1952.

Christian Classics in Modern English. Retold by Bernard Bangley & David Winter. Wheaton: Harold Shaw Publishers, 1991.

de Caussade, Jean-Pierre. *Abandonment to Divine Providence.* Translated by John Beevers. New York: Doubleday, 1975.

Francis de Sales. *Introduction to the Devout Life.* Translated by John K. Ryan. Garden City: Doubleday, 1972.

The Doubleday Devotional Classics. Edited by E. Glenn Hinson. Garden City: Doubleday, 1978.

Fénelon, François de. *Christian Perfection.* Translated and edited by Mildred Stillman. New York: Harper & Brothers, 1947. Reissued by Bethany, 1976.

Fénelon, François de. *Meditations and Devotions.* Translated and edited by Elizabeth Hassard. New York: P. O'Shea, 1946.

Fosdick, Harry Emerson, ed. *Great Voices of the Reformation.* New York: Random House, The Modern Library, 1952.

Guerric of Igny. *Liturgical Sermons.* Translated by Monks of Mount Saint Bernard Abbey. Spencer, Mass.: Cistercian Publications, 1970.

Guigo I. *The Meditations of Guigo I.* Translated by A. Gordon Mursell. Kalamazoo: Cistercian Publications, 1995.

John of the Cross. *Ascent of Mount Carmel.* Translated and edited by E. Allison Peers. Garden City: Doubleday, 1958.

John of the Cross. *Dark Night of the Soul.* Translated and edited by E. Allison Peers. Garden City: Doubleday, 1959.

John of the Cross. *Living Flame of Love.* Translated and edited by E. Allison Peers. Garden City: Doubleday, 1962.

Lawrence, Brother. *The Practice of the Presence of God.* Translated by E.M. Blaiklock. Nashville: Thomas Nelson, 1982.

Lawrence, Brother. *The Practice of the Presence of God.* Spiritual Masters Series. New York: Paulist Press, 1978.

The Little Flowers of St. Francis. Translated and edited by Raphael Brown. Garden City: Doubleday, 1958.

Ponticus, Evagrius. *The Praktikos, Chapters on Prayer.* Translated by John Bamberger. Spencer, Mass.: Cistercian Publications, 1970.

The Prayers of St. Teresa of Avila. Compiled by Thomas Alvarez. New York: New City Press, 1990.

St. Francis at Prayer. Translated by Alan Neame. New York: New City Press, 1990.

Scupoli, Lawrence. *The Spiritual Combat.* Translated by William Lester & Robert Moran. New York: Paulist Press, 1978.

Teresa of Avila. *The Interior Castle.* Translated by Kavanaugh & Rodriguez. The Classics of Western Spirituality series. New York: Paulist Press, 1979.

Teresa of Avila. *Complete Works.* Translated and edited by E. Allison Peers. New York: Sheed & Ward, 1946. Individual titles of the above have been reprinted by Doubleday in its Image Book series. I highly recommend *Interior Castle, The Life of Teresa of Jesus,* and *The Way of Perfection.*

Scripture Index

Topical Index

.